a Country Wife

Farms, Families
and other
Foolhardy Adventures

a Country Wife

Farms, Families and other Foolhardy Adventures

LUCY PINNEY

TED SMART

First published in Great Britain in 2004

This edition produced for The Book People Limited, Hall Wood Avenue,
Haydock, St Helens WA11 9UL

10 9 8 7 6 5 4 3 2 1

Text © Lucy Pinney 2004
Text illustration © Nigel Owen 2004

Lucy Pinney has asserted her right to be identified as the author of this work under the
Copyright, Designs and Patents Act 1988.

First published by
Ebury Press
Random House,
20 Vauxhall Bridge Road,
London SW1V 2SA

Random House Australia (Pty) Limited
20 Alfred Street, Milsons Point,
Sydney,
New South Wales 2061, Australia

Random House New Zealand Limited
18 Poland Road, Glenfield, Auckland 10,
New Zealand

Random House South Africa (Pty) Limited
Endulini, 5A Jubilee Road,
Parktown 2193,
South Africa

The Random House Group Limited Reg. No. 954009

www.randomhouse.co.uk

A CIP catalogue record for this book is available from the British Library.

Cover Design by Two Associates
Text design and typesetting by Textype

ISBN 009189185X

Printed and bound in Great Britain by Mackays of Chatham

Papers used by Ebury Press are natural, recyclable products made from wood grown in
sustainable forests.

PG Wodehouse quotation from *Very Good Jeeves* by PG Wodehouse, published by
Hutchinson. Reprinted by permission of The Random House Group Limited.

'Source' quotation from Alice Walker's *You Can't Keep a Good Woman Down*.
Reprinted by permission of Jeremy Beale, The Women's Press.

Quotation from *Nancy Myles* by Kevin Sheerin. Reprinted by permission of Kevin Sheerin.

Neville Lytton quotation from *The English Country Gentleman* by Neville Lytton. Reprinted by
permission of the Lady Madeleine Lytton.

Pol Tosch, Luxembourg Fox Stew, from: 'Le Livre de la Cuisine Luxembourgeoise © 1982
Hölker Verlag, Münster.

Whilst every attempt has been made to clear all permissions, please contact the publisher with
any ommissions or comment.

Acknowledgements

Certain extracts and themes in this book have already appeared in articles and columns I wrote for *The Times*. I would like to say a huge thank you to them for giving me the opportunity to write these in the first place, and, later, being kind enough to allow them to be turned into a book. I would also like to thank the following publications, where some other stories and ideas in this book first appeared. *The Observer* 'Pigging It', 'Grockle Crop', 'Going Orf' winter 1985; *Cosmopolitan* 'Leaving the City Behind' May 1985, 'My Wild and Woolly Romance' October 1986, 'My Heart Belongs to Daddy' November 1988; *Country Homes and Interiors* 'Ask the Vicar to Tea but Don't Support the RSPCA' May 1986; *Country Living* Magazine 'Carthorse in the Kitchen' January 1987; *She* 'Holiday Pick-Ups' June 1990 'The Delicate Art of Holiday Sex' August 1990.

Thank you, too, to the following, many of them *Times* readers. Dr K.C.Smith for ram-testicle information, R.J. Lewis and

Jackie Stanley for insights into duck eating habits, William P. Boyd for emotional advice, Alan Beat for his black humour, Cassandra Latham for her spell, Roger Morsley Smith for his cockerel story, Karen Eberhardt Shelton for her anecdote about venison, Hilary Joyce for her insight into the porcine sense of humour, Elizabeth Close for her letter about a pheasant, and Lucy Fletcher for hers about a fox-collie. And many thanks, too, to all the farmers and country people whose interviews for my column reappear in this book.

Most of all, I owe a great deal to my editors at *The Times*, Jane Wheatley and Angus Clarke, to Kitty Corrigan who first started me writing about the countryside, to Nicholas Wapshott who accepted my first article, to Marianne Velmans for all her advice, to my endlessly patient agent, Rosemary Canter, and to my meticulous editor, Hannah MacDonald.

In order to make a readable narrative, I have rearranged a few events in this autobiography, and the names of certain characters have been altered to preserve privacy.

This book is affectionately dedicated to
all those who will be annoyed by it:
a long list, headed by
my beloved children, Kathy, Sam and Nat.

Part 1

Chapter One

'Never trust a man who wears spotless white trousers.' Family saying

I came out on to the church porch feeling dazed. My right hand held a contact lens that had shot off my eyeball – probably in terror – as the vicar began his address on the theme of 'Marriage is Martyrdom'. And my left was held firmly in Charlie's large, calloused fingers. I would have liked to have stayed there, in the hot sunlight, savouring the triumph (and amazement) I felt at having nabbed – in the teeth of fierce female opposition – such a brilliant matrimonial prize.

But he rushed me, along with my bridesmaids, into a Victorian milk-cart borrowed for the occasion, lifted the reins and yelled at his stallion, Bob: 'You irritating, bothersome, blithering, vegecidal maniac – get on!' Or rather, he didn't. There is no way I could write down what he said. It was unprintably rude, and consisted mainly of four-letter words. He drove all his horses using foul language, and they responded to it eagerly. Probably because it had a rhythmic lilt, and carried an undertone of affection.

At the familiar torrent of abuse, Bob broke into a brisk trot. The chains on his harness jingled, the cart bounced up and down, and the little bridesmaids screamed. If Charlie stopped yelling filth for more than a minute or two Bob's ears would swivel anxiously, and after a while his step would falter – so the four-letter words were pretty well incessant as we pounded through the narrow Dorset lanes to my parents' cottage. Bob also farted at regular intervals, which, along with the swearing, somewhat detracted from the tastefulness with which both sets of parents had hoped to imbue the occasion.

The relationship Charlie had with his horses was very close, I knew. When left tied up at shows, Bob would scan the crowd for Charlie's face, and pick it out, from hundreds of others, at a huge distance, and he was so trusting that, for a party trick, Charlie would crawl through his back legs on his hands and knees. They even slept together. When Charlie went off to distant ploughing matches with Bob he could never afford hotels, so he would sleep in the lorry – or a stable. He said that though Bob slept lying down, and frequently shifted position in the night, he was always somehow aware of a human presence next to him, and never kicked, or rolled over. A dealer friend of Charlie's had once explained to me that he, too, always slept with his horses when he was away from home. And the only time he had ever got into any difficulty was when, one morning, he had washed his face in the bucket of water one of his geldings was drinking out of. 'He did kick me then,' the dealer said soberly. 'I could tell he thought "Blooming cheek!"'

Carthorses, long dresses and the lush Dorset countryside might sound romantic, but Charlie managed to give them his unique rough edge. For the wedding he was wearing, instead of a suit, a long cotton smock hand-sewn by his mother. It was a difficult garment for anyone – except for, say, Little Lord Fauntleroy, to carry off – but Charlie wore it like a rebel. Within a few hours it was blotched with saddle-oil and mud, spotted with wine and cigarette ash, and he was standing in it up to his waist in duck weed, playfully ducking his small nephews in the ornamental pond in my parents' garden.

The next morning I woke up, on the first day of my new life, in a little white back bedroom with flowered curtains. Charlie was still asleep in the brass bed, so I climbed out carefully, glancing out of the window at the covered concrete yard where, he had told me, the sheep came in every winter to lamb. Beside it was a rough, grassed space where I planned to keep poultry and rabbits.

Pulling on some jeans and a T-shirt, I walked through the huge parlour that ran the whole width of the bungalow we were to live in. It had been converted from an old barn, so had rather odd room divisions. The parlour was a mess: there were glasses and bottles everywhere, and in the middle of the carpet was a heap of horse-manure. This was because, after the wedding, the more hardened drinkers had come back to continue the party, and Charlie had finally got rid of them by bringing two of his horses in through the front door. Though nearly all these guests were farmers, and used to livestock, they were appalled to find themselves so close to it in a domestic setting – and they had fled.

I opened the kitchen door and found myself in a little walled front garden. Near at hand I could hear the horses moving in the stable, their metal shoes clattering on the cobbled floor. And all around me, on every side, were fields rolling up to the horizon, because the farm was set in a wide bowl in the hills. At the bottom of the bowl the fields were relatively flat and that rich green that comes from pretty well incessant drizzle, but as they got steeper they were more and more covered by gorse and bracken and woodland.

On either side of me were barns, outbuildings, old, half-ruined cottages – and towering above them all, visible from every angle, Bettiscombe Manor, where Charlie's parents lived. Slightly too small to be a stately home, it had something of that grandeur and self-possession. Early eighteenth century, with smoky-pink brick walls, slate roofs and a delicate white shell porch, everything about it was immaculate. Its windows dazzled, the tiny lawn enclosed by its front railings was a brilliant, weedless emerald. Even the ten yellow dusters drying on a line in the walled laundry yard had all been pegged out with military precision.

The first inescapable truth about marrying a farmer: your husband is always very closely attached indeed to his parents. If he does not actually live with them, in the bedroom he has had since he was born, he still lives uncomfortably close. And they like to drop in and talk to him all

6

day, and supervise ninety per cent of his behaviour. You may think, as the new wife, that you have more influence over him than they do. You are wrong. Very, very wrong.

It was going to be a scorchingly hot day, which was good, because the hay was ready to be made. When he had planned the wedding, Charlie had hit on the brilliant idea of holding it in early June, because then the guests who stayed overnight could help with haymaking. (We had our honeymoon before the ceremony, to make this possible.)

I had never made hay myself, and had a hazy idea that it involved shady hedgerows, picnics in the sun and riding on laden haywains. And I was sure my friends would like to take part. Especially since Charlie used horses for farm work whenever he could. So though the hay would be baled (by a contractor), it would be fluffed up ready for baling with a horse and tedder and later the bales would be carried into the barn on a cart pulled by Bob and his companion, Ben.

But somehow, as I walked across the drive to the semi-ruined cottage where all my university friends were sleeping, I began to be a trifle doubtful about this idea. And I was even more so when I saw how tired and hung-over they all were. None of them was interested in even having a cup of tea. They just wanted to be left alone to die.

With a great deal of difficulty, I got them all mustered in the hayfield at midday. The sun was blazing by then, and there was not an atom of shade. In the distance the baler was chugging out parcels of hay, and nearer at hand Charlie was hurling bales up on to a wagon. He did this in an effortless, show-off way, using a pitchfork, the sweat barely breaking out on his muscular arms.

I was supposed to stand in the cart, and stack the bales in a neat arrangement that would not immediately tumble to the ground. This was astoundingly, horrifyingly hard to do. For a start, the bales were pricklier than they had any right to be. They had in with them, along with a weeny amount of grass, a huge quantity of thistles, nettles and brambles. And if you managed to squeeze your fingers under the hairy orange string keeping them together, and lift one up, not only did you get blisters, but an incipent hernia, because they were so heavy.

Out in the field, my friends – soft, pale and arty – were supposed to be rolling bales towards Charlie ready to be pitch forked, but after doing this for a pitifully short amount of time had begun standing around in groups complaining, or just slumping on the (prickly) ground in despair. They reminded me of mutinous players in a school hockey match.

When the cart was full they brightened at the thought of a ride, but as it was impossible to climb the steep sides, and anyway the bales kept crashing off (because I was so crap at stacking), they had to walk instead. And even as we entered the barn I could see them sneaking off, in their unsuitable wedding shoes, and making a run for their cars.

It was, strangely, worse inside the barn than out. You would have thought that it would be cooler. But it certainly was not – especially up underneath the broiling tin roof, which was where, for some inexplicable reason, I was supposed to put the new bales. I had to drag them through narrow passageways in a stack of ancient, mouse-smelling hay, and grapple them into position, while, behind me, Charlie made joky references to my incompetence and slowness, and occasionally goosed me by way of encouragement.

Still, the work did become easier once my friends had gone. I found some old gloves to protect my hands, and our best man, Reg – an enormous, woolly-haired countryman – staggered unsteadily out of his cottage beside the barn and offered to help. The horses did not like him much, and rolled their eyes and snorted when he got too close, which was surprising, as he was full of anecdotes about his skill as a horseman. Reg lived with Billy, a pretty blond man who worked as a cleaner for Charlie's mother. And though it was perfectly obvious that they must be lovers – Billy was most affectionate, and they shared a double bed – Reg persisted in the pretence that they were simply good mates. Whenever he could, he talked about all the women he had rogered. Mention any village in Dorset and he would instantly butt in, winking, to inform you that there was a gateway beside the pub where he had given a barmaid a damn good seeing-to. (Or a cosy corner in the churchyard where a female lay preacher had once been pleasantly surprised.)

The work was tough, but there was also pleasure in pushing myself to the physical limit – and surviving. And the banter was fun. Billy came out, in a pair of strawberry-coloured gloves, and while Charlie and Reg vied to see who was fittest, hurling bales unfeasible distances, and springing across dangerous chasms between the cart and the stack, we gossiped or delivered neat put-downs.

At last the shadows lengthened, and I lay, arms aching, on my back, on top of the last load of the day, gazing up at the sky, and then at the tops of the trees as they closed in above me on the turning into the barn. The cart jogged heavily over ruts in the dried mud, and it was very restful listening to Charlie in the distance persuading the horses – in the rudest possible way – to turn and back slowly towards the stack.

The whole romance had been conducted within earshot of horses, and in this valley. I had known Charlie since I'd been a teenager. My mother had been brought up on a Dorset farm, and hated it. (She used to sing a song called 'Misery Farm': 'We're all miserable, all so miserable, down on misery farm'.) And she met my father at a dance given by the Pinneys and married him and moved to London as soon as she could. When I was fourteen they bought a holiday cottage near the Pinneys and I met Charlie for the first time.

I had been carefully trained by my older brother to be a tomboy. His favourite entertainment, whenever we stayed anywhere in the country, was to explore the farms and parkland of insanely bad-tempered landowners. He loved it when a hypertensive, red-faced gent appeared in the distance, shouted 'Hoi!', and started chasing us, pitchfork in hand. Shrieking with excitement and terror (and in my case, wishing desperately that I'd never agreed to participate), we'd sprint across fields, leap prickly hedges and tunnel through ditches solid with mud. So I was initially scornful when, the first day we met, Charlie invited me on a walk and kept opening gates for me and pulling aside barbed wire. Did he think I didn't know how to vault barriers like that?

But after a while I warmed to his courtliness. He made me feel admired and treasured, and I'd never had much confidence. We had a lot in common because we were both the youngest in our families – with a brother and two sisters each – and we both hated being teased.

We went out together, very shyly, for a few months (we only ever kissed twice), and it ended because both families enjoyed ribbing us so much. When Charlie's Uncle Rupert wrote a long comic poem about our romance and read it out to gales of laughter at a Christmas party I felt too ashamed to go on with things. We did remain friends, though.

And then, one Christmas Eve, when we were both in our early twenties, our relationship suddenly developed. He was living with a very pretty woman slightly older than him, in a cottage beside the Manor. I bicycled over and had dinner with them, and when she packed and left to stay with her family for Christmas I lingered behind.

The cottage had barely any lighting, and we sat in the dark, beside a flickering fire, while Charlie played with the two farm sheepdogs. He stroked the ears of one and rubbed the stomach of another, and talked about his horses. I could hear them snorting and stamping while he did this, because the house was set into a sloping field and the animals were sheltering in an open-sided cellar beneath it.

Unlike other farmers in 1975, who were intoxicated by

modern tractors and just wanted to become more and more mechanised, Charlie preferred horse power. This was, it has to be said, largely because he was short of funds. When he had started farming the family farm four years earlier, he had milked cows. He had done this – he explained – in a highly disagreeable manner. As he did not have the money to build a milking-parlour he had bought a second-hand 'milking-bale'. This was a portable, half-collapsing, rusty shack with milking machines in it, which he towed out to whatever field the cows were grazing in. They then had to be reluctantly chased into it, and the milk that came out of them had to be dragged in churns to the top of the farm's bumpy drive by 8 a.m. The only way to get it there was on a tractor, and, of course, because the tractor was rusty and half-collapsing, too, it would never start. Horses were the answer. They were cheap, reliable and, as Charlie was fond of saying, you never go into the barn and find that the tractors have produced a baby – whereas (with a minuscule amount of forward planning) this happens every year with horses.

While he talked, I kept gazing at him. When we had gone out in our teens he had been short – barely five foot three, my height – with huge hands and feet. And though I had liked his character and enjoyed being with him, I had not found him that attractive. But he had changed. He had grown very nearly a foot and lost all his adolescent awkwardness. Now rather scarily sure of himself, he was tall and slender, with long light brown hair, a bony face with a very straight nose, large hazel eyes and a wonderful full, wide mouth. His surroundings, too, had immense, ramshackle charm. The frames were falling out of the tiny wooden windows, there were thick cobwebs on the low beamed ceiling and rain kept hissing down the big open chimney on to the fire. It was the sort of house an impoverished Thomas Hardy hero might live in. In fact, it was *exactly* like that, because the house had only recently been used as the setting for a series of dramatised Thomas Hardy short stories. The film crew had been attracted by the picturesque, old-fashioned buildings at Bettiscombe and the presence of working-horses, and only found fault with the furniture in Charlie's cottage. So a props man had hurriedly run-up some rustic-looking tables, cupboards and settles – which Charlie was still using. As he had also been an extra, and been 'styled' by a make-up artist, he even looked more authentically rural than before, with his heavy sideburns. (His friends had all been extras, too, which meant that they, too, had a theatrical rusticity. In fact that little pocket of West Dorset was pretty much changed for ever by the BBC.)

It suddenly seemed a wonderful idea to go out with Charlie again. After all, I knew already that he was gentle, kind and liked me. The same thought seemed to strike him, too, because, after an hour or so, he strayed on to the subject of how unhappy he was with his live-in partner: how she shouted at him and bad-temperedly threw plates, and the whole relationship was on the point of collapse . . .

Chapter Two

*We were discussing the mysteries of sexual attraction when my oldest
sister Caky told a story about a psychologist she knew. He claimed to
have an infallible system for getting anyone he wanted to go to bed with
him. All he did was place a freshly laundered hanky in his underpants
before he went out in the evening. Then, at the party or night-club or
whatever, he'd start talking to the prettiest woman in the room, excuse
himself, go to the loo, whip the hanky out of his pants and tuck it in his
breast pocket. He said it was the pheromones that did it, every time.*

It was Charlie's stable that did it for me. I loved the smell of
horses, stored hay and grain, old building dust, and the perfume
that came off Charlie when he'd been in there. And I felt safe
for the first time in the calm, companionable atmosphere of the
place. I had been brought up in a highly neurotic, city family,
and the stable provided the perfect antidote.

The evenings were best, when a subdued, golden glow came

from the cobwebby light bulbs and the horses were munching in their stalls. Charlie would climb up into the loft and shake hay down into the mangers, and the horses would look up when he did this, their soft eyes watching him curiously.

Meanwhile, I'd clear muck off the flagstones and fluff up the straw bedding. I was secretly nervous about doing even this because, although Charlie was always telling me how gentle the horses were, experience had yet to convince me. Now and then they would lazily shift position as I was brushing round them, and stamp on my feet, crushing my toes. It looked accidental, but they could have been teasing me, too. Everyone said that horses could tell at once if you were frightened of them – and I was.

I wanted desperately to *be* horsey, but I just did not have the confidence. In the first few months of the marriage I would often saddle Ben up – because he seemed the quietest, being a gelding – and set off to visit my parents three miles away. At first the ride would be lovely. Carthorses have wide backs, so I was less likely to fall off. Charlie always claimed riding them was like sitting in an armchair, but in reality it was more like balancing on an upturned rowing-boat – full of bony ridges and awkward slopes. Ben would amble along past the luxuriant hedges with a look of boredom on his handsomely moustachioed face, and, just as I was beginning to relax, he'd notice a bit of fresh ivy in the hedge and stoop to chomp it up.

'Now, Ben,' I'd say, with what I hoped was an air of command, 'you know you're not allowed to do that,' and I'd haul on the reins. I could almost feel him frown with annoyance.

Sometimes he would raise his head and stop browsing – but only briefly. Down it would go again at the next bunch of blackberries. And there is a definite limit – or so I felt – to the amount of strength you can put into cruelly yanking at an animal's head when all it wants to do is have a light meal. What right did I have to boss him about and hurt his mouth?

One of his favourite tricks, too, was to keep an eye out for overhanging branches and deftly scrape me off. He did this quite benignly, and stood still as I hopped about trying to get back on.

In the end, the only really enjoyable bit of the ride was the return, when we'd amble down the steep drive and Charlie would appear at the bottom and smile up at us through a lock of hair.

'Had a good time?'

'Wonderful. Just incredible. He is such a lovely horse.'

'He is, isn't he? One of the best.' And I'd slide down into Charlie's arms and bask in his approval. I hoped Charlie would not notice how green Ben's lips were (and how much fatter he had got in just an hour and a half). Sometimes I would shyly admit that I still was not very confident around horses and Charlie would say it took time, and add, kindly, that he had never really liked horsey women anyway. They were too domineering. 'And haven't you noticed how even their wrists look bossy?'

Along with Ben and Bob the stallion, an elderly grey mare used to be in the stable every evening. She was called Blossom and had a stained white back with a shallow dip in the middle, exactly like a sagging mattress. She also had a steely streak. She always got her own way. Each year, for instance, Charlie tried to make sure that she foaled in a dry, clean, sheltered meadow. And each year, without fail, she would break through the fence when no one was looking, slip into the stable, and foal into a pile of dung in the end stall.

Soon after he bought her, Charlie made an odd discovery. The stable had a few bricks missing on its inner walls, and these – being at shoulder-height – made useful niches for syringes, or bottles of medicine. But after Blossom arrived the niches became unusable. She made sure they were always filled, right up to the edge, with horse-manure. No one knew how, or when, she did this – she was highly secretive – but she must have indulged in astonishing feats of gymnastics whenever she was alone.

The other horsey activity I was introduced to by Charlie, as autumn ended and winter began, was ploughing competitions. Charlie was wildly enthusiastic about these, and they were generally small events, held in exposed fields, and patronised by a few old, bent countrymen in raincoats belted with twine. Charlie was invariably the youngest competitor by about fifty years.

A typical one would begin long before dawn, after a restless night punctuated by Charlie leaping up to run naked into the kitchen and add to the pile of rusty, odd-shaped – but crucial – tools in a box by the door. Then, very sleepily, and with the woolly mouth one tends to have on cold, damp mornings after hurriedly eating a hard-boiled egg, we would climb into the lorry. There were always far more people than just me and Charlie – there would be other horsemen, or neighbours invited from the pub at the last moment. And I would either perch in the cab, all squashed up between men wearing webbing gaiters and enormous, felty jodhpurs from the 1930s, or sit on a wonky garden chair in the horse-box with even more countrymen (all also sitting uneasily on unreliable deck-chairs which skidded across the floor whenever we rounded a corner). If I went in the box I had to clean harnesses as I went along – it had never been done in advance – which meant that for the whole of the rest of the day I had black hands and forearms and smelt fiercely of oil and Brasso. But I did discover what horses did when travelling. I had always assumed they just dozed. Not so. Bob and Ben were like naughty children. They started by rolling their eyes at each other, then progressed to biting and pushing, and trying to knock each other off their feet. When that palled, they undid their halters with their tongues and did their best to wedge themselves into peculiar positions.

At the other end of the long, long journey I would find myself on a rainswept field miles from any village or farmhouse. In one corner there would be a beer tent that all the men disappeared into. Women were rather frowned at for patronising this – even for the purposes of shelter. The male occupants would fall silent, and stare disapprovingly at them until they left.

And that first autumn, for some reason, there was a man making sheep hurdles at all the ploughing-matches. Since there was nothing else to do, I used to spend pretty well the whole day leaning on one of the hurdles, watching him as he wove bits of bark in and out of thin posts. The first time I did this he was flattered, and smiled at me with his blackened teeth, though I could tell that, as the day wore on, he became troubled by the way I stood there, hour after hour, horizontal rain filling my hood. The next time I saw him (and the next) he flinched when I appeared, and seemed to shrink into himself. He even hid round the back of his pile of sticks – until he realised tht it was no use, and nothing was going to make me go away. My presence clearly cast a cloud over the joy of making sheep-hurdles in a thunderstorm, turning the whole experience from a dreamy, introverted task into something painfully over-exposed and public. Eventually, though, I took pity on him and retreated back to the mildewed interior of the lorry, and, from, say 7 a.m. until nightfall I would generally sit in the lorry cab eating sand-wiches until I felt bilious, and watching Charlie as he slowly inched up and down a sea of mud with Bob and Ben. He had a very distinctive silhouette, with his long legs, wide shoulders and slightly feminine hips. And his fringe kept falling attractively across his face as he leaned over to adjust the plough, so I did not have a bad view – just a monotonous one.

I had only myself to blame if I found the horsiness overwhelm-ing sometimes, because I had known what sort of life I would be leading, well before I had agreed to get married. And it had been the thought of the horses – their beauty, their endearing characters and the romance of living with them – that had always made me certain I was making the right decision when, in the weeks leading up to the honeymoon, I experienced the odd doubt. I liked the thought of cows and sheep, and pigs, too, of course, but, more important, I knew I had a little of the right attitude. When I was six, and stayed at my grandmother's house by the sea, I used to spend whole afternoons catching fish in rock-pools with my hands. Then I'd take them home and boil them up for the cat. My sister Annabel, a fastidious teenager, was appalled.

'How can you do that?' she said. 'It's so cruel.'

'Not to the cat,' I answered.

I also quite liked watching the gardener's wife pluck and draw poultry, and after a while she let me try it myself. These two things made me feel I'd be able to cope with farming.

We had the honeymoon before the wedding, so we would be back in time for haymaking, and Charlie had decided that the very best way to spend it would be for us to travel across northern France, looking for a particular kind of horse: the Ardennes. He had glimpsed this creature in an obscure pamphlet and had immediately decided that it was exactly what he needed. The trouble with using British Heavy Horse breeds for farm work was that they were the wrong shape – and far too grumpy. This had come about, he explained, because no one had worked them for at least half a century. During that time they had become show animals, bred to look flashy. So they had got tall and grown 'feather' (fluffy hair) on their legs. (This looked pretty but was a bad thing. It clogged up with mud and needed lots of grooming.) But in France, different criteria applied. The horses were used for meat, so they were well muscled and chunky – which made them ideal for pulling carts. They did not have any feather. And the breeding stock were unusually biddable – because any animal with a vile temper was simply turned into salami.

The Ardennes horse society was very helpful. They took us to plenty of breeders' farms. But this was a dispiriting experience because *these* horses were always so wild. When we appeared in a gateway wanting to pat them they fled, like sheep. Still, Charlie enjoyed himself because, as I soon discovered, his idea of absolute bliss was standing in a field, drinking fiery local brandy, and talking about horses. He did not mind if it was raining, or snowing, or hailing marble-sized pellets of ice. Nor did the people he was talking to have to be able to speak, or even understand English. They just had to be wildly enthusiastic, and good at hand-gestures. It was the horse/field/alcoholic beverage combo that he found so seductive. He never seemed to tire of it. I did, rather. And so did the Ardennes society officials. After a few days they became fiercely annoyed that he had not bought anything. And finally, in exasperation, they said they would take us to the best Ardennes stud in the country, but we would, of course, be unable to afford any of the horses there because they would be far too expensive.

So we set off for Ferme du Bourbeau, near Verdun. The farm, when we reached it, was tucked away at the end of a long, winding road, in a landscape that was mostly sky and, at the end of May, cold and windswept. It was owned by a vivacious Frenchwoman called Cécile Blaise. She had curly brown hair and the tanned, muscular body that comes from a lifetime of wrestling with large, difficult animals.

Her horses, though, were extremely placid. Varying in colour from pale pink to deep chestnut, they were stockier than any heavy horse I had ever seen. They had a stubby look to their faces, big, curved crests, huge buttocks (made to look even podgier by docking) and manes and tails so coarse, grey and frizzy that they looked as if they were made from wire wool. They ambled good-naturedly about the fields – bending the metal gates into a banana-shape by scratching their bums on them – and came up hoping to be kissed whenever they saw a human.

But it was the air of old-fashioned, deeply practical eccentricity that I loved best about the place. Charlie told me that he had come across the same sort of quality on a farm he had once visited in the West Country, owned by an old gentleman. The day Charlie had called, this character had been sheltering from the cold inside his farmhouse, which had a huge parlour. He was sitting beside an open fire, training a sheep dog by getting it to run up and down the parquet in response to different commands. Against one wall was an ancient, sagging sofa, and sitting on this in a row were a middle-aged sow, a tabby cat and a selection of fancy poultry. They were all watching the dog with a professional eye, swivelling their heads like spectators at Wimbledon as it pounded backwards and forwards.

I was reminded of this story when Cécile showed us the huge stable where she kept her pregnant mares, a few days before they were due to foal. Instead of using a closed-circuit TV system to monitor their progress, like other top breeders, she preferred to install her mother, in a great brass bed, at one end. That way the old lady could sit up all night, watching the row of pink posteriors, and ring a hand-bell for assistance if she thought anything was amiss.

After we had admired every horse on the farm, we were taken into a hot kitchen at one side of the rambling farmhouse. There was a wood-stove, where a kettle steamed over an open firebox, and a big, oilcloth-covered table at which silent, exhausted farmhands, their clothes black with mud, sat eating. It was odd food, too. Mostly, it consisted of huge glass jars full of minced, pinky-grey meat and gobs of white fat: preserved pork from the farm's many pigs. And to go with this there was a paper feed-sack of bread so stale that it exploded when you bit it. We drank Pernod, and red wine, and strong coffee, and Cécile and Charlie talked all afternoon. They became such great friends that Cécile sold him the first of many future horses – two mares called Goguette and Hautaine – for a bargain price. We were still there in the evening, when a different jar of pork was brought up from the cellar. Charlie particularly relished this occasion because he went down with one of the farmhands to choose the jar. The cellar was lined, from floor to ceiling, with jars, all sparkling in the lamplight, and when the farmhand had selected one and taken it upstairs he was greeted with a great rush of incomprehensibly fast, irritable French from Cécile. He paled, and scuttled back for a different jar. Charlie never knew what had been wrong with the jar – they all looked pretty much the same, and the contents tasted equally smooth and

24

bland – but he liked to speculate that Cécile had maybe yelled: 'Not the pancreas, you dolt! I said testicles and ears!'

Neither of us could help wondering, rather naïvely, perhaps, why Cécile was not married, when she was so attractive. Besides, she had a particularly wonderful, rich laugh – the sort only a magnificently fulfilled woman would possess. And, after enough wine, Charlie brought the subject up. 'I will show you why I am not married,' Cécile said, leading the way to a part of the farmhouse that faced a field full of horses. She threw up the window, revealing a starlit night. Then she leaned forward and yelled, 'Fortiche!' There was a silence, broken only by the soft chomping of horses and an occasional squeal from the pigs. 'Fortiche!' she yelled again. And then we heard it. The drumming of hooves. At last, across the field came an enormous stallion, galloping at full tilt. He raced right up to the windows and skidded to a stop, nuzzling at Cécile's outstretched hand. 'There!' she said, turning to us. 'Wherever would I find a man to do that for me?'

Actually, to be strictly honest, after many more visits to her farm Charlie realised there was a man who could loosely be said to behave in a similar way to Fortiche. A formidable-looking suitor of Cécile's, who had to have had some standing locally, he was often to be found hoovering morosely in the smarter, carpeted end of the farmhouse, humbled to this subservient role by Cécile's abundant charms.

Charlie went to collect the horses, that first winter of our marriage, and when he returned and slipped back into my bed before dawn, wrapping me passionately in his chilled body, he told me he'd had a spooky experience. Despite my anxieties, and to make the costs of the trip more bearable, he'd also bought two mares for a friend in Yorkshire, and this meant that he had had a terrifically long drive back from France, up to Thirsk, and down again to the South West. He did the whole loop without a break, and as he finally approached the Dorset county boundaries it was the worst part of the night – three o'clock in the morning. It was not only very dark, but there was a thick mist coming off the coast, and he found himself struggling to keep awake. Suddenly he saw a man walking down the road in front of him. Wearing stout boots, leather gaiters and worn, brown corduroy trousers on his bandy legs, this person was, most eccentrically, carrying an inverted metal hip-bath on his head. Even though it was unlikely that he could see very well, he was walking confidently forward though the mist, his pace fast enough for Charlie to keep going behind him in second gear. Puzzled, but too sleepy to do anything about the man, Charlie just followed him through the narrow Dorset lanes, hardly aware of where he was going, but occasionally glimpsing a familiar landmark. After nearly an hour the man suddenly vanished. Charlie climbed out of the cab – and found himself in our farmyard, right outside the bungalow where we lived.

I was troubled by this story, but I reassured myself by thinking that maybe the hip-bath man was connected to that odd feeling of a kindly presence that Charlie sometimes got when he was ploughing alone out in the fields. A presence that would inspire him to readjust the setting of some rusty, half-seized-up ratchet on the plough – miraculously making the share bite deeper and the earth turn over more crisply. Perhaps the countryside was full of benign ghosts – of farmers and their animals – and I ought to expect to come across them on a regular basis.

Chapter Three

Family dinner at home: We were all sitting round the table, me hiding behind my long black hair, when my father started a fresh argument. He always won family arguments because he was ruthless and bright and had an overpowering personality. So, to enliven things, he had begun putting forward ridiculous arguments. 'Whenever a woman has an orgasm,' he said, beaming round at us, 'she ages visibly. Just a little, but it all adds up over time. That's why Englishwomen look so young for so long, and Scandinavian ones age so fast.' He chuckled delightedly because none of us could rebut the argument. My mother (who has always looked younger than she is) was baffled and helpless, and my sisters and I just couldn't summon the necessary factual resources to defeat him. Besides, I wasn't sure I'd ever had an orgasm.

'Have you started lambing, yet, George?' Charlie asked, before adding, 'Or is it just the way you are sat?' and bursting into laughter.

'I have indeed started lambing,' George said, gravely. 'And I've a present for Lucy, if she would like.' He frowned to himself, as if he was privately sure I would hate whatever he was about to offer. George had enormous dignity, and did not always appreciate teasing. He was an efficient, highly mechanised farmer who lived about half a mile away from us, down a long, cracked concrete drive. He slightly disapproved of Charlie's obsession with horses, but he could be exceptionally kind, too. And he was always dropping in for cups of coffee. It was a January morning, part-way through my first winter at Bettiscombe Home Farm. It had begun with a hard frost, and steam rose from his damp clothes as he sat close to the wood-burning Rayburn. There was a suspicious lump under his brown, stained coat, which I suspected was the present.

I'd been on the farm seven months now, and I was gradually getting used to rural gifts. The first had been a big cardboard box, which arrived one teatime and was left by the back door. It had come all the way from Exmoor, dropped in by friends of Charlie's who were in the area for a farm sale. When I opened it I found that it contained half a dozen bantam hens and a cockerel, packed tightly in together. They were fluffy, and the most beautiful pastel colours: cream, pale coffee, bluish grey – even something approaching strawberry blonde. But I only had a brief glimpse of them, because as soon as the box was opened they flew out, whizzed right over the top of the stable and vanished in the direction of a small spinney halfway up the hill.

So I had to go and confess to Charlie what I had done. He just sighed, and said we had to wait until the evening. When it got dark we set off for the spinney with a feed-sack and a torch, and looked for oval-shaped chicken silhouettes in the branches above us. Then Charlie hoisted me up so I was sitting on his shoulders, and I had to feel my way towards the bantams' legs, and seize them suddenly, before they could fly off. They gave a most piteous, hoarse cry as I grabbed them, which was strangely pleasurable to hear. When they were all caught we put them in a shed in the yard behind the bungalow and kept them penned up for a day, after which they always returned there to sleep, and were allowed to range freely around the farm.

They added a unique atmosphere to the place. I loved the way they minced fussily about, muttering to themselves in little high-pitched, croaky voices. The cockerel was a youngster, and only just learning how to crow, so each morning I would wake to the sound of him going 'cock-a-doodle-aaargh', and then falling silent, probably out of embarrassment. When the hens started laying they chose the most exciting places to do it, too: mangers full of hay that the horses were just about to eat, Charlie's mother's prize asparagus beds, or the insides of prickly bushes. Once I got into Charlie's car and found an egg rolling about in the passenger-seat footwell: one of the hens must have squished herself in through the partially opened window in order to place it there.

George unbuttoned his coat and drew out a tiny lamb, so small that he could cup it in his meaty hand. It was thin and bony, and covered in tight, greyish woollen curls, and it seemed half asleep. It cried miserably on being exposed to the dampish air of my kitchen, but even its cry was small: muffled and high-pitched, like an insect buzzing in a bottle. George explained that early that morning he had found a ewe in difficulty, with an extremely big lamb inside her. After he had helped her deliver it he had felt about inside her out of habit, and to his surprise discovered this creature, which must have been unfairly starved in the womb by its twin.

I tucked the lamb inside my jumper, while George explained that because it was so very weak it was highly unlikely to survive, and could certainly not be reared on the usual powdered milk substitute that orphan lambs were given. If I wanted to have a go at rearing it I would have to come down to his farm every morning and milk the mother ewe out. I hardly listened – I was so thrilled by the trusting way the lamb had snuggled up to me. I even loved the way she smelt: warm, greasy and slightly acrid, with a sweet base note that was similar to the aroma of roast lamb. I decided I would call her 'Samb'.

George had left me a full bottle of ewe milk, and for the whole of the rest of that day I heated up little bits of it and coaxed them down Samb's throat. At night, I put her in a cardboard box by the Rayburn, and I even found it enjoyable climbing out of bed every two hours in my nightie and giving her a feed. She would give her pitiful cry as I lifted her up, and because neither of us had much idea how to bottle-feed, we were soon both covered in dried-on milk and snot, and stiff to the touch.

I was a bit groggy the next morning (and crackled whenever I moved) as I took a jug down to George's farm. He was just finishing up his morning milking, and all around the parlour there were pens of sheep muttering to each other and making wrestling noises in the straw. Samb's mother was in an orchard to one side. George (who had clearly not slept or shaved since our last meeting) took me wearily over there, made a sudden grab for the ewe and, crouching down and holding her firmly with one hand, milked her into the jug with a practised movement of his thick, calloused fingers. It seemed easy.

It wasn't, of course. The next morning, when I went down with my jug, the sheep took one look at me and bolted, her saggy bum bouncing rudely up and down. She hid in a great mat of brambles, and when I got too close stamped her foot at me and squeezed herself even more tightly into the prickles. I had to fetch Charlie.

He had a different technique from George's. He believed in dragging a sheep backwards out of a bramble-bush and milking it in a sort of semi-upright stranded-beetle position, while it snorted with rage. Or rather, Charlie did the holding, while I actually squeezed milk into the jug. While I did this, I apologised to the ewe for putting her to such huge inconvenience, but she never forgave me. In fact, as Samb became fonder of me, day by day, so, by equal degrees, her mother came to abominate the very sight of my distant silhouette.

After three weeks we gave up bothering the ewe for milk – it seemed too unkind. And we mixed up dried powder for Samb instead. She soon began sucking so strongly that the teat shot right out of the bottle. When this happened all the milk would gush on to her head, and she would frisk round the kitchen, sucking air through the teat with a whistling noise. As she grew, so did her voice. It matured to a harsh coloratura, like Maria Callas at her worst, and she learned to push the kitchen door open in the middle of the night, fumble her way along dark passageways to my bed and blare 'Samb!' in my ear.

She followed me everywhere, walking just behind my right heel, so that she bumped softly into it, and if I lay down on the edge of a field, watching Charlie plough, she would climb on top of me and mumble at my face, leaving tiny wet patches. It was the first time I had ever been close to a farm animal, and I began to see why Charlie had such a deep relationship with his horses. I felt less lonely, too, because a great deal of life on the farm involved being on my own and watching Charlie do masculine jobs that I could not join in with. Having Samb was like having my own, wildly enthusiastic (if small) fan-club.

One of the few things I was instantly good at, though, was rounding up animals. The dogs were badly trained and did not know how to do this. (Their specialisms were fighting each other, stealing food, and sitting in front of hot fires, absorbing all the heat. This did not, however, stop Charlie and his parents congratulating them, on an almost hourly basis, on their goodness and intelligence.) Unlike the dogs, *I* understood and obeyed commands swiftly, and was eager to please. I could also run pretty fast. 'Over there!' Charlie would shout, waving his arms at one end of a field, and I would race round behind the sheep or the cows. 'No! Change direction, they're getting away from you!' and back I would whizz. Once, when the postman caught us doing this, he smiled approvingly, and said there was another couple on his rounds just the same, except the wife was in her eighties, and they used the proper sheepdog commands.

On this afternoon there was a thick mist. It rolled across the fields from the coast like a ghostly tide coming in, and within an hour it was up to my knees.

'Just what I wanted,' Charlie remarked mysteriously, going off to telephone. Later, he told me someone was coming to buy the cattle. And by the time they arrived the mist was almost as high as my shoulders, a damp, whitish soup from which cows' heads broke, confusedly, as they thundered out of the gorse bushes where they had been hiding. A tumbling, black and brown and gingery jumble of different breeds, they churned up the mud and flicked turf high in the air as I chased them down the side of the valley. Samb kept calling me whenever she lost touch, and enjoyed all the movement and agitation. Occasionally, through a fainter patch of mist, I'd see her bouncing joyfully into the air.

While the buyer singled out the cows he wanted it grew dark. We drove his purchases up the ramp of his lorry and invited him in for coffee. There was a hushed, Sunday-best feeling in the kitchen, and Samb responded to it by folding herself up neatly next to the fire and assuming a haughty, distant expression. I sensed that I was not supposed to say anything, and simply offered round fruit cake. (The buyer wouldn't have any: 'Got to keep some space for my wife's dinner. She's doing me a full roast in an hour,' he said, glancing at his watch. 'I can't stop long.')

Charlie was at his friendliest, and the buyer seemed flattered, in a startled way. He was a stout man with a pale, sweaty skin and unusually smart clothes for a farmer.

'Whisky?' Charlie asked, pouring a dollop into each cup of coffee. He sprawled the other side of the table, his arms and legs wide, and smiled sweetly. He had a good smile: innocent and guileless. His lips were generous and his whole mouth exceptionally wide and mobile, and when he smiled you saw the soft pink skin inside the corners and rows of perfect, almond-coloured teeth.

It was an odd conversation. Listless and stilted on the buyer's part, gently inquisitive on Charlie's. He was trying to draw the buyer out without being threatening or annoying. After a little delicate probing it emerged that the buyer was shyly interested in motorbikes, and Charlie revealed that he happened to have two in his workshop. 'It's lucky you're here,' he added. 'Because I could do with an unbiased opinion on one of them. Someone who knows what they're talking about and isn't ashamed to come right out and say what they think.' They disappeared, leaving their coffee half drunk. Two hours later, as the penned-up cows thumped impatiently against the sides of the lorry, and I was hauling logs in for the evening in half-decayed baskets that shed wicker hoops all over the floor, the two of them came back in. They were almost arm in arm, and the buyer was flushed with happiness and home-made cider. This time it was just straight whisky in the coffee cups, and the buyer recklessly stuffed a fistful of cake in his mouth before writing out a large cheque.

Charlie chuckled as the lorry wobbled back up the drive, its rear lights like two anxious red eyes. 'It always gets them,' he said. 'Asking for advice. You have to pitch it right, though. Ask them stuff that's too difficult and they feel stupid; too easy and they realise you are taking the piss. There's a real art to it.'

'Wouldn't it have been better if he had come on a clear day? He could have seen the cows properly, then.'

'Exactly!' Charlie unhooked two halters from the wall, and set off to bring Bob and Ben in. 'He wouldn't have bought them at all if he could see how rubbish they were. That's why I waited for mist. Twilight's almost as good. With the two together, we couldn't fail.'

I was shocked at myself for not being appalled. I knew how desperately short of money we were, though, and when I looked at that cheque I felt relief rather than guilt.

Chapter Four

Advice from my father:
Always keep your figure – you never know when you might need it.
Always earn your own money.
Always get your name on the title deeds of any house your husband buys.
Never get divorced – women and children are better off in a marriage.

The financial arrangements on the farm were very peculiar indeed. In fact, I could only bear to think about them from a distance, so when I had nothing else to do I'd climb the side of the valley – up a steep, marshy slope full of bracken and gorse, to where a grey stone the size of a small car jutted out. This was easy to scramble up and as comfortable as a carthorse to lie on, and known locally as 'the wishing stone'. Everyone said that wishes made on it came true: and I believed them, because I'd wished to marry Charlie there.

I didn't take Samb with me on this particular November day because I was finally weaning her. (Even I had had to agree that it was ridiculous bottle-feeding a nearly full-sized ewe.) The trouble was, that last small bottle meant so much to her. It was a real betrayal to stop it. Although she was now out in the fields with the other sheep she kept a sharp eye out for me and ran to the hedge, baaing, if she saw me, or even just part of me, like one arm, or the back of my head. It had got so I had to scuttle about on all fours when I was in the farmyard and dodge from shed to shed so as not to set off that terrible, agonised blaring. Often, it had an especially distressing, thick tone to it. I discovered why the first time I crept up on her unexpectedly. Her fat, woolly legs were firmly planted in a field while her face was buried in the hedge, and she was greedily stripping out wild flowers in between throwing back her head and wailing with a full mouth.

When I was sitting on the stone I could see a great deal of what was happening in the valley below – and hear most of it, too, because the air was so clear and still: whole snatches of conversation would sometimes float up intact. That day, eighteen months after our marriage, I was worrying about money as I watched Charlie standing in the sunken field where the horses were, a halter hidden behind his back. It was a sunny morning with threads of dew sparkling in the hedges, and all the pastures very fresh, as if seen through eyes newly washed by tears, and he was trying to get hold of one of the new French mares, so he could carry on breaking her in. He did not believe in catching horses by bribing them with sweets or buckets of feed – he felt that spoiled their tempers. Instead, he preferred to follow them slowly around a field until they let him slip a halter over their heads. Sometimes this took hours. His patience and gentleness were astonishing. Time after time, the horse he was after would wait until he got within touching distance, and then shy away with a naughty toss of its head and trot out of range. When that happened he would light up a cigarette, lean on the fence and watch it for a while, before quietly resuming his pursuit.

'Little tease. I'll get you in the end,' I heard him say softly, as he pinched out the end of his cigarette, and got up to try again. Hautaine – a strawberry-roan with a delicate head and porky thighs, who exactly fitted Reg's description of the perfect cart-horse: 'face like an angel, body like a barrel and girt big arse like a farmer's daughter' – turned her head to study him before ambling off. You could tell she had worked out, most precisely, what the safe distance was, and was keeping to it.

I could even see right into the walled garden at the back of the Manor, though there was nothing much going on there – just a gardener digging over a herbaceous border. On warm days Charlie's father, Michael, would be out under the fig tree, writing poetry at a little table. He took this very seriously indeed, and regularly published it himself in small booklets. Sometimes, too, he would put on staged events, at which his lines were read out in ringing Shakespearean tones, while mysterious, blurry photographs flashed on to a screen and dissonant music played. I'm afraid I had quite the wrong attitude to these performances because my sisters found them so paralysingly funny. They liked doing imitations of them, and whenever I went home one or other of them would suddenly pick up a tea-towel, fling it round her shoulders in a dramatic way and pretend to do a Pinney poetry reading, complete with arm-gestures and spooky music. Some days my sister Annabel would only get as far as putting on her 'Michael Pinney face' – sensitive, yet haughty – before falling about, snorting with laughter.

Billy was in the laundry yard beside the kitchen, scrubbing down the flagstones so vigorously that his thick blond hair shook. Above his head, striped dishtowels and silk knickers flapped in the wind.

There was a van parked by the railings at the front, which meant that the deliveryman from the local delicatessen was in the house. He arrived every fortnight and stood politely just inside the kitchen door with a notebook and pencil. 'Any bacon today, Madam?' he would enquire, a quizzical look on his raspberry-coloured face. 'Half a pound of the finest back? Thank you very much, Madam. Any lard today, Madam . . . ?' His bill was never paid. And it was a mystery to me why he did not seem to mind, and kept on visiting and delivering, year after year. But then, none of the servants was paid, either. The electricity and telephone companies were less understanding about the family's reluctance to pay bills. Quite regularly the Manor would be plunged into darkness, relieved only by the glimmer of candles from the delicatessen (which, fortunately, stocked almost everything a person of quality might want). At those times my mother-in-law would call at our bungalow and ask to see Charlie. They'd have a discussion that excluded me – as if financial matters had to be dealt with in a distant, patrician manner I was incapable of assuming – and afterwards I'd see that he had made out a cheque to her on his already disastrously over-drawn account. Or, if for some reason this was impossible, she would hurry away distractedly and, shortly after, Michael would climb into the car, an anxious expression on his beaky face, and set off up the drive in search of a friend he could touch up for a loan. Every other stratagem to raise money had already been tried – even Charlie's remaining cows were mortgaged to the hilt.

The situation had not always been so desperate – in fact, the Pinneys had once been wealthy. Michael came from a grand family, and often talked about his childhood, which had been spent with nannies in a nursery wing. The Christmas he was six he was allowed to have lunch with his parents, as a special treat. Unfortunately, the cook and butler were drunk. Michael was delighted to be served roast turkey with brandy butter on the side, but when it got to the Christmas pudding – which came with a horseradish sauce – he burst into tears and was sent back to the nursery in disgrace.

In the 1930s he had been left a large inheritance, which he spent on buying Bettiscombe, and the farms around it (all later sold off). It was a clever move: back then land had been so worthless you could snap it up for five shillings an acre. He and Betsy even furnished the house from local auctions, where antiques were going for nothing. They soon established them-selves as intellectuals and gave glamorous parties. Charlie told me that once, when he was a child, he listened at a door when Michael was entertaining Ted Hughes, and heard Hughes declare, in a voice hoarse with strain, that he had to return to Devon soon 'because the light in Dorset is simply too intense'.

Whenever I asked how the money had vanished I got slightly different answers. It had drizzled away gradually; it had been lost in a succession of ill-judged court cases against lawyers administering the inheritance; or pigs had consumed it. Apparently the farm had once been one vast outdoor piggery: the animals had succumbed to pneumonia and died in battalions, incurring a nightmarish debt. Charlie had even spent an entire school holiday, on a hired bulldozer, burying them. It was odd to think, looking round at the sloping fields, that the whole place was a pigs' graveyard.

I wished on the stone, squeezing my eyes up tight, that we could make a decent living out of the farm and be safe from debt. Opening them again, I couldn't see how we would do it. We didn't have any animals that could make us money – only a few sheep and horses, and though I'd got some severance pay when I left my job as a copy-editor in London, we wouldn't be able to live on that for ever. The very thought of money made me hot and restless because I'd been brought up in a family where it was considered so important.

My mother and father – who both worked – used to argue about it as they drove down to the West Country on Fridays: 'I paid the telephone bill, so that cancels out you paying for the wine, and I bought a brace of pheasants, so you owe me 2s 6d from Tuesday, when you got that lavatory paper . . .' They'd actually riffle through pockets and bags and hand change over to each other, count it out carefully and be cross if it was threepence short. So the Pinney casualness tormented me.

I knew there had to be a sound financial basis to the farm —
we had to make more cash and have less outgoings. But even if
we made it work, how would we stop Betty and Michael taking
the profits? They had such a strong influence over Charlie, and
they were convinced that anything he owned belonged to them,
too. Often, I'd find bananas or tinned food I'd bought mysteriously missing from my cupboards, and after a long, pointless
search, would discover from Charlie that 'the Manor had needed
them'. A month earlier I'd even burst into tears and begged him
to leave Bettiscombe altogether. When Betty and Michael got
wind of this they called us both in for a serious talk.

'Who would look after the farm if Charlie left?' they'd asked
sorrowfully. And Michael explained that we had a lifetime tenancy of the place, and so did any children we might have.

'So, you see, there's nothing to worry about,' Betty had
smiled. 'It'll all come right in the end. There *is* money — we just
can't get at it at the moment. It's only a matter of waiting until
all this business with the Birmingham solicitors is settled.'

Afterwards, when the men had gone, Betty and I had had one
of our intimate talks, while we made meringue doves, using an
icing nozzle. Whenever I had a go, producing something that
looked like a lop-sided duck, she'd lean forward and scoop it
back into the bag again.

'Almost good enough,' she'd say kindly. 'But you need to
develop an eye for detail.'

'Don't you get panicky about the finances?' I'd asked.

'I leave it all to Gaffer,' she'd said, as she sculpted two elegant
wings and stood back, puffing on a Gauloise, to admire them.

'He has a very balanced attitude to life. Besides, I did a dreadful thing to him once, and he forgave me. I don't feel I have a right to criticise him.'

I didn't have the courage to ask Betty for details of the dreadful thing. She wasn't the sort you challenged easily. Behind her frail exterior was the steeliest will, and I was beginning to doubt whether I'd ever be able to unravel Charlie's finances from hers and Michael's.

The second inescapable truth about marrying a farmer: they have no money. The money is in the land, which, for obvious reasons, cannot be sold. They wouldn't be farming then, would they? If there is any money produced from keeping animals it is generally snaffled by the folk mentioned in Inescapable Truth No. 1. (The parents.)

The van had gone when I next glanced down, and Charlie had caught Hautaine and was walking her to the stable. For days he'd been harnessing her and making her drag an old telegraph pole backwards and forwards across the meadow, just to get her used to the idea of pulling a weight.

An unfamiliar noise started up, somewhere in the distance. I couldn't see where it was coming from, even though I stood up and carefully scanned the valley. It sounded as if someone was turning a rusty wheel slowly and monotonously. Charlie had heard it, too. He took the mare into the stable, and then ran out, towards his workshop. The noise grew louder, sounding more like a multiple chorus of yelps, but I still could not see what was making it. Charlie came out of the workshop pushing one of his trials bikes. He started it up with a roar, only getting properly hunched down in the saddle as he bounced over the ruts at the entrance to the field nearest our bungalow. Then he was off up the grass track, his loose jacket puffing out like a cushion in the wind.

I suddenly saw what he was heading for. A mass of cream and brown dogs had appeared over the skyline and was streaming towards the field in the middle where the sheep were. They yelped as they ran. Samb might be in danger! I jumped off the stone and began running down the hill towards the sheep.

I glanced up to see what was happening whenever I could, though the going was so rough that I had to pay attention as I jumped over marshy bits criss-crossed by springs, and tore my way through brambles and gorse. The dogs were in the sheep field when I next looked, and the sheep bunched convulsively, a cloudy mass against the green pasture. Then they broke into clumps and scattered along the hedgerows, but the dogs didn't chase them for long. They streamed through the field and across the hedge the other side, making for a little wood halfway up the valley.

Some horsemen had appeared now, at the very edge of the farm. They were wearing black jackets and black hats, and I saw a flash of scarlet at the back. It was the hunt. And I could see, too, that Charlie was aiming to cut them off as they made for the hounds. The hounds had reached the wood now, and slipped inside, though a few ran in and out, appearing and reappearing, like bees working a hive.

I'd reached a hedge and had to run up and down it, looking for a gateway, and couldn't see anything at all for a while, though I heard a hunting horn. When I was through, and on short, nibbled grass, untidily scattered with sheep droppings and bits of wool, Charlie was not that far away. He was on a rise two fields off, talking to the huntsmen, and two of them had dismounted. The dogs were streaming back and running round the group, and there was something distinctly unfriendly about the body language of the humans. One of the horsemen in black jackets was dangerously close to Charlie, his thoroughbred horse fidgeting and dancing underneath him, its tail held high. Charlie had got off his bike, and was pointing back towards the edge of the farm, when there was a crackle and Samb forced herself through a hedge, and bounced towards me across the grass. She stopped to pee with happiness at the sight of me, then butted my leg hard.

'I haven't got anything for you. I'm so sorry.' I bent down and cuddled her, but she wasn't pleased and kept shoving at my leg with her head, and bleating insistently.

As I crossed into the next field, with her following, I saw two ewes lying up against the hedge, breathing heavily. The rest were bunched up in the far corner. I was climbing the gate into the field where the men were, when the conversation there seemed to come to an abrupt end. Charlie shouted (it sounded like 'f★★★ off') and the tall horseman in black, who had been looming above him, leaned down, raised his whip, and struck Charlie across the face. Then the hunt turned and trotted off towards the farm boundary and it wasn't long before they all rode out of sight over the rim of the valley, and there were just a few straggling dogs left. Even those had gone by the time I'd run up to Charlie.

He was standing, gazing after them and clutching his cheek.
'Bastards!' he said.

'Why did they do that?' I asked, horrified.

'Because I told them I didn't want them hunting across the farm.' He took his hand away and looked at his palm. 'Is it bleeding?'

'No, but it looks very red.'

'I've told them over and over again not to come here, but they don't take any notice. So bloody arrogant. They think they can do what they like. The other farmers round here don't dare tell them to get lost: they're too scared. The hunt are so powerful; lots of them are JPs. It's too easy to find yourself up in court against one of them.'

Samb butted my leg again. It reminded me. 'There are two sheep back there lying down. D'you think they are all right?'

Charlie rubbed his cheek again. 'Unless we're very lucky the sheep will miscarry now they've been chased, and all we'll get out of them will be soup and bones. It's not as if the hunt ever say they're sorry, or offer compensation. They're like the bullies at my school. Sods.'

Whenever he felt particularly angry about something he would always compare it to school. He'd been sent to a boarding prep school when he was only seven, and found himself in the hands of the sort of people who punished children if they wet the bed in distress. It was a subject he rarely discussed, but it had clearly had a savage effect on his personality. He'd discovered early on that the only way to survive was to hide his feelings completely and never, ever cry. It seemed odd that

Betty, who obviously loved him, had been able to bring herself to do this to him, but it was simply what her family did. Charlie – and his brother and sisters – had had to go to boarding school to learn stoicism and independence. I found her attitude hard to sympathise with because my own parents had gone to boarding schools. They'd both hated it so much that they'd sworn bitter oaths never to send any of their children there. So I – along with my brother and sisters – was sent to an ordinary day school (which was quite bad enough).

'I can't believe it,' my mother said, sitting in my kitchen, looking doubtfully at the deep brown tea I'd made her. She preferred the scented, dishwater variety. 'You must be mistaken. I know the people in the hunt and they would never behave like that.'

'But they did – I saw them.'

'Well, there has to be another explanation, then.'

She decided to risk it, took an experimental sip, and then peeled a dog hair from her tongue and placed it politely in the saucer. Ever since I'd married she'd got in the habit of bringing parties of friends round, without warning, to admire Bettiscombe. I found it difficult to cope with, because I couldn't quite get a grip on housekeeping. It wasn't that my mother's house was that tidy – but unless I made a huge effort mine was horribly messy: full of dogs, mud and little animals. Charlie hated the intrusion. He'd smile charmingly at her, apologise for being too busy to stay, and scarper.

This time my mother and her friend, a novelist, had been invited into the Manor and given a ghost tour. The Manor was famously haunted. Honoured visitors were always shown into the little front parlour, where Michael would pull an old shoe-box out of a cupboard and open it with a flourish to reveal a human skull. Then he'd explain how, according to legend, if anyone ever took it out of the house the skull would scream, the house would fall down and the person responsible would die.

'One Hallowe'en,' Betty would add, between drags on a Gauloise, 'I came home from shopping to find a photographer on the porch. He'd talked Billy into letting him hook the skull over one of the iron railings, and he was taking pictures. I was furious. I stole up behind him and said quietly: "Do you realise you'll be dead within the year?" ' She always took another lengthy puff before concluding. 'We didn't know his name, so we never found out if he *did* die.'

Betty was small, white-haired, bent, and cadaverously thin, so being tapped unexpectedly on the shoulder by her would be alarming in itself. While her audience was still visualising the scene, Michael would launch into a scholarly history of the skull. (It was rumoured to have belonged to a slave, but had probably been dug up from the Iron Age fort up the road.) I was always more interested in the other hauntings. There were ghosts bowling skittles in the attic; and a horse-drawn funeral cortege that rumbled down the drive on moonlit nights and waited by the front door, complete with the sounds of harness and carriage creaking, and horses stamping and blowing. But it was the little touches that unsettled most. Betty liked to spend wet afternoons refurbishing an Edwardian doll's house in a room beside the back staircase, and she said she often heard phantom children playing softly outside: a sound that she found both comforting and peaceful.

Charlie came in to fetch a halter, and left again hurriedly.

'He's not Betty and Michael's son, is he?' my mother's friend said.

I was taken aback. 'Why do you say that?'

'Because his eyes are brown. Theirs are blue. Blue's a recessive gene.'

'Mmm,' my mother said. 'There was talk when Charlie was born. Betty used to take him out in his pram, and I remember hearing that when people asked her if she thought he looked like Michael she'd say "Of course not! Michael isn't his father." But she had a sophisticated sense of humour, so no one took it very seriously.'

Chapter Five

My father talked about an old countryman he used to know, whose parents had, as the rural custom was then, indulged in 'bundling' when they were courting – i.e. petting in a bed, fully dressed, with a bolster between them. He was conceived during one of these thrillingly frustrating sessions and, later in life, when he became maudlin about his lack of success, he'd remark, 'Well, what do you expect? I was strained through a sheet.'

It was past midnight and I'd just finished work. Unable to bear the money-anxiety a moment longer, I'd got myself a weekend job at the pub at the top of the road. After I'd changed sheets and cleaned upstairs rooms for bed and breakfast visitors I'd pull pints, but it gave me a dismaying insight into village life. Neighbours I'd always thought of as sweet old countrymen became alarmingly grumpy and obscene when I was serving them across a bar with a low-cut shirt on.

I put my bag down and peered over the gate into the front garden. As I'd suspected, there was an enormous dark shape the other side. It finished urinating and gave a small, soft grunt of satisfaction. Then it wandered slowly up the path, the light spilling from the kitchen's frosted window revealing its body to be ginger with a metallic gleam along the backbone. This was our Tamworth pig, Henrye. Charlie had given her to me as a present back at the end of the summer, but she had such a genius for escaping that, so far, she had spent remarkably little time on the farm.

The first day she arrived, as a small, naked-looking creature, only just weaned, we put her in a loose box beside the stable. This had an unusually pretty floor made of blue and pink bricks arranged in a herringbone pattern. We gave her a dish of scraps and a bowl of water, and she looked so forlorn that I put in a blanket as well, and an old golliwog of Charlie's (which Betty had given me as a memento).

When we checked on her a few hours later, we found that she had bitten the golliwog in half, eaten most of his wool stuffing, rootled up the floor, dug a neat, piglet-sized tunnel – and vanished. Although we searched the farm, we did not hear any more news of her until a week later, when Betty gave a smart tea party, and all the guests arrived twittering with excitement because they had seen a bizarre animal at the top of the drive. When they described it as being red and moving horrifyingly fast, we knew it was Henrye. (The name had been chosen by Charlie to tease Betty, who had a close female friend called Simone.)

Over the next few months we never managed to see Henrye ourselves, but we heard plenty about her. The local bee-keeper described a charmingly friendly piglet that had frisked up to him when he'd been mending a skep, and other neighbours said they'd surprised her eating their compost heaps. At last Charlie heard about a farmer two villages away who regularly regaled his friends with stories about the small wild boar that lived on a hill with his sheep. By the time we managed to corner Henrye and drive her into a borrowed cattle-lorry she was considerably bigger. So Charlie decided the safest place to put her was the garden of the bungalow. There was no way she could get out, because it was walled with a small latched gate in one corner. Besides, it was very neglected, and badly needed digging. 'It's perfect timing,' Charlie exclaimed. 'Why not get animals to do all the boring jobs we can't be bothered with ourselves?'

So we ushered the hefty adolescent Henrye in, built her a makeshift shelter under the only tree and left her to it. The first week she dug very industriously, truffling up a wide hole under the tree. She even pulled out all the couch grass and dock roots, and laid them on the path in an untidy – if workmanlike – heap. The postman was most impressed. The next week she was marginally less active. She simply occupied herself with finishing off the edges of her hole in a thoughtful, professional manner. At the beginning of the third week she rolled herself into the hole and fell into a deep slumber. And we realised that all she had been doing, the whole time, was *making herself a bed*. Thereafter, she only got up to go to the lavatory noisily by the gate, or to whiffle her nose in through the cat flap in the kitchen door, looking for treats. As time went on, and locals began calling in to look at the mess she had made and have a good laugh at our expense, she grew quite irritable about the intrusion and would lurch to her feet menacingly whenever she heard the gate squeak open. She never hurt anyone, but she certainly deterred visitors from the Manor from calling, and my bananas were safe at last.

I unlatched the gate and walked up the path, and Henrye wandered over, grunting, and sniffed – playfully, with her mouth open, as if thinking about biting – at my leg. I bent down and scratched her behind the shoulder blade, and she stood stiffly, with her snout up, relishing the experience. Her eyes closed in pleasure, so that they no longer sparkled in the light from the door.

I always envied farm animals their ability to lose themselves in the moment and get the most fun out of every experience, however trivial. They were especially good at lazing around. I felt mysteriously jealous whenever I saw the bantam chickens contorting themselves into strange shapes in the dust at the edge of the yard, getting extreme sensual pleasure from even the tepid rays of a November sun. I couldn't enjoy doing nothing myself: I always felt I had to jump up and bustle about, improving the farm or earning money.

Henrye's hair was extremely coarse, her skin was scurfy and she was getting wattles of fat round her neck. They trembled like jelly as I scratched. She gave off the sweet, warm scent of a pig kept on straw, and I could see Charlie had given her a fresh bale for her nest in the hole under the tree. A gust of laughter came from the kitchen. Charlie must have friends in.

When I'd left the house in the morning, he'd been on the hill breaking a horse, and I'd felt the usual worry about leaving the place unlocked. No one in Bettiscombe believed in locks. They never had. In fact, no one in the entire Marshwood Vale seemed to worry about being burgled or about psychopaths creeping up on them while they slept. Coming from London, I found their breeziness in this area quite unacceptable. After a few weeks in the bungalow, I discovered an old key that fitted the front door and started locking it. This lasted until I went off shopping one morning, leaving a note (and lunch) for Charlie on the kitchen table. When I got home the door was as securely locked as when I had left, but Charlie had eaten all the cheese and written on the bottom of my note, in his spidery handwriting: 'What is the point of writing this when I can't get in to read it?'

To save him having to force a window each time he wanted to have lunch, we compromised: I would lock the door, but leave the key on a hook in the stable. His friends soon got to know where the key was, and not only let themselves in whenever they wanted, but even took to absent mindedly wandering off with the key still in their pockets. So I had to get more keys cut, and in the end so many assorted ruffians in the area had the key to our bungalow that I might as well not have bothered with security at all.

I was just getting tired of scratching when I remembered the sheep. They were on the point of lambing, and Charlie had said they needed to be checked regularly. I'd do that first, before going in the kitchen. So I walked down to the lower yard, which had been turned into a maternity ward. We had two varieties of sheep: some had bony, curved foreheads, with ears set well back, giving them a noble – even intellectual – air, like distinguished Oxford dons. The others had stupidly low, curly brows and looked as if they were wearing fluffy pantaloons and high-heeled shoes. Both kinds bulged and sagged with unborn lambs, and each morning the yard where they were penned was littered with half-masticated hay that had been spat out of almost completely toothless mouths. (Charlie could only ever afford to buy the cheapest sheep in the market – the ones other farmers had rejected as too old.)

As I climbed in with the ewes I saw that the hay in the feeders had run out and the water-buckets were dry. A haughty-looking intellectual with one swollen cauliflower ear dipped her head into one of the buckets and licked the side thirstily as I approached. She lifted her head and looked directly into my eyes, as if willing me to give her more water. Samb was in the shed, too, but when she saw me she turned her head away. She was finding it very hard to forgive me for weaning her.

I quickly fetched more hay, but filling the buckets took longer, and I slopped water all over my shoes. When I had finished I walked among the ewes, looking for any that might be in trouble. Most were lying down comfortably in deep straw, chewing the cud. A couple had already lambed, and been singled off from the rest in neat pens made out of wooden pallets and baler twine. Their lambs were tiny, with legs like knobbed sticks. They trembled, backs bowed, and wool still slightly damp, against the flanks of their mothers, and the ewes got up and stood protectively over them, their eyes fierce. A ewe in the back made a low, conversational noise that sounded like 'bleugh'.

Over in the far corner a woolly-bloomered sort with a bramble trailing off her head was looking miserable. Her head was down, she was taking deep breaths, and every now and then she gave a sound halfway between a groan and a scream. Something black was sticking out of her rear end; it bobbed in and out as she strained. A sheep I could help! I'd recently been on a lambing course in the village hall, to prepare for a moment like this. Along with other farmers' wives, I'd taken it in turns to push my hand inside a sheep made out of a plastic drum, with a bit of rubber tubing standing in for a vagina. Inside had been two freshly dead lambs floating in soapy water, and you had to get them into the correct position (front legs outstretched, head flat on top, as if about to do a dive) by feel only before pulling them through the tube. It had been easy. The instructor had given us loads of useful tips, too (the most bizarre being to use 'any old vibrator we had hanging about the farmhouse' to widen the cervix if the sheep got 'ring-womb' and it didn't open naturally). And he had been stern about cleanliness, so I washed my hands thoroughly at the yard tap before rubbing lubricant over them in the correct manner. Then I pushed the ewe right into the corner, so she was trapped, and knelt in the straw behind her. I screwed up my nerve – and eased my hand gently into her vagina, next to that black thing, which looked hard and shiny and was probably a little cloven hoof.

It was the first time I had ever been inside a real sheep. There was no room at all – I really had to force my way in. And, surprisingly, it did not smell bad. I shut my eyes and tried to visualise what was going on in there. If it was a hoof, was the leg it was attached to a front or back one? I couldn't find a tail when I eased my hand beyond what was definitely one leg. But then I couldn't feel a head, either. Just a mass of something that was covered in slime and wool; and it was quite hard to feel even that, things were so impossibly squished up in there. The sheep kept flinching, and trying to struggle away, too, and I hated hurting her. She gave deep groans, and her sides clenched convulsively.

The wet wool went on and on until it suddenly dropped away, and I found an assortment of legs, all pressed together at different angles. The sheep cried out in despair, and I felt like doing the same. As my fingertips explored the woollen lump again they slipped into a sort of crevice. There were tiny teeth inside and they bit me. It did not hurt, but there was an edge of hostility there. The mouth was clearly annoyed by my fingers. A mouth! That meant that something in there was alive. I moved backwards and discovered a soggy nodule that could have been an ear, but no matter how hard I concentrated, I could not work out how the legs went, and who they belonged to. The sheep struggled and bounded sideways and my arm popped out wetly. It became freezing cold almost at once. 'I'm sorry,' I said to her, as she pressed herself into a group of other expectant mothers. When her face was securely hidden among all their woolly legs and stomachs she stopped moving, no doubt imagining that she was invisible. 'So very sorry to have bothered you. I'll fetch someone who knows what they are doing.'

I raced back to the house. Henrye snuffled at the back of my legs as I flung open the door. The small kitchen was full. There was a warm heap of dogs beside the stove, guns, boots and ammunition piled beside the door, and every chair was occupied by a muddy stranger. A shout went up as I appeared. They had obviously been there for hours: smoke hung in layers in the air; there were cold cups of tea on the table, and all that remained of the cake I had baked that morning was a few crumbs.

'There's a fish for you in the sink,' Charlie called out. I looked round. An enormous brownish fish lay there, so long that its tail poked right out of the sink, wound through the dirty cups and plates and finished up in the soap dish. It had rows of evil-looking teeth.

'It's a pike,' he added.

One of the other men in the kitchen mumbled shyly: 'We catch them when we get the salmon and no one wants to buy them.' He didn't look directly at me, and I realised with dismay that, yet again, just by being there, I had spoiled the party. They were already starting to shift in their chairs and look round for their guns. It was difficult socialising with Charlie's male friends because they did not feel comfortable talking to women. (It wasn't just me: one local farmer put his hands over his ears and screwed up his eyes whenever his wife spoke.) Often, they would not reply at all if I asked them a question: pretending they hadn't heard. And if they did answer, they did so with such dismay that it seemed unkind to force them to make further conversation. So generally I would listen with my back turned –

while doing something feminine and housewifely like making dough – and act as if I was hardly there at all.

'There's a sheep in trouble,' I said to Charlie. 'And it feels all peculiar inside her. I can't work out what is going on.'

'Put the kettle on, I'll be back,' he said, and got up.

I followed him. Nothing much seemed to have happened since I had gone, except that the ewe was now grinding her teeth and the foot had slipped back inside. Charlie did not bother to wash. He just squeezed a huge amount of lubricant on to one palm. I held the ewe by the head, while he deftly felt about inside. 'F***ing tight,' he said quietly. And then: 'Twins. First one is big, and it's got a leg back.' He explored some more, and pushed his arm deep inside until it was buried up to the armpit. The sheep gave a high-pitched blare and tried to leap away. I grabbed her by her wool and she snorted phlegm into my skirt. Then there was a grunt from Charlie, and a lamb slithered out on to the straw. It had a jet-black head, and it steamed in the cold night air, its eyes wide open, with a faint look of terror, as if it had just come from the underworld. Charlie wiped its nose with a wisp of straw and put it by the ewe's head. Then he sat down beside me and lit a roll-up. 'Better see if she can get the other one out by herself,' he said, settling down for a wait.

The new lamb shook its head so its ears slapped together wetly, and the ewe nuzzled it, giving a throaty purr that sounded like a faulty hairdryer being switched on. The sight of them bonding so lovingly reminded me of Charlie's doubtful family background.

'Did you ask your mother?' I said.

Charlie looked at me enquiringly before turning to the ewe: 'Come on, lick the lamb, you silly old fool.'

'You know, about your father,' I prompted. 'You said you were going to see her today.'

Charlie sighed. 'She says it's true. He was a friend of Gaffer's called Jordie. He and Gaffer met in the desert, when they were both fighting against Rommel. Jordie didn't have anywhere to go when he was demobbed, so Gaffer suggested he came back and lived here. And he and Ma fell in love. She said she remembered looking out of an upstairs window and thinking how much she fancied him.'

I struggled to imagine Betty having a passionate love affair, and failed. It wasn't because I didn't think she was lovable, but because she looked so very old. And she'd conceived Charlie in her forties, which seemed ancient to me. 'Did she say how it ended?'

'Not really. Only that she ran away with him and came back when she'd had me. I think they both thought I'd have a better life if I was brought up here.'

It was obvious Charlie didn't really want to talk about it, but I did. I ventured one last question. 'Are you going to see your real father?'

He pinched out his cigarette and got up. 'Come on, fatty,' he said to the ewe. 'I can tell you're determined not to squeeze that lamb out.' He bent down and felt inside. There was a costive, faraway look in his eyes. I'd seen the same expression when he was adjusting the fan-belt deep inside his car. 'It won't be difficult to find him,' Charlie said suddenly. 'He only lives five miles away.'

Charlie and I sat at a table in the smoky corner of a Bridport pub holding hands. Every so often the door would flap open, letting in a stranger and a rush of cold air, and we'd look up through a mass of tightly packed bodies to see if it was Jordie. I couldn't imagine what it would be like to discover that the person you had thought of as your dad all your life – wasn't. My whole identity was bound up in who my dad was. I idolised him, even though he could be a bully at times. When I'd been a teenager, I'd wanted to be exactly like him. He was famously successful with women; so I had lots of boyfriends. As I got older I wanted to be a writer like him – though I ended up working for a publisher instead. And I always loved it when anyone said my eyes looked like his or I told a story the way he did. In countless ways I tried to please him and live up to what he was.

Michael was a good father, too, though his style was very different from my dad's. He was tender, and loving, and always called Charlie 'darling' – which I thought odd and unmanly – and had always treated him like the other children in the family. How torn Charlie must be feeling.

'Do you know what he looks like?' I asked.

'Yes. At one time he was around quite a lot. A big bloke with black hair. I always liked him – and it was funny, I felt close to him, too, without knowing why.'

'What does he do for a living?'

'Sells animal medicines.'

The door opened again and Charlie half-rose, then sat down again, disappointed. 'He's a salesman. But he used to run Revelshay, the farm just down from Bettiscombe.'

'What happened to him after he stopped being with your mum?'

'I'm not sure. I haven't managed to find out exactly. I think he farmed for a bit, and then he moved to Bridport and got married and had children.

A voice said, 'Charlie?' delightedly, and Jordie was in front of us. He was a tall, heavy-set man with a low, carefully combed black quiff, and a face I instantly warmed to: vulnerable and merry. He had the air of a much-loved stand-up comedian, anxiously awaiting that first laugh that would restore his confidence. He raised his eyebrows at us. They were exactly the same as Charlie's: finely drawn, long and tapered. His nose was the same shape, and his forehead. As they waited at the bar for their drinks they looked oddly identical, like a cartoon showing the ageing process with, on one side, a long-haired, thin, triangular-torsoed youth, and on the other a lined, mature man, with a hint of a belly.

I could tell that Charlie was longing for a silence to fall so he could broach the subject of his paternity, but Jordie kept relentlessly telling silly jokes and puns. Everyone in the pub seemed to know and like him, and he stopped mid-flow to call to a crowd at the other end of the mirrored bar and offer them drinks. After a few moments, they came back and sat down, making light conversation.

'Have you tried fixing the grandfather clock at the Manor yet?' Jordie asked.

'It's hopeless' Charlie answered. 'Sometimes I can get it to work for a bit – I don't know what I'm doing wrong. Maybe it needs rebalancing, or tilting at an angle.'

'I spent a whole summer fiddling with the blasted thing. Never got anywhere,' Jordie reminisced.

I cleared my throat. 'Charlie said you used to live at the farm just down from Bettiscombe.'

'Mmm. I ran it with Michael for years.'

'Why did you leave?' I asked timidly.

'A financial problem. They had to sell it in a hurry.' He giggled. 'As you've probably discovered, they run into these trifling difficulties from time to time.'

That was the closest we got to anything personal. After that he just cracked more jokes and bought us more and more drinks, and left in a haze of cigar smoke, saying he was expected home for lunch. When he'd gone it felt as if the sun had just gone down.

'What a lovely man,' I sighed. 'I can see why you always felt there was something special about him.' I knew it was disloyal, but I preferred him to Michael.

'Yes,' Charlie agreed, gazing at the door Jordie had left by.

Chapter Six

Letter from Caky: 'As you know, I'm now working for the John Lewis Gazette, and I spent all last weekend writing a carefully researched article about the late John Lewis, grandfather of the present Chairman. I had to suppress most of the information known about him. He used to sack on sight any shop assistant with fair, curly hair (they would cower behind the counters when he came in), and he'd drive down from Hampstead in his coach and pair and go through the pig-bins at the hostel where his assistants lived. Any piece of meat he felt had been unjustly thrown out, he'd retrieve and send up to be served again in the canteen. Well, my article was a masterpiece of whitewashing, but, when shown to the Chairman, it provoked a vituperative two-page memorandum: I hadn't been fair to the old boy, shouldn't we emphasise the nice side of his character, etc.'

Hearing about my sisters' new careers was unsettling. Annabel had joined the BBC and Caky was a journalist, and here I was, two years on, in an increasingly tattered, muddy coat, cutting my hair myself, and still trying to grasp the basic principles of farming. I suppose I was now slightly more confident about lambing – provided it was an easy problem – and I could herd horses in and out of fields on my own. (Charlie had told me not to worry if they charged me, as carthorses hated squashing humans underfoot and always turned aside at the last minute. It did seem to be true.) But it was always a worry when he went off anywhere and left me in charge of the farm – because the unexpected and bizarre always dished me. And when things go wrong on a farm they do so in squirmingly horrible ways.

That day in early February when Charlie went off to market with a load of calves started out fine, for instance. I let the chickens out and shook down hay for the horses in the stable. And then I set off across the fields to have a look at the mares, Hautaine and Ironie, who were in a sheltered field behind the Manor, waiting to foal. It was a lovely place for them, sheltered by overgrown hedges full of beech and oak and hazel, and with a little spring that bubbled across the grass in one corner.

It was difficult to tell how close a horse was to foaling, but Charlie did not think either of these two were very near. He had told me that they had not got swollen teats yet, and they had not 'waxed up' either (got gummy stuff on their nipples). I bent down and peered at their undersides, just in case, although I had no idea what I was supposed to be looking for.

After that, I wandered uphill and had a go at counting the sheep – something else I was no good at. They moved all the time, and they never lined themselves up neatly. So my total kept coming up different. The only way to get them to stay still was to lecture them. If I stood on a high point – like a gate, or the top of a round silage-feeder – and talked very loudly, they would stop whatever they were doing and gaze at me with a look of good-humoured wonderment. And it was, actually, an excellent way of honing my skills as a public speaker because, after few minutes, one or two would inevitably become restless and start to turn away. If I let them get away with it, the others would do the same. So I had learned to pick on the fidgety ones and stop the rot fast. 'What do you think you are doing?' I would shout, pointing at them. 'Yes – I do mean you, with the clods of mud dangling from your bum, standing over by that tree.' When I did this, they would turn and stare at me with a vaguely shifty expression, and stop moving. It was just a bit difficult to give a really interesting speech while counting, but I did my best.

The only problem with this method was that sometimes George's head would pop up above one of the hedges dividing our farm from his. He would gaze at me with no particular expression on his face, though I was sure he was wondering inwardly whether I was deranged – before giving a neighbourly nod and disappearing again.

This morning's talk was about Charlie's visit to market. 'So,' I ended. 'If you could please arrange to do absolutely nothing today? No mass breakouts, no getting stuck upside down in blackthorn bushes, no mystery ailments?' I made it 184, which it always was without Samb and her twin grown-up daughters, and then patrolled the hedges looking for these three. They were grazing happily on George's land and seemed a bit miffed to be caught, although Samb gave me her usual blare of greeting, muffled by a mouthful of greenery. I was just chivvying them back in with the others when I heard a piercing cry from the farmyard. It wailed on and on, and it seemed to be coming from the pigs.

Feeding these was supposed to be my next job. They were Henrye's latest offspring, and they were fattening in an airy, concrete-floored shed. It had an odd drain down the middle, which ended in a square hole opening on to the yard. The hole was roughly the size of an extra-large tub of margarine, and the pigs liked pushing their noses down it and sniffing the sunshine and fresh air that came through. They also enjoyed whiffling stray potatoes and bits of bread along the central drain and in and out of this hole, in a porcine version of golf. You could often hear them doing it in the afternoons, encouraging each other on with little grunts and slaps.

I ran back over the hill and instantly saw something moving in the yard beside the pig-shed. It looked like a paper-bag fluttering in the wind, but as I got closer I realised it was a head. A piglet's head, protruding from the drain. It was a male piglet: I knew this because:

1) Male baby animals were always the ones that got into trouble.
2) When I looked inside the shed there was a plump little male backside sticking out from the wall, like a stuffed trophy.

The other piglets were highly amused by this development.

Some of them were charging around in excitement, biting their straw bedding and tossing it in the air. And some were snuffling and licking at the trapped pig's legs. Each time they did this he squealed louder. He was making an incredible sound. It felt as if someone was slicing into my brain with a circular saw.

The problem was – as I realised when I knelt down beside that panicky, sweaty little head – that the drain was so tight that squeezing through in the first place must have been a job requiring quite exceptional effort and determination. And what had made it possible was that, at the time, his ears had been pointing backwards, giving his head a streamlined look. Now, of course, they weren't. They were also red and puffy from being squidged through the drain. I tried pushing the piglet back but nothing moved; he was stuck too fast. All that happened was that he opened his eyes and screamed even more dementedly than before. So I dropped the idea. If pushing was out, so, too, was doing nothing, because the piglets inside, realising that their trapped brother could not retaliate, were snapping at his legs and bum a lot less playfully.

Food. That was what I needed. I ran off and filled a bucket with pig-mash and warm water and tipped it into their trough, and then I sat down beside the trapped head and tried spooning little bits of mash into its screaming mouth. It did not really calm him much. I would never have thought it possible, but this did seem to be one of those rare occasions on which a pig did not feel peckish. I even put segments of crumbled-up chocolate biscuit on his tongue, and he was not interested in those, either. They fell out untasted. Beads of sweat rolled off his skin as he squealed on and on. And a crimson flush of rage suffused his neck and head when the other piglets, having finished their food, began biting his legs again.

I gave them more mash – and then more – until they just looked at me cynically when I appeared with a bucket, before laying about their brother with heavy, bulging stomachs. I leapt into the pen and began shooing them away with a brush. Outside, the piglet screamed, never seeming even to pause for breath. 'Please come back, Charlie, Please come back,' I said to myself, over and over again. In the end I put the brush down, climbed out of the pen and sat down beside the piglet, completely defeated. I stroked his head affectionately. It didn't stop the squealing, but it made me feel better.

When Charlie got back he solved the problem in thirty seconds. I do not know what he did, because I was inside, pulling on the piglet's legs as instructed, but there was an extra-loud squeal and then the little chap popped through, fell back on the floor, shook himself and trotted off to eat some mash. After five minutes you could not tell him apart from the others. The silence was incredible, though I could not immediately hear what Charlie was saying. I seemed to have gone a bit deaf. I hit my ear with the flat of my hand to clear it.

'Have you checked the mares?' he asked again.

'Not for a while.' He turned and ran for the field. 'They were fine last time I looked, though,' I called after him.

When I caught up he was kneeling in the corner where the spring ran over the grass. There was a little foal there, and its head was resting limply on his hand.

'Hautaine's foaled,' he said. His voice trembled. 'She went and had it in the one place where she shouldn't. It drowned in the spring. In two bloody inches of water.' Hautaine was standing near him. She bent her head and sniffed uncomprehendingly at the foal. 'And it was a filly, too, damn it.'

The next day the weather changed. Snow began falling from a grey sky. It matched our mood. Everything seemed utterly hopeless. I felt unbearably guilty that I had not broken off from the pig problem to check the mares again. Charlie felt terrible for stopping to have a pint in the market pub. Things were not helped by George, who sat down heavily in his usual chair by the fire and, when we brought up the subject of the foal, told us a long, grief-stricken tale about a calf. The gist of it was that, the previous week, he had been up and down, calving and lambing, night and day, with only an hour or two of uninterrupted sleep, and during one of these brief, well-deserved naps, a calf had got trapped inside its mother and died. And he could never, never forgive himself for not being there. 'I should have been,' he kept saying, hitting his forehead with his fist – he had one of those kind, very weathered brown faces, like an overcooked oatmeal biscuit. 'I let that calf down and her mother, too.' He shook his head. 'Farming is about being there. Being in time. Never letting the animals down.' Every word was like a hammer blow. We all sat silently, choked up with emotion, until he roused himself and brushed away what could have been a tear. 'This will never do. I've sheep to bring indoors. The weather's getting worse. I've no desire to dig them out of drifts.' When we opened the kitchen door to let him out it moved stiffly – there was an inch of snow behind it in a wedge.

'You know what I hate about farming?' Charlie said, as we watched George's solid figure disappear up the drive. 'The way so much of it is about guilt, and the puritanical avoidance of pleasure.' He took a Mars bar out of the emergency chocolate tin on the dresser and crammed it, whole, into his wide mouth. 'What is the point of being alive,' he mumbled indistinctly, though a mouthful of toffee, 'if you spend every waking hour mentally ticking yourself off?'

I woke with a start in the brass bed. I could hear the wind howl outside. Something knocked a bucket over in the yard below, the sound muffled by snow: it was one of the sheep. I felt quite contentedly warm in the bed until I remembered how badly things were going. We had got all the animals off the hills, and the snow had got heavier, and last night Ironie had foaled in the stable. We had got there very quickly and the foal had come out safely, but it did not seem to have any strength. It would not get to its feet, or drink on its own, though we tried over and over again to encourage it to.

In the end Charlie brought it into the kitchen and bedded it up near the stove. I fed it with a lamb bottle full of mare's milk but it just let most of the metallic-tasting, sweet stuff ooze out of the side of its mouth. It was a little colt, about the size of a rocking-horse, with a tiny, coarse grey mane and tail like its mother and a strawberry-roan coat. And it was delightful being able to cuddle it, because usually foals are so skittish – they learn to trot out of human reach within about half an hour of being born.

Needing old blankets to keep it warm, I asked Betty if there were any I could borrow, and she took me up to the attics and turned on the dusty light up there. She was making pastry, and had to click the switch on with one elbow – she left me to find bedding on my own, while she retreated downstairs to Radio 4. The Bettiscombe attics were enormous: high enough so you could walk upright with ease, and properly planked underfoot. Everywhere were old bookshelves and cupboards and great chests full of folded curtains. It smelt only faintly of damp, though you could hear the wind, and see tiny cones of snow forming where it was forcing itself through cracks in the tiles.

I was wary of the skittles-playing ghosts, so I didn't explore very far, but the attic went on and on, into a twilit vastness, each section devoted to a different aspect of Pinney history. There was a whole roomful of paintings, canvases, easels and portfolios marking the years Betty had spent as a successful artist, before she had children. There was a furry mountain of discarded toys, each with distinctive, pointy, prickly faces and shiny eyes. There was a section like a shrine to broken china: entire dinner sets with each plate and serving dish neatly split in two. (I found out later this was the legacy of one of Billy's predecessors, a maid who panicked whenever she washed up.) And there were ghostly stacks of unread books, brand new and glossy. Each stack had the face of an unusually beautiful young man on it. I slipped a book in my pocket.

'What's this?' I asked Charlie when I got home. The poetry was not strikingly good. One effort contained only seven lines, each of one word: Monday, Tuesday, Wednesday, Thursday, Friday, Saturday, Sunday.

He laughed. 'It's Gaffer's. He used to print other people's poetry.'

'Why?'

'Why do you think?'

I turned the book over. The poet was lovely: he looked like the lead singer of a rock band. 'Because he found the writer attractive?'

'Could be.'

'Is he gay, then?'

Charlie opened his eyes wide, thinking. 'Bisexual, I think. He's always liked women too.'

I put the book down hurriedly. I was shocked, but Charlie acted as if he hadn't said anything out of the ordinary. I'd im-agined the countryside was a place where lives were more strait-laced and old-fashioned. Clearly I was wrong.

There was a faint dinging noise, as a telephone was replaced in the depths of the house, and quiet footsteps. I felt across the bed. The sheets were still warm on Charlie's side, but he had gone. I pulled on a dressing-gown and went out to the kitchen. The light was on in there and the fire burning so fiercely in the Rayburn that the water pipes rattled on the wall; the foal rustled in the blankets beside it, like someone in the grip of a night-mare. Then the kitchen door opened and Charlie came in covered in snow.

'Ironie has cleansed,' he said. 'It should be all right. But you remember that Cécile told us, when we were in France, that these mares found it hard to cleanse properly? And that we had to be sure to get every single bit out?' I nodded, though I had not actually heard this before. Still, I did know that it was important for the complete afterbirth to come out of any animal.

'Well –' Charlie tugged at his pocket, and pulled out a supermarket carrier bag wrapped round something. 'Here's the cleansing. I'm not sure if it is complete.' He unwrapped it and spread it out on the table. It looked like a pair of tights designed by Damien Hirst: it was fleshy, purplish, pink and grey, and it had scabs and smears of blood clinging to it, and two definite feet with long, finger-like toes. 'It's this one, here, that I'm not sure about,' Charlie said, pointing to the end of one of the toes. 'There could be a bit broken off.' As I bent to look, the lights abruptly went out, and the ancient fridge gave a sigh and switched itself off.

Charlie lit a match and checked the circuit box. 'Power cut,' he said. 'Still, it doesn't matter. I've rung the vet, but he won't come out. Says it is too risky, because of the blizzard.'

'What are you going to do?' I asked into the darkness. 'I'm going to take the cleansing to him,' Charlie replied. 'I have just been on to Reg, and he left his car on the main road by the pub. He says the snow plough has just been through up there, so we're going to give it a try and drive to the vet.'

'But won't it be dangerous?'

'Maybe.' Charlie's voice sounded more cheerful. And I remembered he liked challenges and danger; it was the routine and humdrum that he could not stand. When we were shovel-ling a year's worth of dung out of a yard together he would always break off halfway to go and buy a special implement to make things go faster, or fetch a friend who might be persuaded to help and jolly us along with funny stories.

'Reg is putting some concrete blocks on the boot of his car, to give it a lower centre of gravity – and if it slides off the road – why, I'll just walk to the vet.'

'You could die,' I said. 'If the snow is as bad as you say you could get lost in it, and get hypothermia. Please don't go.'

'I've got to. Ironie might die if I don't.' There was an edge to his voice that made me back off and stop arguing. I hated it when people got annoyed with me. Perhaps it was something to do with having a domineering father. 'Can I come with you, then?' I asked timidly.

'No.' There was a rustle from the other side of the room as Charlie felt for the coats. He lit another match to find his motorbike gloves; I saw his face looking very intent – almost happy – in the golden light. 'It's too dangerous for you and, besides, someone has to stay and look after the animals. I won't be gone long.' He opened the door.

'Can you kiss me goodbye?' I called. I thought he had not heard, because the door opened and snow and freezing air came in, but then I felt him catch hold of my face in the dark and give me a fleeting kiss. 'Don't worry,' he laughed. 'Though I know you will.' And he was gone.

Chapter Seven

'You know how it is in these rural districts. Life tends at times to get slow. There's nothing much to do in the long winter evenings but listen to the radio and brood on what a tick your neighbour is.' The Ordeal of Young Tuppy – P. G. Wodehouse

The pub was stuffed with farmers. Charlie was leaning on the counter, telling the story of his heroic journey across a snow-bound landscape, while, over by the fire, Reg was telling a slightly different version. In this he was the experienced older man, giving sensible advice which a lunatic hothead recklessly ignored. Without his firm handling, he implied, the whole expedition could have ended in disaster – even death.

'And then the car skidded, and Reg started screaming in terror, in a shrill falsetto,' I heard Charlie say, before a gust of laughter from his companions blotted out the rest. Someone squeezed past me, spilling beer on my coat, and I turned to talk to Billy.

'It's funny how everyone in the Vale made for the pub the minute the blizzard stopped,' I said, and went on to marvel about all the little paths I'd seen worn into the snow on top of the hedges, each one leading inexorably to the Rose and Crown. (You could not walk along the lanes, the drifts had completely filled them in.) 'It must be a very close community here.'

'Either that, or a boozy one,' Billy agreed. His hair was freshly blow-dried, and he was wearing a wool jacket that looked as if it had just been pulled out of a dry-cleaning bag. He smelt of lemony cologne, and I was unpleasantly aware that I had a dung-stain on one side of my coat, and a piece of straw (complete with marble-sized sheep-dropping) dangling from my fuzzed-up hair. But then, Billy had always made me feel like an amateurish female impersonator.

He was so well groomed, and so feminine in the old-fashioned sense of the word – gentle, kind, an expert cook, superb at home-making and cleaning. Charlie had told me that when Billy had first arrived in the village three years earlier his neighbours had simply assumed that he was a woman. They had brought him presents of flowers, eggs and cakes, and sat for hours in his scrubbed blue and white kitchen, filling him in on the more *outré* details of village gossip. And it had come as a shock to them to discover he was gay – although, because they were so fond of him by then, they swiftly accepted it.

They had assumed he was female despite the fact that he never wore dresses, or make-up, or even had breasts. You might think this was odd – if you had never seen the other women in the area. For instance, two miles away there was Rose, well over six feet tall, 46-inch waist and muscled like a stevedore, who not only looked exactly like a man (complete with moustache and light goatee), but could beat most males easily when it came to farm labour. Her monolithic figure was often to be seen on the skyline, cutting mangel-wurzels all day in the rain, and she could throw bales an astounding distance on the end of a pitch-fork. All this did not make her less appealing to the opposite sex, though, who regarded her with flirtatious awe. Once, the post-man attended a wet local funeral in too-smart shoes, and when he hesitated in front of a wide, muddy gateway, Rose waded forward in her wellingtons, picked him up and carried him over her shoulder to dry land. Ever afterwards, he could never refer to the occasion without blushing with pleasure.

'I bet Reg did panic in that snow,' Billy said, glancing across to where Reg was pretending to punch Charlie on the chin. 'What a wuss he is.' His tone was affectionate.

Charlie was talking to a man with very sharp, dark brown eyes.

'Who's that?' I asked Billy.

'That's Ken. He and Charlie used to go out drinking at night. They'd get to the pub on Bob the stallion. And then, on the way home, Charlie would push Ken off into his yew hedge, and Ken would roll down it and creep indoors on his hands and knees. It did not matter how pissed they got, because the horse always remembered the way home.'

'What did Ken's wife think about it?' I asked.

'Oh – Ken's not married. He's a wizard.'

'A wizard! Can he actually do magic?'

'So they say.'

'What sort of things?'

Billy bent forward to whisper in my ear. 'He put a curse on someone once.' While I tried not to stare, Billy told me how Ken had fallen out with one of the farmers near us, and been seen on the hill, stretching out his hands and muttering. The next day the farmer's sow and piglets were found stone dead. As the weeks went by there was a further catalogue of misfortune, all of it with an unpleasant twist. The family's pet pony was found dead, too, straddling a low wall, and when the farmer's wife went out to shut up her chickens, her torch was mysteriously dashed from her hand and she was lost for an hour and a half in her own back yard. She was so horrified by the experience that she refused to go out there ever again, and a fox ate all the poultry.

'I'd loathe that,' I shivered. 'I'm scared of the dark anyway, and I never like getting the chickens in. What happened in the end?'

'They left. The farmer started going blind, you see. They say Ken was dancing on the hill the day the removal vans came.'

All the way home across the snow I thought about this story. It seemed quite monstrous of the wizard to take a neighbourly disagreement so far. When I asked Charlie about it he just laughed. 'But there is no need to get in a flap. I get on very well with Ken, and he'd never put a curse on me. In fact, if there is anyone you've got a tick against I'm sure he'd oblige.' I must have still looked worried, because he squeezed my hand and added: 'What happened to that farmer wasn't a curse. It was just farming. Sometimes things go wrong for no reason at all.'

When we opened the kitchen door we found the foal had died. I did not realise at once, because it was in its usual, sprawled-out, sleeping position, but when I touched it, it was cold. It was a blow, but we had almost been expecting it. What was worse was that its mother, Ironie, seemed unwell now.

She was lying on the floor of her stall with her head down, and though she looked comfortable to me, Charlie was instantly alarmed. He clicked his tongue at her and she tried to get up, but somehow she couldn't quite manage it. She gathered her hooves under her obediently, but didn't seem able to summon the energy to pull herself completely upright. She stumbled and slipped. Charlie half pulled her, and urged her, but she still couldn't manage it, though she struggled to. After half a dozen goes she was too weak to even do that any more, and blood trickled lazily from one leg, where she had grazed it on the floor. She was not interested in hay or water, either. Her pink coat looked yellower than before, and blotched with sweat, and there was melancholy in her large, dark eyes.

'We've got to get her upright again,' Charlie said. 'She'll get pneumonia if she stays down too long.' He tried hauling her up with the halter again while I pushed from behind, but it was no good. We'd get her a little way and then she would simply slump again. She closed her eyes and rested her head gratefully on the flagstones. Their chill seemed to soothe her. Perhaps a big sling was the answer. Charlie sent me off to find hessian sacks and stitch them together while he got out a drill and fitted an old pulley to the stable ceiling. Sawdust drifted down over Ironie. She seemed exhausted, and even all the activity around her did not arouse her interest. She closed her eyes and slept.

We spent an hour searching for nylon rope in outbuildings and stitching the sacks together. When the contraption was finally assembled it was tricky getting the mare into it. She was so heavy, and her lassitude made her harder to handle. We pushed from one side until our joints cracked, then squeezed the sling under and pushed from the other. She felt slightly damp and cool, and her breathing was heavy. It was getting harder to encourage her to open her eyes. I had a very strong feeling that she was wishing herself into another world, absenting herself, but I did not like to say so.

Still, the sling worked. When Charlie and I heaved on the end of the rope Ironie slowly inched upwards. Unfortunately, she was so enormous that she kept sliding ponderously out of the back . There was something elephantine about her. All her grace had gone: she had just become a heap of ungainly flesh. We carefully winched her down, rearranged her and tried again. After a while I could not pull any more. I felt drained by the hopelessness of it all, and the hard work that just went on and on. I stopped to rest, but Charlie went on hauling, ropy muscles standing out on his back and arms, his body slick with sweat. There were cobwebs and dust on him from the sacking.

The pulley was an old rusty one, and squeaked. The other horses put their ears back when they heard it. They stopped eating and looked round fearfully, the whites of their eyes showing. But Charlie kept hauling and stopping, hauling and stopping, accompanied by that dismal, rusty squeak, and eventually Ironie's hooves brushed the ground. She looked like a giant puppet whose owner had let go of the strings. And the sight of her huge buttocks dangling so uselessly was obscene. She did not even attempt to struggle upright. I tried putting her hooves into position, but she let them tip sideways. Charlie tied the rope up and stopped to rest, taking great gasps of air, and the sling slowly sagged so that Ironie's hocks were resting on the flagstone floor.

'I can't understand it,' Charlie said breathlessly, as he started to haul her up once more. 'We got the afterbirth all out. She should be getting better.'

He would not come to bed when it got late. He stood beside Ironie, stroking her head and talking to her in a low, comforting murmur. Outside the stable the wind had got up and it was snowing again. I rang the vet but he said he could not get through. I fed the other animals and then came back to the stable again with some sandwiches and tea, but Charlie would not eat. He was hauling on the pulley. I hated that steady squeaking noise. I felt so useless. I was not strong enough to take over and give him a rest, and I knew next to nothing about animals. I was just an irritant, alternately trying to comfort him or begging him to get some sleep. In the end I crept off and sat down in the pen with Samb and the other sheep. I'd slept with them the previous night, too, but they were a bit restless. I liked being snuggled into their warm bodies, though, and hearing them breathe and mutter to each other. At least they were merrily and companionably alive. I didn't even mind when Samb peed noisily by my ear and woke me just before dawn.

I stumbled outside and found thick snowflakes were still falling from the grey sky. They caught on my eyelashes and melted when they touched my cheeks. The stable yard was silent when I reached it. I could not hear the pulley squeak. The door was open a little bit, and Bill and Ben were sleeping on their feet, their bedding wet and dirty. In the end stall, Ironie was back on the floor, sprawled out on top of the collapsed pulley, one side of her coat stained dark with liquid. The floor was very wet, and Charlie was sitting against the wall, his legs stretched out in front of him, his eyes open.

'How is she?' I asked.

'She's dead,' he said. 'She died a long time ago. The pulley was pointless. It just hurt her and upset her. All I did was torture her for the last hours of her life, when she needed to rest.' I slipped in beside him and held one of his huge, calloused hands in mine. It felt like a glove made of pumice stone. His arm was bleeding from a great scratch, and he was terribly cold. I picked up his coat and put it round his shoulders. His eyes grew damp, but he pushed the tears away with his wrist and they stopped.

'Life's a bastard,' he said forcefully. 'Everything's such a bastard.' He swallowed. 'I wanted so much to make this work,' he said. 'I really, really thought I could, and we would make money from the horses. But it's like there's a curse on me.'

It seemed like that to me, too, but I denied it. 'It'll be all right,' I insisted earnestly. 'We'll make money out of the farm somehow, and buy more Ardennes.' I thought desperately. 'I could run the bungalow as a boarding-house, I suppose.' He wasn't listening to me any more. He turned his face away. I went on gripping his hand and thinking. I was sure I could do bed and breakfast – after all, I knew roughly how to go about it from helping up at the pub. Charlie's mouth turned down and his eyes closed, and I snuggled into him. He had a habit of retreating into himself whenever there was a crisis, but I didn't mind. I liked it. There was so much I didn't understand about him. He was a constant, fascinating puzzle. Sometimes I would ask him what he was thinking about and it was always something totally alien, like: 'I was just wondering whether to grease the lorry's prop-shaft.'

The snow had melted a little by lunchtime, allowing a different vet from the practice to come out. He did an autopsy outside the cider-house, so that pink water trickled across the ice in the stable yard, and announced, with the air of a man pulling off a complex trick, that there was a little piece of afterbirth the size of a fingernail inside that had gone bad. The mare had died of septicaemia. Charlie glowered at him, but he did not explain why, or protest about the other vet. He seemed sunk in hopelessness. 'What's the use?' he said, when I asked him. 'Ironie is dead. There's no point suing anyone over it. This family has lost enough money by going to court. I'm certainly not making that mistake myself.'

I tried to cheer him up by cooking. Or at least this was what I told myself. Actually, baking was my personal method of getting over trauma. Whenever I was worried I made fat little rolls tied in knots and sprinkled with butter and poppy-seeds, or trays of chocolate sponge, or comforting vegetable curries. The problem was that the dead foal rather got in the way. I kept stumbling over his legs as I wandered backwards and forwards with bags of flour and greased baking trays. It was only a tiny kitchen, and he took up well over a third of it. There was no way I could shift him on my own, either: I had already tried.

Charlie was in his workshop, squinting at a model aeroplane, and painting its wings with a fine brush. He seemed less gloomy, but preoccupied, not inclined to talk. (He didn't want to eat rolls and cake, either.) It seemed that his family's way of coping with problems was to retire to a miniature world. I went into the Manor, where I found Betty upholstering a doll's armchair with a jeweller's glass in one eye and a Gauloise smoking in an ashtray beside her. 'Can I borrow Billy for a few minutes?' I asked.

'Of course you can,' she said, putting her work down and smiling. 'And would you like me to brush your hair first? There are animal droppings in it.'

Billy was amused, rather than horrified, by my bizarre domestic arrangements. He helped me edge the foal out of the kitchen door, past the racks of cooling cakes and pies, but it took us a lot of joggling and fiddling. The poor creature was as awkward to handle as a baby grand piano.

'What do you think, Billy?' I asked, as I manoeuvred a stiffly outstretched hoof past the light switch. 'Do you think I could make money out of having people to stay here, in the bungalow?'

He stopped halfway into the garden. (He had the foal's head; easily the best end.) I could see he was struggling to be tactful. Behind me, the cat leapt gracefully on to the table and knocked a pile of buns into the dark green foal diarrhoea I hadn't yet got round to cleaning up.

'You could,' he said kindly. 'But they'd have to be a very special kind of person.'

Chapter Eight

Conversation with my friend TJ about our very different family background: There are three household objects only found in the country homes of Bohemian intellectuals born before WW2:

1) A small, plastic, triangular container by the sink, used not for its true purpose (storing washing-up brushes) but as a repository for compost. (A friend's little sister used to stir this with a spoon and call it 'making pogee'.)

2) A mini-table, made of soggy wood, laid across the bath and containing items too unappealing to use, like mildewed sponges, rusty loofahs and slimy pumice.

3) A meat safe, cosily inhabited by flies, mice, silver-fish and ants, that all the nicest foods are put in. (TJ's brother called this 'the rancidiser'.)

Of course, anything like this has to be ruthlessly eliminated from your home if you are going to run it as a guest house. I was glad I had spent so many hours cleaning the local pub. It had given me an inkling of normal standards of cleanliness.

'Dear Mrs Jiggins,' I wrote, making my handwriting look as comfortingly flowery as possible. 'Thank you so very much for your deposit. We will expect you from midday next Saturday.' I put my pen down, doubtful as to what should come next. 'Yours sincerely?' Or was that off-puttingly formal? My right hand was curled in a loose fist on the table and at the sight of it the little brown chick that had been pecking about in the sugar bowl leapt down, ran across the table and squeezed himself inside. Soon, all that could be seen of him between my thumb and forefinger was a little fluffy round that was his backside, and two tiny legs, facing forwards. Instead of cheeping, he gave miniature purrs of pleasure at being once more in a warm, dark, safe place.

I had rescued him two days earlier when I had found him abandoned in a muddy puddle by his feckless bantam mother. He was barely alive, but after a good warm in the bottom oven of the Rayburn he quickly became an exuberant – and extremely demanding – member of the family. He made such a noise if he was left alone in a box that he had to ride in my bra when I was working in the yard, occasionally poking his head out of the V-neck of my jersey to check up on what was going on.

I annoyed the chick by taking my hand away to put at the bottom of my letter, 'Looking forward so much to meeting you.' (A lie – I was dreading it.) It was 5 p.m. and my first guests were due any minute. A guest house was the ideal business to run because we needed to earn money fast and it required no qualifications and, best of all, no savings or loans. When you advertised, you asked people to send deposits of, say, £15 a person, and with that money you bought all you needed in order to entertain them: beds, linen, china, food. I had had a bad moment in the local auction rooms two weeks earlier when I had just had to buy (at a hugely inflated price, because another desperate would be landlady was after it, too) a bunk bed. It was the only way I could turn my bedrooms into the 'family rooms' I had advertised. (Both rooms were far too small for a double bed, two singles, a wardrobe and a chest of drawers to fit in. Even with the bunk beds you could not open the doors properly but had to squidge through sideways. I was desperately hoping none of my guests would have paunches. And I kept having dreams where my rooms magically expanded. I'd always wake feeling so disappointed that it wasn't true.) The only conceivable problem with running a guest house – as far as I could see – was that I only knew how to make the beds and the breakfast. The finer details were a mystery. So I went round visiting all the local farmers' wives, asking for advice.

Ruby had been doing it for over twenty years, and I turned up at her farmhouse at 10 a.m., just as her small, subdued husband was finishing his post-milking breakfast. He was eating purple, gristle-threaded bacon accompanied by circles of fried pastry.

When Ruby's husband had gone out and started slowly scraping the yard, punctuating each sweep of his brush with a piteous, hacking cough, she explained that she gave him fried pastry each morning, not because he liked it (he didn't) – but because she did not believe in throwing food away. The pastry was left over from the enormous apple pie she made each Monday, using apples from the farm orchard. 'He doesn't care for apple pies, either. Never has. But I make him eat one every Monday. Otherwise, what would I do with all that fruit? It would be a waste, and I can't abide waste.'

Long-standing farming marriages always worried me. I'd never come across one yet that I envied. They had a grimness about them, redolent of slow-burning resentment. I tried not to think about this as Ruby led me into the part of her house reserved for guests. We left a warm, steamy zone, smelling of fried oil and wet sheepdog, and entered one that was chillingly aseptic. There were stiff white lace covers on the arms and backs of all the chairs, and the classic West Country farmhouse odour of mildew and damp plaster had been almost entirely smothered by spray-polish. (Though the icy, clammy feeling, as if one had just stepped inside a giant, frozen bath-sponge, remained, of course.) While I admired the plastic freesias on the mantlepiece – which ponged fiercely of disinfectant – she looked round approvingly. 'This is what you want,' she said, wiping the television screen with the damp cloth that always seemed to be in her hand. 'You mustn't be homey and comfortable. They take advantage, then. It's better if they feel awkward.'

'Why?'

'Because otherwise they never stop wanting things – and running hot water,' she said fiercely. 'I just show them the hand-basins and don't tell them about the bath – it is in a separate room at the end of the passage. If they ask, I give them the key, but I do it slowly. I make sure they feel bad about asking.'

She looked at me warningly. 'Don't be too soft with your guests. You'll regret it if you are.' I could not help feeling irritated that she automatically assumed I was going to be far too anxious to please. She was right, of course. I couldn't imagine ordering anyone about or laying down rules. I'd have to get Charlie to do it.

As she went on giving me tips, I was struck by their eccentricity. Some were completely mad. For instance, she told me to save money by buying one pair of sheets only for each bed, in nylon. She washed and dried all hers between one group of guests departing, and another arriving. How was I going to make that work, with freak rain squalls over Bettiscombe practically every day, and less than two spare hours on changeover day to get them all dry? Besides, everyone knew nylon sheets were vile. And she insisted that I had to give my guests an evening meal as well as breakfast.

'But I thought I would just take elderly couples – one at a time – and give them breakfast only. Then I could fit it all in with the farm work.'

She gave a mirthless laugh. 'You will not get enough visitors booking in if you do that. People only go to farms because they have got kids and they want a cheap holiday. It's family rooms and an evening meal – or nothing.'

'But I have only got one spare room and it is very small', I said doubtfully.

'You won't be sleeping in your bedroom,' she said. 'Me and Will use the old chicken shed in the season. Mind you, it needs a good clean first, or the poultry lice are troublesome. And you know that couple down by the crossroads? They don't even use an outhouse – they lie down in the corridor after their visitors have gone to bed.'

She started to close the door. 'Advertising!' she said, looking startled, as if she had nearly forgotten the most important thing. 'The people you don't want are the uppity ones, who give their children fancy names. Dreadful, they are. You want nice clean ordinary families with well-behaved children called things like Debbie and Sharon and Paul and Adrian. So advertise in *Daltons Weekly*.'

Back in the kitchen she explained about the cooking. Guests were picky about food. You could not give them anything you liked. 'They won't eat pigs' heads, trotters, offal, that sort of stuff,' she sounded regretful. 'It's roasts with all the trimmings. Trifles, blancmanges, ice-cream. Coffee and mints for afters, and soup to start with.'

'But isn't that rather a lot of cooking? Soups as well?'

'It *is* bothersome, but I always say it is worth the effort. They like their soup,' and she proudly showed me her store-cupboard where rows of packages and tins were lined up. There was not just instant soup in there but instant blancmange and trifle. Tinned fruit and vegetables were piled up to the ceiling, but at least her freezer was full of real meat from her farm. Apart from roasting joints, all she seemed to have to do was heat and assemble stuff. 'Is this really what they like eating?' I asked, worried.

'Oh yes. Their favourite meal every week is the tinned ham salad I do on Friday.' She pulled a piece of paper out of her pocket. 'I've done you a list. It's what I cook every week during the season. Sunday, roast beef and peach flan, Monday, lamb and rice pudding . . . after a while you can tell the days of the week by the smell in the kitchen – and the look on the dog's face.'

'What if they stay longer than a fortnight?'

'Never, ever, take anyone for that long.' Her mouth set in a thin, resentful line. 'I reckon a body can stand anything if they know it is only going to last seven days. But even that does not hold true for some. You'll see.'

Remembering this remark now, the hair on the back of my neck stood up on end with fear. In the distance, I heard a rumble as a vehicle negotiated the thin gravel at the top of the drive. Maybe it was Charlie. He had gone to market that morning to buy more sheep (using some of the deposits). The deposits were a wonderful, refreshing fund of cash pouring into the farm. I was glad the older Pinneys had not heard about them yet. They had found the whole idea of me taking paying guests rather comical, and kept teasing me about it, as if it was a bizarre habit I had suddenly developed.

My parents, on the other hand, were appalled. My father even offered me money, assuming I must be quite desperate. I tried to explain to him that we were not starving: but we needed a regular income – and running a guest house was the only way I could think of to get one.

The drive down to the farm twisted violently as it went over a tiny stone bridge. Those who whizzed up and down frequently knew that at this point you had to put two wheels on the verge or your exhaust got ripped off by a series of pointed stones. Strangers did not, of course. So when I heard a sharp impact, and then a loud roar, I knew my guests were on their way.

When they finally arrived on the doorstep the new arrivals – though fretting about their exhaust – did not look too alarming. All of them, even the two children, were painfully thin and very reserved. I showed them into a family room and they did not mention its embarrassing smallness at all. They actually seemed relieved, as if they had been expecting something far, far worse. The mother even put out her hand and felt the cotton sheets with a look of wonder on her face. (I had bought them all in charity shops, but they had been crisply laundered and ironed.)

The other guests (who arrived half an hour later) were less agreeable. The wife was heftily built and muttered a great deal about the difficulty of getting into her bedroom. But then, she also complained bitterly about her damaged exhaust, which I felt indicated the sort of character she had. Over tea and biscuits she explained that she was a mental nurse. She did not refer to her husband's occupation, and it was difficult not to suspect that he might have been one of her patients. He looked odd: so tall and thin that he folded over at the top, and shockingly pale, with a lopsided haircut. He was also not the slightest bit interested in exploring the farm with his children. He lingered indoors, his favoured area the gloomy passageway outside the bathroom, where he would grumble to himself about the impossibility of getting inside to have a wash or a pee. There was some basis to his dissatisfaction: our bungalow had only one bathroom (with the only lavatory in it) and, with ten people installed, there was rather a queue. In fact, I quickly got used to using the muck-heap in the yard myself. (Although sometimes I would steal into the Manor and use one of its five washrooms instead.)

Charlie was a huge hit with the guests. As soon as he got home he welded up their exhausts, and then, smelling strongly of angle-grind and engine oil – with a soupçon of sheep manure – he took over the role of waiter. The oxtail soup was terrible. I followed the instructions on the packet, but nothing could make it even halfway palatable. It was so glutinous that it resembled a semi-liquid pancake, and it smelt like an old gym shoe, but when Charlie handed it round, everyone had a stab at eating it. They visibly enjoyed the ham salad, though, and were thrilled by the trifle with its hundreds and thousands. I had scattered them over a thick layer of double cream. I felt so guilty about the poky rooms that I decided to be extravagant with cream. Besides, I got it cheap from a cheese-making business up the road.

As I was stamping the soup box into the dung heap later, Charlie sidled up and explained that there was a small problem with the sheep. One of them had died on the way back from market. It hadn't had anything wrong with it, just got trampled underfoot and suffocated, and as it seemed a pity to waste the meat he had cut its throat and hung it up at the back of the tool-shed. He thought that we should cut it up and freeze it quickly, though, before the flies got to it.

Neither of us was sure how you butchered an animal. 'It can't be that difficult,' Charlie said firmly, sharpening our biggest bread knife and stabbing at the sheep's stomach with it. Enormous quantities of tubing and offal tumbled out on to the ground. Glancing out of the shed, I noticed that the father of the nice family was sitting in his car reading the instruction handbook. It seemed a peculiar thing to do in the evenings, but no odder, perhaps, than eviscerating a sheep.

When I turned back to see what Charlie was doing I found him peeling the wool off the sheep, and for a while we both grunted with exertion over this task. The next step was to bury the skin, along with the offal and the severed head. So, after checking that our guest had gone indoors, we set off across the fields with a clutch of gruesome buckets and buried the contents just beyond the wall of the Manor garden.

The carcass was very heavy and extremely hard to cut. After we had hauled it into the kitchen, Charlie chopped at it with an axe, in a series of heavy, thwacking blows. Shards of bone flew everywhere, and there was plenty of blood. Later, while Charlie parcelled the joints and labelled them, I started clearing up. There was a lake of blood under the kitchen table, and it was so extensive that it even lapped against the door to the hall. In order to clean properly, I had to open this door, but I listened first, to be sure there were no guests out there, waiting to use the toilet. On my knees, and very cautiously, I swung it wide. There, staring down at me, with a look of bewildered terror on his face, was the psychiatric nurse's husband. I suppose I did look a bit unpleasant, with my face and clothes splattered with blood and bits of bone. He gave a cry, and fled.

When Charlie and I were warmly tucked up in the large cupboard near the back door (we had discovered we could fit a double mattress in there) I realised what I had done. 'He must think I've murdered you, and been chopping you up all night,' I whispered. 'He probably thinks I'm going to go in and have a go at him next.'

'Don't worry, I'll take him his tea in the morning,' Charlie murmured sleepily. 'That'll reassure him.'

It may have – momentarily. The only problem was that when Charlie put down the tray of tea and drew the curtains in the guest bedroom he revealed an unappealing – if authentically rural – scene. During the night the farm dogs had dug up the sheep's head, and left it, half gnawed, on the lawn.

It wasn't too bad, taking guests, though the hours were long. I'd rise before seven to wash and make trays of morning tea, and after doing all the farm chores, washing-up and scrubbing down the kitchen I rarely went to bed before eleven. And even then, there would often be an apologetic tap on the door as a guest asked if they could have hot cocoa or a fresh light bulb for their room.

Their tastes in food were just as conventional as Ruby had suggested. One day I came back from shopping to find a freshly caught pike in the bath, and cut great steaks from it, which I fried in butter for the guests' tea. They couldn't eat it. But they loved frozen supermarket fish and always congratulated me on it. And I had to admit that it was useful, having had a bit of an unusual upbringing (my father was a part-time restaurant critic, and never allowed things like chips, white bread or ketchup to be served in his house) to discover what people outside my family enjoyed eating. They were delighted by pastry made with lard, and Yorkshire puddings with every roast, but regarded hot, vinegar-free beetroot as a worrying curiosity.

Letter to Caky: 'I've just had the best afternoon. I went and read a thriller in the steep field leading up to Sliding Hill. The autumn sun was out, and after a while Samb ambled over and nuzzled me, so we dozed off in each other's arms (and legs, and hooves). I feel as if I have just come out of prison (complete with the famous pallor, due to spending the whole summer indoors cooking and cleaning). You'll be pleased to know that my pet chick has turned into an adolescent cockerel. It now likes climbing on our feet and hiding inside our trouser legs. Unfortunately it is also sexually fixated on human hands. Charlie has been getting cross because every time he tries to work in the yard it gets tremendously excited, flies over, grabs his wrist in its beak, and attempts to seduce his index finger.'

Chapter Nine

'There is nothing like having a virtuous drudge at home, sir; depend upon that. It gives a zest to one's enjoyments in the world, take my word for it. No man of sense need restrict himself, or deny himself a single amusement for his wife's sake: on the contrary, if he select the animal properly, he will choose such a one as shall be no bar to his pleasure, but a comfort in his hours of annoyance.' The Memoirs of Barry Lyndon – William Thackeray

Furniture vans had been outside the Manor all morning, and I watched them with a strange mixture of triumph and unease. I was cleaning out the goose-pens, standing up to the top of my wellington boots in feathers, guano and rotting straw, and attempting to haul it, layer by layer, out to the dung-pile in the yard. It was a truly terrible job: the inside of the pen was swarming with small black flies that bit, and, besides, there was so much to do that it was inconceivable the work would ever be finished. It suited my mood, though, which was murderously grumpy. I was nine and three-quarter months pregnant: a condition not covered by the booklet given to all expectant mothers by the health centre. There, the pregnancy diary stopped in the fortieth week, with a thrilling dash to hospital.

I kept going to see the doctor, hoping that he would induce the baby, but he thought I had simply got my dates wrong. So, like a giant black beetle standing on its back legs, I blundered around the farm, full of ill humour and wind. I kept getting stuck in shed doorways, and there was absolutely no position I was comfortable in – sleeping, standing or sitting. I couldn't bear to socialise or answer the telephone, either, because the only thing anyone ever said to me was: 'Haven't you had it yet?' And since (on principle) I never swore, there was no way of adequately replying. The only conversations I wanted to have were with other people who had been through the same torment and had useful tips. Why wasn't there a magazine on the market called *Monstrously Late Baby*? I'd tried eating curry every night, hot baths and plenty of sex. (Which Charlie had become uncharacteristically reluctant to supply.) And none of them had worked. So, in desperation, I thought I'd try violent physical exertion – and the goose-shed did need a clean.

We'd reared the geese for the Christmas market, so we'd killed them in late December, as carols floated out of the Manor and partygoers could be seen at the windows biting into mince pies and drinking sloe gin. Charlie had done it by laying a heavy bit of iron piping on their necks, standing on it, and pulling. He'd killed his first chicken aged six, and was quite hardened to the sinister side of farming, but each goose-execution left him trembling with horror and guilt. And then the plucking! There were layers and layers of feathers, each of which had to be pulled out deftly or the creamy-yellow, fatty flesh underneath tore, and the bird would sell for less. You couldn't stop when you got fed up, either, because the feathers only came out easily when the bird was still warm. (Once a goose has been executed you have to keep going for approximately two hours until it is picked clean.) And the whole flock of geese grieves, pines and loses weight from the moment their first friend goes outside for an unpleasant encounter with a length of piping. So they all have to be killed one after another, as swiftly as possible. Every night we were still murdering and plucking long after the last guests at the Manor had said cheery goodbyes in fruity, cultivated voices and roared up the drive.

When I tired of pitchforking I'd emerge into the yard dripping with liquid dung and lightly frosted with leftover goose dandruff and watch the removal men. There were four of them, and they had edged down the drive in two articulated lorries soon after dawn, and begun stowing away the entire contents of Bettiscombe Manor. The family's debts had finally become so pressing that the only way to avoid ruin was to sell all the furniture.

I had put them in touch with a reliable antique dealer – I knew him because I'd worked for him as a teenager in London. And when he arrived with a couple of friends to do a valuation I tried to warn him about the fatal charm of the Pinneys by taking him aside and whispering, 'Whatever happens, don't lend them cash, will you – please?' But it was no good. Dazed by four different kinds of cake, and a selection of amusing anecdotes about the West Dorset literati, he made Betty and Michael an offer: he'd loan them the money they needed immediately. And they could have it, interest free, for six weeks. Only if they failed to raise it elsewhere in that time would he take the furniture away. When he left that afternoon he positively glowed with altruism – and he told me, in a reproving tone, that my parents-in-law were wonderful, charming people and deserved all the help they could get. 'You could almost call them the salt of the earth,' he said. 'Except that wouldn't get across how very special they are.'

The removal men were bringing out the 'Golden Bed' – the huge carved and gold-leafed wooden bed in which Charlie had been born. It was a beautiful thing (it had originally come from Blenheim Palace), and I knew I should feel desperately sorry for the family, but I didn't, not entirely. Looking after paying guests for two years had somehow worn away my ability to feel sympathy for people who spent money without going to the bother of earning it. There had been a lot of vomit involved this season – mostly my own, because I had had morning sickness. And there is nothing quite so difficult as preparing a full English breakfast for eight people while awash with queasiness. The kitchen swaying around me, I'd brown the sausages at arm's length and quickly hide them in the oven with the tomatoes. Then I'd grill the bacon (so I didn't have to look at it), but the difficult bit was the eggs. The way they wobblingly coagulated

in warm fat in the pan, and those odd little bluish–white nod-
ules, resembling phlegm, that trembled on the edge of the yolks
. . . They invariably had me racing out of the front door and
crouching over a bucket hidden inside a fuchsia bush. (I had to
throw up in the garden because if I didn't the guests would
knock politely on the kitchen door and say they had changed
their minds, and could they have a continental instead?)

It was not just my body functions I was haunted by, either.
Sometimes when I made beds I would discover that my guests
had left me grisly surprises. When I called in at Ruby's for sympathy about this she didn't give me any.

'Oh yes,' she said, rubbing lard vigorously into apple-pie
pastry. 'That's guests for you. That's why you get paid for having
them. I hope you've a good detergent. They do extra-strong
down at Mole Valley. And personally,' here her voice lowered to
a whisper, 'I always keep a pointed stick handy for picking up
unmentionables.'

Now the grandfather clock was being carefully stowed. It was
one of Betty's family heirlooms. It had a gold filigree clock-face
and bonged every quarter hour so enthusiastically that it was
almost impossible to sleep through. As it disappeared, Charlie
hurried out of the Manor, leapt into his car and whizzed up the
drive. I wandered back into the goose-pen and communed with
the flies again. I loathed the way the Pinneys were always in
debt. I felt ashamed each time I drove past the little garage
where they owed £500, and was sure I could sense the
disapproval of the owner. I was hoping – prissily – that this

disaster with the furniture might shock them into changing their ways.

When I came out with my next load of dung the grand piano was being brought out in pieces. Each was carefully stowed away in a wrapping of green baize, and when it was all done the men fastened up the back of the lorries. They'd finished. I glanced across at the Manor and noticed how lifeless and forlorn it looked. There was no washing flapping in the laundry yard, and none of the usual cheerful morning aromas of fresh coffee and thin toast. What must it be like in there, in those echoey empty rooms smelling faintly of lavender soap? I felt a chill round my heart as the enormity of what had happened to them suddenly hit. Even I couldn't help admiring the simple elegance with which Betty and Michael lived. The way they would sit bolt upright at the scrubbed white kitchen table and eat hardly anything at all – a small poached egg – off the most delicate china with heavy silver knives and forks. Would they even have any tables and chairs left?

The gravel on the drive crackled, and Charlie skidded across the yard in his car and leapt out. He waved a bit of paper at the furniture men.

'I've got the money!' he shouted. 'You can put it all back again!'

'I don't know that we can,' one of them muttered. 'I've never heard of such a thing.'

Charlie dashed into the house, and back out again to argue with the men, and I hid in the goose-shed. I wanted to bury myself in the dung. What was my antique-dealer friend going to say? How much had it cost him to hire all those vans and men?

I wrapped my arms round my head in despair.

'Lucy?' Charlie said behind me. 'What are you doing in here?'

'Just the usual: groaning and snarling to myself.'

'It's a miracle!' Charlie smiled properly for the first time in nearly a week, all lines of worry smoothed from his face. 'I went to see George and I managed to talk him into lending Ma and Gaffer the money.'

I walked up the side of the valley to escape. There was no point in ever sitting on the wishing stone again. I was tired of asking for the money troubles to be over and the baby born. I wandered in the opposite direction, towards the cows. As I got closer I saw that one of them was grossly pregnant and standing on her own, looking uncomfortable and sniffing the wind. A kindred spirit at last! I sat down in the hedge, wrapped my coat around me and watched her, and after a while I dozed off.

I woke with a start. Her front legs on the bank near me, she was beside herself, alternately biting chunks out of an oak tree with a splintering noise and throwing back her head to bellow. The other cows in the field, and all the little calves in the barn, were bellowing back – it was a tremendous racket. I scrambled further into the safety of the hedge and watched as she began kneeling down in the grass and then getting up again. Each time she would carefully smell the place where she had been resting, before going off to savagely attack the tree. A little balloon of liquid appeared at her rear end and gradually elongated, and after a while I could see two hooves, protected by a yellowish pad that looked as if it was made of plastic.

I got to my feet and began walking down towards the Manor to get Charlie. There was still one removal van in the yard, and he was talking to the driver, and I recoiled from the thought of getting involved with the arguments that were going on down there. I'd wait a bit longer. When I got back the cow was alternately standing up and sitting down, and bellowing more mournfully. I found an old bit of rusty machinery sticking out of the hedge a little further down, and sat down on it to rest my stomach. I could feel the baby leaping about inside, and something knobbly, like a little fist, was pressing against the skin near my hip.

When the cow crumpled to her knees with the air of someone who had finally come to a decision I got up and approached her. It couldn't hurt to try pulling on the legs, surely? I crouched and caught hold of them, and I did not even have to use much effort: they slipped free easily, encased in a thick membrane.

The bag lay on the grass with a dark shape inside. It wasn't moving. Not another dead animal, surely? I stood indecisively beside it for a moment and, glancing round, noticed that the sheep had broken out of their field and crowded through the hedge into this one, and were watching the birth, too, along with all the other cows, the whole lot enthralled and silent.

The calf needed to breathe. Everything newborn needed to breathe fast: I knew that from helping with the lambing. So I fell to my knees and broke the bag with my hands. The calf slithered on to the grass in front of me in a pool of watery, scarlet blood. And it suddenly opened its eyes and was very definitely alive – an almost spooky sight. The cow did not seem at all interested in it; instead she bent her head and sucked up the blood, with a sound like someone rude slurping soup.

I ran, then, down across the fields towards the Manor. The financial muddle didn't matter any more because I had good news.

'Charlie!' I shouted. 'There's a calf been born! It's alive!'

I remembered this scene when, two days later, my own baby was finally induced. I was as violently angry as the cow – I ripped a light-bracket completely off the delivery-room wall, kicked the bed to pieces and used shamefully filthy language. But my labour took far longer – twenty-four hours – and at the end of it I clasped my new daughter and felt the purest, most powerful love I had ever felt for anything in my life.

And the very next morning we were told we had to leave the farm. The bank – which held a charge on the house and land – had discovered that Michael had illegally given us a tenancy. This time, the only way to fend off disaster was to evict us.

Part 2

Chapter Ten

'For years of her marriage there had been so little panic she'd fallen asleep. So that if you asked her what she did between 1965 and 1968, she would probably recall only that those three years amounted to a day, really, and that on that day one of her neighbours had invited her to go fishing, and she had declined.' From 'Source' in *You Can't Keep a Good Woman Down* – Alice Walker

The big windows in the front room of the bungalow, where we had always given our paying guests their meals, were open to a clear, blue September sky. Two swallows came in and dipped and swooped playfully around the room. When they had gone I sat on the windowsill and gazed out at the fruit trees I'd planted as tiny whips over a decade ago, the year we left Bettiscombe. They were enormous, now, and jostled for space with each other, their branches tangled up together and weighed down with apples and quinces.

I glanced back at the room. It was so different from when we'd been there. It was now painted a subtle, expensive cream, and had Turkish rugs on the floor. It was also extremely untidy, and crammed with towering piles of books, trunks and boxes, because ever since Betty had died of cancer, Michael had lived here on his own. He'd sold the Manor and its farmland to Terence Conran's wife, Caroline, and she'd allowed him to stay on in the bungalow as a sort of absent-minded caretaker. It was interesting talking to her about the Manor, because although she'd repaired and redecorated it the ghosts had remained. They'd become far more malevolent, too. She described how she kept seeing the flames of candles being carried along the passageways by invisible beings. And, worse, how the cupboard in her bedroom had once opened in the middle of the night, and a woman in eighteenth-century clothes, complete with mob-cap, and clutching the hand of a little girl, walked slowly out and approached the bed with a very unpleasant look on her face.

There were shouts from the kitchen, where Michael was overseeing the making of lunch by Charlie's two sisters, Prophecy and Susannah, and I leapt up guiltily and went over to one of the boxes. I was supposed to be sorting them out, because Michael was moving – to stay with one of his cousins. I'd just got the lid open when Charlie stormed into the room.

'Really!' he said. 'It's like clearing up a house when someone's died, except that instead of being six foot under they're still wandering about, making a thorough nuisance of themselves.'

'What's he done, now?'

'He's been washing and drying some broken eggshells very carefully with a tea-towel. And he's ordered Prophecy to take all the rubbish out of the skip and sort through it again.' He wandered over to the window and leaned out. His expression was wistful, and I knew he was wishing we still lived here. Leaving had been dreadful for him. He'd found a part-time job on a rare breeds farm in Gloucestershire, but he'd only been allowed to take two Ardennes horses with him. Everything else had had to be sold. At the time he'd been most distraught about what was going to happen to his Shire stallion, Bob. After months of panic he found a dairy farmer called Nigel Johnson who agreed to buy him. Nigel provided regular updates on Bob's progress, and as he belonged to the same horse societies as Charlie, we even saw Bob regularly at ploughing matches and shows. He was kept entire, and bred from, until the year he died – though his tastes grew more finicky the older he got. 'He was rather timid by the end,' Nigel said, the last time I spoke to him. 'When we had mares in for him to serve we would put out bales of straw so he didn't get kicked, and he would peer round to see what the new arrival was like. If she was lively he'd jump back, as if saying: "Good grief – I can't be expected to do this!"'

At least Bob – and Ben, and Blossom – went to good homes where they were cherished. The same could not be said of the other farm animals. I would never forget the day that the sheep were rounded up and sent to market. Samb knew from first light that something bad was about to happen. She hid round the back of a hedge and had to be stalked and grabbed, and carried the way we always had to do it when she was being stubborn: in a wheelbarrow, her legs tied with baler-twine to stop her leaping out. When I pushed her up the ramp of the lorry she had looked at me disbelievingly, as if to say, 'Not me. You can't mean to do this to *me*.' But I had to. What else was I to do with her? We were moving to a cramped two-up, two-down in the middle of a village and I couldn't keep a mature sheep there.

When the back of the lorry went up and was fastened in place Samb found a chink in the side and gazed at me through it with one golden eye, the pupil like a horizontal date-stone. She blared heart-rendingly the whole way up the drive, and I could still hear her harsh coloratura as the lorry rumbled and turned for Axminster on the brow of the hill. There were no excuses for what I'd done. It was wrong. Maybe I should never have made a special pet of her in the first place – but then I'd thought I would be able to keep her for ever.

Inside the box I'd opened were letters. Stacks and stacks of them. They weren't folded, and the paper was still crisp and pure white. The top one began: 'My dearest, knowing that you are the other side of the Vale makes everything about Betty and Jordie easier to bear . . .'

'Who do you think these were meant for?' I asked Charlie.

'No idea. They clearly weren't sent, were they? Who knows what he used to get up to? I opened a mouldering copy of *The Seven Pillars of Wisdom* this morning, and found a letter inside from Ma, dated 1938. It said the land agent had told her if they sold two particular fields they'd be able to pay off all their debts and have money left over. She ended it by saying "Please can you reply soon?" Well, he didn't. He just hid it in a book.'

I said nothing. I'd just discovered a pleading letter we'd written to Michael, tucked inside a copy of *The Hunting Wasp*.

The contents of the house were being roughly divided into stuff Charlie, his sisters and his brother wanted, stuff to be taken to a car-boot sale, and rubbish. But Michael insisted on another category: stuff he wasn't absolutely sure about. That went into a no-man's-land in the sheep pen inhabited by broken wardrobes, all his army kit from the desert war complete with tin dishes, salt and pepper pots, and uneaten hard-tack biscuits – and laundry hampers filled with Betty's silk dresses, each one veiled in mushroomy white mould. This was where he ordered me to put the letters. When I took them out, a telegram announcing Charlie's birth fluttered past me along the concrete, coming to rest against a pile of unpaid bills from the delicatessen (wrapped beautifully in white silk ribbon).

Halfway through the day we stopped for lunch in the garden, and Charlie's sisters sat side by side, both tall, slim, pretty women with blond skins and high cheekbones.

'Did you mind terribly,' I asked them shyly, 'when Betty ran away with Jordie?' Susannah said she hardly noticed, because they only ever saw Betty for an hour after tea, anyway, when they were brought downstairs, clean and smart, by the nanny.

'What I *do* remember,' Prophecy said, 'was when Charlie was two. I've such a vivid memory of being in the dining room, watching Jordie play with him. He adored babies and was very physical with them, in a way that Gaffer isn't. He was blowing raspberries on Charlie's arm, and Charlie was laughing and laughing with that lovely soft, fat chuckle that babies have.' She finished her tea. 'Maybe the reason Jordie left Bettiscombe in the end was that he just couldn't bear a situation where he loved his son so much, but couldn't acknowledge him, and had to watch him call another man "Daddy".' She got up to go indoors but Susannah lingered at the table.

'It must have been a great love affair,' I said.

She leaned forward. 'Prophecy will never believe this,' she whispered. 'But I'm sure Gaffer and Jordie were lovers during the war.'

It was so hard to take in, let alone believe. Maybe that's what Betty had meant, though, when she told me she had done 'a dreadful thing' to Michael. What odd marriages people had had in the past, where they did such complicated, cruel things to each other and yet went on living together. I was glad I had such a simple, straightforward relationship with Charlie.

When everyone had gone, he and I piled all the furniture he'd chosen on to a trailer behind our van. These included a self-portrait painted by Betty – where, very young and dressed in a starchy canvas smock, she gazed levelly out, as if judging others and finding them severely wanting – some delicate, spindly tables and chairs from the parlour where the screaming skull was kept, and the old grandfather clock. Up until now Charlie had always rejected everything to do with his parents' culti-vated, intellectual lifestyle. He'd often poked fun at it. When he was in the mood he even could effortlessly pastiche Michael's poetry:

Belgian
Chocolate dribbles
o'er
marble teeth and
slivers lava-like on cracked lips
where once passion played its wanton joyous games . . .

but now those lips can only mutter
'Who filled the soap dish with peanut butter?'
'Who clogged the bog?'
'Who filched the last, soft, leaf of toilet paper?'

And he'd always teased Betty with the farm animals: rudely mating his carthorses right outside her bedroom window. (And it *was* a rude sight. Carthorses have to be helped to breed, and the person who handles the fiddliest part of the business – Charlie's invariable role – is called 'the penis man'.) Once – before we married – he'd bought a whole lorry-load of sickly featherless chickens from a battery farm and they'd escaped and run in through the open door of the Manor on a hot summer night when Betty and Michael were hosting a grand dinner party. He used to double up with laughter as he described how the room had gradually filled with these panicky, disagreeable-looking birds and the guests had risen in alarm from the table. It sometimes seemed as if he'd begun farming simply in order to rebel against everything his parents believed in.

The packing done, we decided to pay a last visit to the wishing stone. On our way we passed the back of the walled garden and saw that Betty's fig tree had dropped a branch, laden with fruit, on the wrong side. Most of the figs had been turned into edible palaces by the wasps, but a few were still intact. We ate them guiltily, while a blackbird called a warning. The evening was chilly, but they were still warm and tasted of honey.

We struggled up Sliding Hill, getting scratched by brambles, and I was shocked to discover that the stone was now almost entirely hidden by bracken. It looked smaller than I remembered, too. We climbed up together and sat on the top, looking round at all the fields that the Pinneys had owned and lost, as one by one they were swallowed up by shadows and sea mist. Holding Charlie's hand, I made my usual secret wish, for financial security. But I doubted very much that it would be answered.

You could always tell it was spring at Egremont without opening your eyes. First thing – even before dawn, and the cockerel started his muffled crowing from the chicken yard – you'd hear a very particular noise. A heavy patter of feet on the roof right above the bedroom, loud mutterings, and a scrabbling, scratching noise, as of someone cack-handedly working a knobbly stick into the top of a chimney. This was the resident jackdaws. Listening to them was like eavesdropping on a gang of incompetent builders. There was the same worrying sound of falling bricks and plaster. The same long pauses while new strategies were thought out, or refreshment breaks taken, the same determination to proceed with a botched plan of action, and, of course, the same ruthless disregard for the feelings of the house-holders. Charlie and I did not dislike jackdaws. We just wished there was a way of reasoning with them.

Egremont was a small farm on the outskirts of an east Devon village. Surrounded by flat fields full of seeding docks, and a ramshackle collection of yards and sheds, the house itself was covered in unsightly pebbledash and had a roof that shed tiles in any strong wind. There were a number of large trees in the garden, too, which jackdaws were welcome to nest in, and there was even another chimney the opposite side of the house that we never used (largely because it was jammed solid with old jackdaw nests). They did not want to build in either of these places, though. They preferred the front-room chimney. It was regularly brushed and warm: ideal for baby jackdaws to grow up in.

As we had no central heating, and the only heat sources in the house were a rusty Aga in the kitchen and the fire in the front room, this was a point we were unwilling to give way over, either. And each spring always saw a renewal of hostilities on the matter. After living there for seventeen years we had grown increasingly exasperated by the way the jackdaws always won, so at the end of February Charlie wobbled about on the end of a ladder and cemented a piece of netting in the top of the disputed chimney. He hoped this would settle the question once and for all, and stop them wedging their sticks and blobs of mud inside, because usually we not only had smoky fires from March to September, but were pestered by teenaged jack-daws. They'd fall out of their nest, tumble down inside the chimney, and emerge, bewildered and covered in soot, into the front room. There they'd bounce anxiously on the sofa, scuffle about in the ironing basket and hide behind the books in the bookcase, crapping in terror when I tried to dislodge them. And that's not to mention the trouble they caused in the farmyard, where they ate cowcake, poultry food, eggs, chicks and duck-lings, along with more specialised items like pea seedlings and fresh window-putty.

Still, I used to comfort myself by thinking that we were at least better off than our friends in Cornwall. They lived next door to a woman who put huge quantities of bread out for the birds on her lawn every day – and as a result, their jackdaw-infested chimney was always stuffed to the brim with burnt toast.

But on that spring morning in 1998, I lay in bed blissfully free of the usual jackdaw-dread. I wondered idly what they would do, now that they couldn't use the front-room chimney any more? Which would they choose to nest in: the trees or the clogged-up chimney?

The stamping noises up above became more agitated, and there was plenty of shrill conversation. Then I heard the famil-iar sound of a bird landing on the roof with a knobbly stick in its mouth. This was followed by a dreadful grouting noise above a completely different part of the bedroom, and then a soft, falsetto caw of triumph. What on earth were they up to?

When we ran out into the garden we saw that they were car-rying out a two-pronged attack. One lot were stuffing sticks hopefully through the chimney-mesh and the others were burrowing through the crumbling eaves of the house, and hauling bundles of twigs into the attic.

In his book *Farmer's Glory* the countryman Arthur Street maintained that the best thing to put in a catapult and lob at a bird was a small potato, but we disagreed. Over the years we'd been living at Egremont we'd found that Cadbury's Mini Eggs made far more aerodynamically efficient missiles, and also, in the spring, there were always an awful lot of them lying about the house. Mind you, it was difficult to hit a jackdaw with them – the birds were so good at side-stepping in mid-air – but at least a hail of chocolate eggs slowed down the nest-building a little bit.

This morning, though, Charlie wasn't interested in getting out the catapult. He was so maddened by the sound of jackdaws dragging large amounts of flammable material into the attic that he decided to go up there and confront them in person. This was a mistake, because he didn't take into account the fact that they can walk upside down on their elbows and have exceedingly sharp beaks. Soon after he swung up through the attic trap-door there was an anguished cry, and his legs appeared through the ceiling of our oldest son's bedroom.

'It's time to get up, anyway,' I said soothingly to Sam, as Charlie released a further storm of laths, plaster and horsehair.

'Are you OK?' I called up to Charlie.

'I'll be out in a minute,' he said indistinctly. 'The good news is I've found that old Chuck Berry LP I was looking for.'

'The bad news is, he's wrecked my bedroom,' Sam said crossly.

It was true. I wondered anxiously how much it would cost to put right, because plastering was probably too technical for Charlie to manage on his own. Normally, when something went wrong in the house he had a stab at fixing it himself. So we had strange taps in the bathroom that made a sound like the QE2 docking in heavy fog whenever you turned them on, and, for reasons I had never fully understood, all the doorknobs had been mounted on thick cubes of wood. But the most striking feature of the house was the home-made wood-burning stove in the front room. Charlie had had the idea of constructing this a year earlier, infuriated by our children moaning on about how cold they were. He also disliked the way everyone in the family except him wore coats, hats and gloves indoors all winter. Although this gave a slightly formal feel to meals and TV watching, it did have a useful side. It meant that if someone you didn't like called in hoping for a cup of tea you could say, quite convincingly, that you would have loved to talk to them but, unfortunately, you were just on your way out to an important appointment.

An enormous object made out of leftover scrap iron, the wood-burning stove was changed and adapted at irregular intervals. Charlie would suddenly have a brainwave about making it better, heave it off its plinth, and trundle it through the house on an oily trolley. Hours later it would return, differently shaped and with shiny weld-marks like slug-trails all over it, and Charlie would explain the new features.

'This,' he'd say proudly, manipulating an odd-shaped wedge of metal, 'is a baffle for increasing the air-flow. And you have to be careful . . . damn.'

'What?'

'It wasn't supposed to come off when I did that.'

'Will it still work?'

'Of course it will still work. You'll just have to hold it in place with an oven-glove until I get round to re-welding it.'

Then he'd fire it up, and heat would gradually diffuse through the room – though, oddly enough, it rarely got hotter than an open fire. In fact, sometimes I wondered whether he had simply managed to create a device for blowing heat up the chimney. Or – and this was the bit I dreaded – there'd be an agonised shout from the front room, followed by the sound of a bucket of water hitting red-hot metal. I'd rush in to find Charlie kneeling in front of the fireplace, in a front room that resembled the smoke-box of an early steam-engine, its walls barely visible through a pall of smuts and soot.

Officially, Charlie was now an inventor. When Betty got ill we had moved from Gloucestershire back to the West Country, so Charlie could spend his mother's last year sitting by her bed, talking to her and holding her hand while she gradually faded away. Egremont was a 'dealer's farm' – too small to be economically viable, best used as a fattening station for calves, bullocks and sheep while prices went up (or down – which was what usually happened to us). But it was ideal for what Charlie had decided he really wanted to do: designing, testing and building horse-drawn machinery. He had begun this because he got tired of pulling old machinery out of hedges and mending it. His designs were modern, used hydraulics and hi-tech gearing systems and won awards at the Royal Show – but though he got plenty of press interest it was the wrong sort. No matter how long he spent explaining his ideas to journalists the resulting feature nearly always showed him cuddling a carthorse under a headline like 'Back to the Past!'. Still, it was interesting talking to these folk, and discovering how little they knew about the countryside. The best question they ever asked was: 'What do the animals do at weekends?' Though 'How do you tell when a lamb is dead?' came a close second. A specialist agricultural journalist called George MacPherson (who did get the details right) told me that all the rural inventors he had ever met were the same: they lived in tumbledown shacks and had wives whose eyes blazed with inner rage. He added, kindly, that I was the only wife he'd met so far without that distinctive look.

Just before eight, I took Sam, aged seventeen, off to the station to catch the train to his sixth-form college. (Kathy, nineteen, was at university.) And when I got back the first visitor of the morning, a policeman, arrived. He unbuckled his belt, poured himself a coffee and set his radio down next to the biscuit tin. We were a regular stopping-off point for him whenever he was patrolling in the area.

'What was that thing I met out by the gate?' he asked. 'It was small and woolly, and for a moment I thought it was going to speak to me with a human voice.'

'Oh – that's . . .' I began, and fell silent with embarrassment, leaving it to Charlie to explain about the lamb. Recently, our latest purchase, Holbein, had reached adolescence, and like many young stallions, developed an evil streak. Charlie always called this 'playfulness'. 'He'll grow out of it in time,' he used to say, cheerfully, about an earlier stallion, which liked sidling up and biting me savagely on the bum.

If Holbein had been human, he would have been a football hooligan, but as he was a horse he spent his time opening gates with his tongue, letting himself into forbidden fields and bullying the sheep. He liked to single out a timid ewe and kick her in the head with a hollow crack that could be heard half a mile away. And he often trotted dangerously close to lambs. A week earlier, he had finally gone too far and stamped on a lamb, and we found it dragging itself miserably across the grass, while its mother blared in distress. It was no good simply moving the sheep to a different field, because Holbein would have got at them again. The only safe place for them was the garden, which had layers of netting round it to stop animals getting in, and our toddler from getting out. (The garden at Egremont, like the one back at Bettiscombe, was always being sacrificed in the interests of the farm.)

The day we put the sheep there I was surprised by how uninterested they were in the lawns. They only wanted to eat the flowers and shrubs.

'That's the blackcurrants gone,' Charlie said, the first morning, as he came in for coffee. As he went out again he observed that we would not be having any figs in the summer, either: a sheep was stripping the buds off with awesome efficiency. They did not slow down at night, either. We could hear them chomping and tearing at vegetation even at 3 a.m., and sometimes, just to enliven the hours of darkness, they bowled garden tables along paths and kicked over dustbins.

Within a few days the place resembled a miniature version of the African veldt, grazed by a succession of animals from warthogs to giraffes. To be fair, they had also done their best to improve the fertility of the place: everywhere you looked there were black pellets. Or, as Charlie put it: 'The garden looks as if a very short, demented drunk with a strimmer has gone beserk – and then crapped himself.' The weeping willow had been nibbled into an art deco shrub with just one upward-facing sprout at the top. And we even saw sheep running, reared up on their back legs, past the cherry tree and biting off leaves as they went.

I quite enjoyed the way their behaviour altered as the days went by. In the beginning they were wild and flighty, and disliked being approached or looked at. Then, gradually, they became fascinated by us. A gang of them began following me, enthralled, as I hung out the washing. Often they would wipe their faces on the sheets, or taste the toes of pairs of tights.

Another lot took to staring rudely in at the windows at us while we ate dinner, and a former pet lamb started chasing me round the side of the house and attempting to squeeze in through the front door before it shut. If he succeeded he'd do a victory dance round the kitchen table.

But after a week most of them were so blasé about being in a garden that they did not even open their eyes when a car revved nearby. This was inconvenient because their favourite snoozing point was just inside the gate, and we had to add ten minutes to every journey, just to allow time to roll sleepy matrons out of the way, and heft stout lambs about.

Among all these happy families, the ewe with the injured lamb stuck out. She was always fretting over the way he could not follow her. She'd stop halfway through stripping bark off rhododendrons, and blare at him to come over. When he didn't, she would stand next to him, sniffing his back, and nudge him with her nose. He'd make an effort, then, and haul himself up on his front legs. He had an engagingly cheeky expression, and he tended to live in the front flowerbed, where he took a keen interest in visitors. As they came in he would sometimes drag himself a little way towards them, stare into their faces, and bleat. And it was hard not to think, as the policeman had, that he was trying to communicate. But we'd been feeling increasingly uncomfortable about him. In the past, the children and I had nursed countless injured or sick lambs, usually in boxes in the kitchen. We'd fed them every three hours, and moved them frequently on to fresh bedding to stop them getting pressure sores, but they never got better: they simply took longer to die. (In some cases, months.) And it felt cruel keeping them alive because normally a young lamb is a living incarnation of joy — racing and springing round the fields in the sunshine, leaping into the air with pure happiness. There was something almost obscene about a lamb that could do none of this and just watched from the shadows. It was clear this latest one was never going to recover, either. Because he couldn't feed, we had been milking out the ewe and feeding him in bottles, and he was getting weaker.

Explaining this to the policeman made Charlie decide to take action. He looked up the number of the local lamb-bank (a local introduction bureau for sheep farmers, putting people desperate for lambs in touch with those just as keen to be rid of them), and discovered there was a smallholding two miles away that had a spare lamb.

Meanwhile, though, it was time for 'crib'. This is a useful extra meal that people in the West Country go in for. It fills that painful chasm between breakfast and lunch, and there's a pleasant irresponsibility about it. You do not have to have anything specific for crib, like egg and bacon – it simply consists of any old snack you happen to fancy. This morning it was cheese on toast and hot cross buns, and just as we had finished making a fresh pot of coffee, Seymour, a sheep farmer from half a dozen fields away, turned up to collect his lamb castrator. He had to have chocolate cake for his crib because his wife had recently put him on a diet, and he was feeling deprived and gloomy. (I always kept some in the fridge for him.)

'What really gets me,' the policeman said, launching into one of his favourite topics, 'is the way young mothers let themselves go. My heart sinks to look at them, outside the primary school at three-thirty, with their unbrushed hair, rolls of flab and baggy tracksuits. And when you think that it's only a few years since they were coming out of school themselves, looking gorgeous in those short uniforms . . .'

It was a bit of a puzzle to men, I supposed, but not to anyone who had devoted any time to looking after a toddler. While I listened, I kept an eye on our three-year-old, Nat, who had stuck his head out of the cat flap, impatient to be outside, playing with the animals.

'Sheep lose their glamour fast, too, ' I remarked, going over and picking Nat up. He writhed, all solid-packed muscle, like a piglet. 'I'm always so impressed by the way rams don't mind that their wives are all saggy and covered in bits of dung, and still find them attractive.'

'You wouldn't be if you knew as much about rams as I do,' Seymour said. 'Ours even eye up the old gardener who comes in to prune the orchard.'

At this point the police radio announced that a severed hand had been reported by the roadside in Cullompton. The policeman sighed and got to his feet. 'It'll be a rubber glove – it always is – but I've still got to check it out.'

The hippies who owned the spare lamb lived down a long, overgrown lane, and were doubtful about us. They wore hand-knitted trousers with very high waistbands and quizzed us about our lamb-rearing skills as earnestly and worriedly as if they were social workers and we were fostering a child. The lamb (whose real mother had no milk at all) was bony, grey-wooled and lively – but smelt dreadful. It had mild diarrhoea and an eye-watering personal odour (and a look of apology in its eyes, as if it sensed that it was a bit socially unacceptable). We immediately named it 'Pongo'.

When we got back home Charlie picked up the injured lamb and disappeared round the corner to the woodshed. After a few minutes I heard the sound of the axe hitting the block. I felt guilty – but what good was that? Over the years I had learned that when you have a farm it is like ordering your own personal universe: it is up to you to arrange matters so that you make money out of the animals without being cruel. I soon realised what an active virtue goodness is: laziness, inattention and stupidity quickly led to suffering. After all, if we'd discovered what Holbein was up to more quickly, the lamb never would have got hurt in the first place. While I tried to stifle my inner townie, which still fretted over the ethics of killing anything handicapped, Charlie fetched a craft knife and skilfully flayed the dead lamb. Then he dressed Pongo in the skin and we pushed him and the injured lamb's mother into the stable and left them there, imprisoning the mother in a version of the stocks, so she couldn't do him any serious harm. At first, she kept sniffing him suspiciously and sitting down whenever he tried to drink, but after a couple of hours the skin slipped, tangling Pongo's legs so that he could only move with difficulty, and you could practically see her relax. Of course it was her lamb – it couldn't walk!

By the next day we could let them out. Pongo had visibly fattened, there was a milky rim to his mouth and his evil smell had lessened. Charlie rearranged the lambskin so it hung from Pongo's neck like a cloak, and he wore it with a casual, throw-away elegance, like a young prince. And as for the ewe, she was so proud. She kept ushering Pongo in and out of the deepest parts of the rhododendron bushes and stamping her foot at the other sheep. You could sense her thinking: 'See – I knew he'd come right in the end.' It was hard not to think that – despite the doubtful morality – we had done the right thing.

Meanwhile, I saw Charlie weighing the axe in his hands and looking at the jackdaws. 'Do we know any circus knife-throwers?' he asked.

Chapter Eleven

'It is perhaps only when women are too poor to keep servants that they taste to the full the joys of motherhood. For the first two or three years of the infant's life it is a tyranny and a slavery to the mother, but out of this slavery there comes an infinite tenderness . . .' The English Country Gentleman – Neville Lytton, 1925

It *was* a slavery and a tyranny, looking after Nat: following him wearily around all day trying to make sure he didn't injure himself. He didn't sleep much, either, and when he did it was in my arms. So he was always in our bed. But apart from the fact that he woke me three or four times a night, by singing monotonously or poking me with his tiny rubbery feet, I enjoyed this. I'd always loved the easy sluttishness of domestic life: cuddling down in the warm nest of an unmade bed with an affectionate baby and a slightly nettled husband.

I felt happiest as a mother. I'd enjoyed sitting for hours in

Sam's room in the evenings reading to him and discussing stories, or bicycling at top speed along country lanes beside Kathy as she haughtily rode her latest borrowed pony. My relationships with my children were the first I'd ever had which were entirely natural, where I hadn't had to conceal part of my personality – the side that occasionally felt angry or frustrated – in order to avoid giving offence. But then, from Charlie's point of view motherhood had probably not improved me. I didn't go with him to many shows now, preferring to stay at home with the kids – and I spent any money I had on new clothes for them and wore their cast-offs. (They took the place of all my old London clothes, which had fallen into rags: I wore one of Kathy's old school coats for years, and once Sam grew out of his urban camouflage trousers they became a staple of my wardrobe.)

Nat snuggled hotly into my side and began singing his wordless night-time song: 'Mmm. Oooeer. Mmm.' I rolled him over to make him stop, and heard a noise I'd been dreading. It came from the front room immediately below, where we'd put the new furniture from Bettiscombe, and it sounded like an old-fashioned party in progress: educated voices raised in conversation and breaking into polite laughter, and music. Some nights it was piano-playing, but tonight there was a flute. I went out on to the landing, telling myself that I was imagining things, and stood in the pitch dark leaning over the stairwell, the draught from the ill-fitting window in the bathroom fluttering round my feet and making the loose carpet levitate. The flute recital was clearer out here. Accomplished and unearthly, it floated directly up from the open front-room door. I was too cowardly to go down – I just ran back to bed and squeezed myself back in between Charlie and Nat, and hoped the sound would go away. It generally did after an hour or two.

I was used to the house making odd noises, and good at explaining them away. Often the stairs would creak stealthily, as if someone was walking up them, and I'd tell myself that it was the wood contracting in the cool night air. But it was harder to explain this, and when it first started I hadn't liked to mention it to Charlie in case he thought me idiotic. As the months went by I began to hear the sounds in the day, too, and they always stopped when I reached the threshold of the room. Had I left the television on by mistake? Was a car or tractor parked up in the road outside the garden with its radio playing loudly? No. There was no reasonable explanation for the noises at all.

And then one afternoon when I was playing upstairs with Nat, I heard them louder than usual. I ran down and saw Charlie standing in the front-room doorway looking puzzled.

'Can you hear it, too?'

'Yes, I've heard it for weeks, now.'

I sat down on the stairs, relieved. 'It scares me, especially at night. What do you think is causing it?'

'No idea.' He laughed uneasily. 'Maybe it's ghosts, and they've moved here from Bettiscombe.'

Letter from Caky: 'Now I'm working at Cosmopolitan *I think I've worked out why you're finding it so hard to write for women's magazines. It's because of their very nature. You see, you and I know full well that the world is — let's say it's orange. But all women have a deep craving for a world that's pink, so they'll pay £2 or more for a magazine that tells them the world is pink, and they've been right all along. People like you are hired to write articles imbued with the utter conviction of the pinkness of the world.'*

I'd been supplementing the family income by writing ever since Christmas 1986, when I heard that a friend from university was editing a small section of the *Observer* and looking for new writers. So I sent him an article about the farmers I knew, and the dodgy turkeys they sold to make ends meet. The next week I opened the paper and found my article printed inside it. The shock nearly stopped my heart: I felt as if someone had shoved a spear in under my ribs. After that I began writing more and more, but I never made much money, largely because I had no confidence at all, was always sobbing to myself about how bad my work was and only managed one article every three months.

'I can't even show it to you,' I'd say to Charlie, after sitting up all night rewriting a single paragraph over and over. 'It just won't come out right, however hard I try.'

He'd dodge round me, snatch the article out of my hand and read it with a frown on his face, occasionally snorting with concentration. 'It's perfectly all right. Send it off! And for God's sake stop having a nervous breakdown every time you set pen to paper.' Then he'd storm out of the back door, and a little while later I'd see him bowling past the window in a cart with our wildest horse bucking and rearing in the shafts, and trotting crab-wise as it approached the gate. Although he loathed the emotional state I got into when I wrote, Charlie could be supportive, too. When I started a novel he bought a computer with the compensation he got for a motorbike accident and insisted on typing each chapter into it as I wrote, so that I was forced to keep going. (He couldn't spell, so the book read rather strangely.)

After a while I stopped writing just about the countryside and got commissions to discuss emotional problems for women's magazines. I'd spend hours in cow-stalls, poultry yards and converted barns, talking to my friends about their marriages. And then I'd memorise what they'd said, rush home, write it up and painfully shape it into a piece on 'things you would prefer not to do in front of your husband' or 'holiday sex'. According to these researches there wasn't much sex on holiday – not when you'd been married for ten years. In fact, I tapped into a rich seam of dismay about the whole subject. One friend, remarked, typically, that 'When it's his birthday he insists on having sex; but my special birthday treat is always *not to do it at all.*'

One afternoon we were in the village playground (trying to ignore the aroma of pig-dung that always hung about the place) when another mother started talking about a friend of hers whose marriage had just broken down.

'Oh dear, what happened?' We leaned forward, concerned.

'She said she got on OK with him but she had to leave because the earth never moved.'

All of us spontaneously burst into laughter at the absurdity of this remark.

Strange anecdotes would get thrown up in these long conversations. One neighbour revealed that years earlier, when she had been working as a nurse in a private hospital in London, she had been approached in the middle of the night by an auxiliary and asked if she wanted to see Roger Moore stark naked? He had only just become famous and was recovering from a minor op downstairs. My friend was led into a softly lit room where warm air was coming through an open window, and Roger Moore was lying asleep on a bed with his arms folded behind his head. She said that he looked very much more handsome than he ever did on screen, with a powerful animal magnetism and skin so perfect that it appeared polished. The two of them gazed at him in awe for some minutes, briefly lifted the sheet across his middle to satisfy their curiosity (nothing unusual to report) and then crept away.

I hated the idea of not being wildly enthusiastic about sex. But something strange had happened to me when I had children. Before then, I just worshipped Charlie and I felt about him the way the nurses did about Roger Moore. I would often think back wistfully to the first time we slept together, in the little bedroom at the top of his cottage, with its tiny window furred with cobwebs and dead flies, its tarnished brass bed and its oil lamp throwing a warm, yellow circle of light. He was so beautiful then, his body magnificent with its heavy muscles and long legs, and I could never get enough of him. I'd tremble with excitement just at the very thought of touching him. But somehow, when I had children, those feelings got transferred. It was their faces and skins that seemed unnaturally perfect; and it was them that I longed to hold.

Every now and then, though, I'd come across a friend whose experience of sex was completely different from mine. It was like hearing a language I couldn't understand, then. I was always telling myself how happy and lucky I was, but when I spoke to these women I would feel unsettled.

'I was very shy when we wed,' one said, as we waited in the rain at the end of a muddy lane for her husband's cows to appear, so we could steer them into the correct field. 'It took months for it to work. But now it keeps getting better and better. More inventive. Deeper. You know?' I didn't. I sensed something was wrong with my own relationship but I thought it was just that I wasn't trying hard enough. Unlike my other female friends, though, I tried never to reject my husband physically, just because I wasn't in the mood. But even this made him unhappy. 'It isn't the same,' he used to say. 'When the other person doesn't really, really want to.'

Along with the writing – and freelance copy-editing for different publishers – I used to do bed and breakfast and evening meals, too, because Charlie had started teaching other farmers how to use carthorses. A whole group of students would come and stay for a few days at a time and I'd glance out of the windows at them while I fluffed up pillows and scrubbed egg off breakfast plates. Even after all these years I still wasn't confident enough to help with breaking or teaching. I could clean the horses out, feed them and take them out to pasture – and that was all. But then, someone had to earn the money. And it was so difficult to earn anything significant from rearing animals or making farm machinery. And besides, as I often said to Charlie, if we'd both been horsey all our income would have been spent on stallions and mares and there would have been nothing left over to pay the electricity and food bills.

Mostly, the students stood about in knots on the windiest field on the farm, hunching into their coats and stamping to keep the frost off their toes while Charlie made them take turns guiding a matched pair in and out of old traffic cones. The horses would twitch their backs and tails mutinously while this was going on, and steal covert glances at Charlie. They didn't obey the students at all, just followed Charlie's voice-commands. And they walked so slowly up the field away from the farm that it bordered on being insulting. (On the way back, they'd always gallop.)

Charlie was immensely popular with these students. They'd almost fight to sit next to him at break-times, and they ordered quantities of his machines. One married couple were especially keen. They bought the whole range of equipment, and a pair of horses, and they kept ringing up for advice. They'd drop in frequently, too, to stay the night or catch a meal on their way to visit family in Cornwall. They were both very blonde: the woman, Sophie (or 'Sofe' as her husband called her), curvy and strong-minded, with those half-shut eyes that keen horsewomen always get from squinting into the sun. Her husband, Peter, was shyer and quieter and always seemed to walk a few paces behind her.

Somehow, I invariably ended up talking to Peter while Charlie and Sofe argued about horses.

'You should brush this poor thing more often,' she'd say. 'Look! He's getting rain-scald.'

'Rubbish,' Charlie would growl. 'Too much grooming removes natural oils.'

'And the dust in this stable!' she'd exclaim, running her finger along the dividers. 'It's outrageous.'

Often Peter and I ended up in a café with my children while Charlie and Sofe examined horseflesh on a nearby farm, or we'd share a pew in a country church while the other two struggled outside to stop the wedding cortege from bolting. I both liked and disliked being with Peter. Sometimes it was embarrassing: he was the sort who sings very loudly in the wrong key in church, drowning out not only the congregation, but the vicar as well. And he had a rather bland character, compared with Charlie. But his physical appearance was glorious. Fine bone-structure, artfully tousled hair, small almond-coloured teeth, a feminine beauty blurred by day-old stubble. Even his nostrils looked as if they had been shaped by a master-sculptor. But while it was lovely gazing at him, it was troubling, too, because I realised that, against my will, he was beginning to fascinate me. He always seemed to be standing and sitting a fraction too close. If we all went out in a car I had to go in the back with Peter and my children while Sofe and Charlie, in the front, bickered about whether using blinkers was sensible or cruel. And each time we rounded a corner at speed (Charlie driving recklessly because he was so annoyed) Peter's shoulder would accidentally rub against mine. And at each contact I felt as if my body was about to burst into flames.

I didn't like this, because I'd always felt strongly that marriage was about unconditional love and total fidelity. If one of you had an affair without the other's knowledge how could you have a proper, deep, close relationship? There'd be deceit at the heart of it, and a whole section of your life you could never discuss with your spouse. And an open marriage, where you both had lovers, was even worse. One of my parents' friends had had that kind. I didn't care for the emptiness and bitterness I saw in it. Besides, damaged marriages created unhappy children. I didn't often have strong opinions about anything, and usually fell in with what others believed or wanted. But I couldn't have felt more fiercely about this. As far as fidelity went, I was on the extreme wing of the Spanish Inquisition.

Somehow, though, it was impossible to avoid bumping into Peter and Sofe. On my birthday, Charlie said he would take me on a mystery tour, and we ended up at Peter and Sophe's farm. We crept through fields of grazing ponies, and surprised them in their kitchen, where they were very touchingly curled up on the sofa together, fast asleep. All they had to eat in their house was an iceberg lettuce seething with greenfly. (Charlie ran his finger across the top of the fridge and when it came away black he raised one eyebrow quizzically at Sofe. 'Everyone knows only dull women have tidy homes,' she said, nettled.) So we went out to a chippy and on to a fairground. While, in one way, it made a perfect outing, because I got to go on all my favourite rides with Kathy and Sam, it was unsettling, too. Peter actually touched my arm with his fingers in the back of the car this time, tentatively, as if trying out the opening bars of a tune. I moved away sharply, but my heart was beating too fast and my face had gone hot. I hoped he didn't realise the effect he was having on me. And I told myself his touch hadn't meant anything, and I was just being foolish. Why would he fancy me anyway? I wasn't nearly as pretty as his wife, and they seemed contented, though once, when we were talking about our marriages and I said that although mine had lasted fourteen years it had all gone by in a blur, like a single happy, exciting day, he was surprised. 'We've been together eight years,' he said. 'But it feels far, far longer.'

One wintry teatime, I left Kathy and Charlie at home in bed with the flu and drove off to collect Sam from his best friend's house. Once there I got deep into conversation with his friend's mother, TJ. She had a freckly face, reddish-brown hair and green eyes sprinkled with gold.

This evening she was laughing about the way her female relatives kept giving her lace teddies and silk knickers for Christmas.

'They think I need to be more glamorous,' TJ said. 'But they've got it all wrong: they ought to be giving my husband the ritzy underwear, because he finds me irresistibly attractive even in sloppy old sweaters and jeans. If I wore lace teddies *I'd never get any peace*!' I laughed because it was such a familiar story.

'I do feel guilty about being such a frost,' she said. 'I really wish I *was* more wanton.'

'What does wanton mean?' her son asked suddenly, from the doorway. He was always listening in on our conversations.

'It means arbitrary and capricious,' I replied.

'Gosh, how nice it would be if I was more arbitrary,' TJ said, to put him off the scent, as he ran off to look it up in the dictionary. 'And capricious! Mmm, mmm, that's exactly what I need.'

When I got home Charlie was pacing the kitchen, smoking furiously. He poured himself a Scotch, drank it down in one and pulled me upstairs. He told me he'd been asleep in the bed when a mouse ran across the room and jumped into the brief-case I took with me when I went to see editors in London, and which always lay open, because the catch was faulty. While scrabbling in this briefcase for the mouse, his fingers had closed on a foil-wrapped condom, and he'd instantly assumed I'd bought it so I could have wild affairs when I went to London. Since I had never in my entire life had the nerve to buy a condom in a shop, and anyway had never wanted to have an affair, the whole accusation was preposterous. (It was more likely that the condom had fallen off the top of the wardrobe, where he'd put some out of reach of the children.) Nothing I said would calm him, though. I swore on the Bible that I had always been true, but he wasn't convinced.

I'd almost managed to reassure him by the time we went to sleep. I had a nightmare: Peter, dressed in a fox-suit, broke into my chicken run and tore my poultry to pieces with his teeth. When I woke, sweating with horror, I found Charlie was already awake. He'd had a disturbing dream of his own, where he caught me and Peter having sex. We clung together tightly for comfort, and I thought it better not to tell him about those ambiguous touches in the back of the car.

The next day Sofe and Peter dropped in to ask if they could stay the night. I didn't want to say yes, but Charlie was his usual expansive self. They'd brought a bottle of cherry brandy with them, and his eyes lit up at the sight. And while I cooked dinner he explained to us all how the shape of the carthorse has altered like the shape of women, responding to different historical fashions. For instance, in the 1920s powdered resin was rubbed into their feet to make the hair stiffer and whiter, and back then a good horse was one with feather from its knees to its feet, sticking out like a bell. (Resin was banned in the thirties because it actually deformed horses' legs, causing great knobbly growths under the feather.)

After dinner we watched television with Kathy's three pet goslings. These lived in the conservatory, in a mound of guano, and when they were let out, flailed after her wherever she went, squeaking and holding out their little featherless wings. From behind, they looked like a row of pale yellow, fluffy bottles as they bobbed from side to side in her wake. And when she felt like it she would roll them in towels (so they didn't crap on the carpet) and sit them in front of the TV. Farm animals love television, and lambs, especially, will watch it for hours. A woman once wrote to me to say she lost a penful of sheep on her farm, one day, and after an extensive search, discovered they had wandered through her open front door and ended up in front of

the television, watching the Test Match from behind her husband's armchair.

I hurried through the washing-up and went off to bed when
the children did. I wanted no more flirtation. I was sick of the
trouble it caused. The others didn't seem to notice I had gone.

I woke suddenly at 1 a.m., with a sense of wrongness. Charlie
hadn't yet come to bed, and I couldn't hear his voice. Instead
there was just the sound of one person walking very slowly
through the downstairs rooms. I checked on the children and
they were both asleep, Kathy surrounded, as usual, by a heap of
old Bettiscombe stuffed toys. Their eyes reflected the landing
light, so it looked as if they were watching me doubtfully. And as
I came out of her room I saw Peter coming up the stairs.

'What's happening?' I asked.

'Charlie and Sofe drove off to buy cigarettes hours ago,' he
said. 'And I can't sleep.'

'Oh. Have you everything you need?'

'Yes.'

'Good night, then.'

I went back to bed, and to my dismay he wandered in after
me. He sat down on the duvet, breathing sickly fumes of cherry
brandy in my direction. 'Charlie and Sofe went off in the car
together ages ago,' he said, slurring his words slightly. 'You'll be
glad to know Sofe was driving.'

'You've just told me that,' I said, a little waspishly.

He leaned forward and kissed me. His lips felt harder and more
individually distinct than Charlie's. 'No,' I said, pulling away. 'I've

never been unfaithful and I never want to be.' I went on in this vein for some time, feeling ridiculously uptight and Mary Poppinsish, especially as a small part of me had guiltily fantasised about this moment and longed for it to happen. He listened to my homily with a smile playing over his face. In the distance a familiar partially ruptured exhaust could be heard getting closer. There was a roar as it negotiated a sharp turn in the road.

'If that's your husband I'd better go before I give him something to be jealous about,' he said cockily, as he left. It was Charlie: after a short while I heard his voice in the kitchen.

I drifted in and out of sleep, then, until Charlie climbed into bed, reeking of cherries, and put his hands round my waist. 'What a well-groomed little wife,' he said in a pleased tone. It seemed as if the whole night different men, ponging violently of cherry brandy, had been interfering with me. I didn't dare tell him what had happened. The next morning I discussed the incident with Kathy instead. And we both marvelled at the oddity of a world where people casually broke their marriage vows and tried to kiss others when they weren't the slightest bit in love with them, and probably didn't even like them much. It was curious when you thought about it. What had Peter been offering me, after all? If I'd kissed him back all I'd have had at most was a few minutes of hurried sex. It was an insult, really. What kind of person would have accepted?

The next morning Sofe was obscurely upset. 'I heard you and Charlie laughing in bed last night,' she said with a hurt look. 'What was that about?'

'Noah's Ark,' I answered, mashing cornflakes into left-over

gravy for the goslings. 'Kathy wrote this poem at school.' I held it out, but Sofe didn't bother to look at it. It started:

Winter cold and dark, and I remember the ark
A ship against the golden sky, with animals that rush and fly . . .

It went on in much the same vein for lines and lines.

'Anyway, Charlie was annoyed by it, feeling it was dull and pretentious, and last night he came up with a new version. I've written it down. It really made me laugh.'

She looked at Charlie's poem, but she didn't even crack a smile, and she wasn't mollified.

Peter darted back from the car just as they were about to leave and gave me a last quick peck on the lips, so fast that I couldn't dodge him. He never visited again. And, in fact, the couple's interest in us seemed to wane from that moment, although from time to time over the next few years Sofe would drop in on her own and spend a day with Charlie and the horses. Sometimes I'd think about it all with puzzlement. I felt I'd missed something – that there was some extra meaning to the whole sequence of events that I had signally failed to grasp. But I didn't know what it could be.

The animals went in two by two, but what did they do with all the poo?
Old Noah roared out to his missus: 'The bilges are awash with pisses.'
There's no time for a p.m. nap. 'Give us a hand to shift this crap . . .'

Chapter Twelve

Country tip – How to tell if the locals like you:
'When I first moved here I noticed that my sheep kept vanishing. I thought
of going to the police, but I didn't want to upset the neighbours. So in the
end I asked a local official, who knew the moor well. His first question was:
"How many sheep are you losing a year?" When I said it was a steady
10 per cent, he said. "Well, your neighbours obviously like you. If they
wanted you to leave they'd be taking half . . ."' – Dartmoor farmer

'The thing about village life,' I said to TJ, 'is that you always get
a label.'

'A label?'

TJ was my very best friend now. We'd met years before when
she'd moved from London to a large house in the West
Country, and had a son, Josh, the same age as my Sam. She had
a little daughter now, Grace – an afterthought, like my Nat –
and the shared madness of having another child late in life had

made us closer. Her daughter was two years older than Nat, but she didn't mind playing with him. It was a relief, because all my other old friends had gradually discouraged me from calling. I'd had to make a completely new set out of the mothers at toddler group. And none of them understood, the way TJ did, exactly why I'd longed for another, last child. She knew I'd wanted him for conversation and company, for going to cinemas and fair-grounds and cafés with, because Charlie didn't like doing any of those things. I'd had Nat, just as she'd had Grace, for a particular kind of very close relationship that I couldn't get elsewhere. We often discussed our unease at being both happy and strangely dissatisfied with our spouses, and she had the knack of express-ing what I stopped short of thinking.

That morning, for the first time, I noticed she had lost a lot of weight. The baggy clothes she wore hung even looser. When I asked her if she was dieting she said, taken aback, that of course she wasn't. She was just walking the dog a bit more often, and had lost some of her enthusiasm for doughnuts. (I had noticed that the brief lists she kept on her kitchen table no longer con-tained the word 'chocolate' followed by three exclamation marks.)

'Yes,' I went on. 'A little mini-biography that everyone in the village gets to hear except you. Like – you know that man with the odd face who lives near Hembury Fort? I always forget his name.'

'The one who looks as if someone's sat on his head?'

'Yes. Well, his mini-biog is: "Got drunk at the harvest supper, and French-kissed two members of the football team." '

'Yes – it is.' TJ smiled. 'I remember being told that!' She was ironing: she paused to squirt more water on the sheet in front of her.

I'd become extra aware of these mini-biogs because I'd been going to so many toddler groups and play-schools, and had quantities of new people described to me swiftly and maliciously. At one I'd met a woman who had only recently moved to a village near Cullompton and had a truly dreadful mini-biog. (Which, unusually, she had heard.) Divorced, with a small baby, she explained that she had bought a cottage off a sweet old couple. And after less than a month the drains had blocked solid. So she called in a local plumber. She thought that was the end of it, until she noticed that people in the village had odd expressions whenever they greeted her. And then, one dreadful evening, she overheard herself being discussed in the pub. Apparently, when the plumber had cleared her system he had discovered thousands and thousands of used condoms clogging it up, and had assumed (because the sweet old couple couldn't possibly be responsible) that she had done it herself in three weeks' occupancy.

'Isn't it awful!' this poor woman had said, staring at me while she clutched her baby. 'How can I explain that they've got it wrong? Do you think I could take out an ad in the parish magazine?'

'That's exactly why my mum selected her cleaner so carefully,' TJ said. 'Because, as you know, village cleaners are the ones who supply the most obscene biographical detail. It's a brave woman who has one at all – unless, of course she does what my mum did.'

'And what was that?'

'She hired an imbecile. You wouldn't believe the things this woman did. She'd iron one leg of each pair of trousers with a crease in it, and the other flat, and once she found a very old mess the cat had made, that had gone dry, in the corner of the kitchen, and buffed it to a high shine with the floor-polisher. But she never said anything rotten about my mum.'

To be honest, though, if there was one thing I had learned in nearly quarter of a century of living in the country, it was that it didn't matter if your fellow-villagers did know the odd painful detail about you. They were very forgiving. They had to be, because there is so little privacy in the countryside. If you enjoy going out at dawn, say, and dancing about in your secure, well-hedged garden dressed only in a pair of Calvin Klein underpants, you can be sure that within a few days every single person within a radius of about five miles will know all about this harmless quirk. Fields and roads are no more private than gardens. Anything you say to a companion while rambling along an isolated footpath or bicycling down an overgrown lane is bound to be overheard by a farmer crouching behind a bush. Sound carries remarkably well across an empty landscape, and even if your comments are not caught by the person they would most enrage or interest, they are likely to be helpfully passed on.

But this intense curiosity of country folk as to the true nature of their neighbours is not, ultimately, unkind. It is all part of a lengthy weighing-up process, at the end of which an astute assessment will be made of your weaknesses and strengths.

Recently TJ had been earning a fine label of her own. When her husband lost his job, interest rates went up and they couldn't pay the mortgage. They were forced to sell up and move to a tiny rented cottage on the outskirts of the village. And now she was doing her best to keep the family solvent by stacking shelves at the local supermarket in the evenings, and doing other people's ironing during the day. She bore everything with stoic good humour, and recently, she complained to me, whenever she walked her dog along the roads, older villagers would come shyly up and shake her hand, mumbling something incoherent about decency.

'I do wish they wouldn't,' she said. 'It always makes me cry, and I can't bear that.'

I didn't know what label Charlie and I had, but I suspected it might have something to do with the way bills were always paid so late, our hedges were chaotically overgrown, and a police car was parked worryingly often in the drive.

When I got home I found Charlie in the kitchen, having a long, rambling conversation with one of his friends, John, who ran an engineering business nearby. It could hardly ever have been open, judging by the amount of time he spent in our kitchen. He had shoulder-length hair, sexily shadowed eyes, and a rumpled, oily look.

'Can I borrow the van to do an interview?' I asked. The two of them were leaning back in their chairs, feet on the table, discussing the list of ingredients on the back of the cheap biscuits I'd bought. They were enjoying the pleasant *frisson* of horror induced by the words 'unspecified animal fat'.

'What kind of animal fat would you least like to eat?' Charlie asked John.

'It has to be . . . dog fat.'

'Let's pinpoint it more exactly,' Charlie said. 'What dog fat would be worst? Poodle, Pekinese or corgi?'

'Basset hound kidney fat,' John said firmly. 'Real cack, that'd be.' He was fond of the word 'cack' and used it often.

Charlie riffled through the great pile of newspapers and letters on the kitchen table, and frowned at one inviting him to give a talk to a group of retired farmers on the topic of his choice.

'Maybe I could rustle up a half-hour chat on dog fat for these people,' he said. He had been trying to make money lately by giving talks. He never made notes ('Bugger that! I'm not doing any preparation when they're only paying £20!'), spoke casually and naturally, and told plenty of jokes. His talks were surprisingly popular. His only problem was that he had rather run out of audiences to give his standard speech on 'Farming on a Shoestring' to. Unless he wanted to travel out of the West Country he urgently needed a fresh topic.

'Everyone else's talks are so boring,' he said. 'I can't believe what they get away with. It's all stuff like "The Story of Taxation" or "Photocopiers I have Serviced". Actually that's quite a good subject. I've been fiddling about with our photocopier quite a lot recently . . .'

'What about "Fashion and Me"?' John said, giggling. 'You could just stand there. You wouldn't even have to say anything.'

It was true. Charlie's clothes were highly unusual. 'I have

always been grateful,' he was fond of saying, 'that I have never had "an innate dress sense".' He bought most of his stuff from a poky discount shop in town that was a favourite with all the local countrymen. There were his socks, for instance, which were made of a fuzzy maroon synthetic fabric, stitched all over with black bobbles, and which never seemed to wear out. His boiler-suits – astonishingly cheap – came from the same source. They had been cut to fit a short farmer with an exceedingly large bottom, and sat uneasily on his tall, lanky frame. And the jeans he wore underneath were even stranger. Whenever he got a hole in one leg he'd snip it off with scissors and sew on the leg from a different pair in its place, achieving a bizarre *trompe l'oeil* effect, as if he was wearing semi-invisible bloomers. The children were uneasy about being seen in public with him whenever he wore these jeans but he pretended not to understand why.

But then, they were even more embarrassed by his van. Old, dented, and covered in animal hair because the horses liked rubbing against its sides and the cat slept on the roof, it had recently received a fresh indignity. A couple of months earlier South West Water engineers had been in the area, relining our pipes with resin, and Charlie had wandered up in his boiler-suit to have a chat, and ambled back a few hours later with a bucket of resin. A little later on I noticed him painting it over the rustier bits of the van.

'Is resin a good filler, then?' I asked.

'Don't be silly,' he said. 'It's *free*. That's why I'm using it.'

After a full week it still hadn't dried properly, and the van had turned into a sort of mobile yellow flypaper, its sticky surface covered with struggling beetles and bluebottles. In desperation, Charlie attacked it with his sander, and then painted it all over with green metallic paint. Sadly, the paint and the resin didn't agree. They slowly reacted with each other. Day by day, more and more mottled blisters appeared on its surface, as if the poor thing was succumbing to a dreadful vehicular smallpox. And then the blisters began to leak and dribble. Everywhere the van went it would leave small, but embarrassing pools of green froth. It even got to be quite celebrated, in a small way. Whenever Charlie went to motorbike scrambles in it people would come up to him on the course and ask to see the famous oozing van they'd heard so much about.

And when I started interviewing people for *The Times* I often used to drive it off to remote farms. It created an excellent impression, because it established, right from the start, that I wasn't a posh, show-off city type, rolling in money. However scruffy the farmer's vehicle might be, mine was infinitely worse – so it set the tone nicely for the whole encounter.

Sometimes I would arrive to find a farmer barely out of his twenties, fiercely intelligent, pale-faced and bespectacled, who resembled an accountant or a university professor, and had reams of figures to prove that what he was doing was bound to succeed. Often there was a desperate bravado to his spiel, as he laughingly explained what good exercise it was running away from a psychopathically enraged sow, or cleaning out pens. 'Whenyou scrub out a water trough the trick is *not* to stand in it, fall over and grab the electric fence, because humans, water and 7,000 volts definitely do not mix. I've only done it once.'

The pig industry was slipping into crisis (largely due to the strong pound, and a world oversupply of pork), which made such interviews extra painful. I'd heard of piglets for sale at 50p, of producers going into voluntary liquidation because it was the only way they could be sure their animals got fed – and worst of all, that so many desperate farmers were sending their pregnant sows to abattoirs, that at some places two tonnes of aborted piglets were being thrown away every day.

Today's farm was both modern and full of odd animals. It belonged to Paul Worden, who kept just under a thousand wild boar on Bodmin Moor. And soon after I arrived he rolled up his trousers to reveal a nasty curved scar on one calf. 'See that?' he said. 'One of them bit right through my wellie, my boiler-suit *and* my jeans.'

I gasped. 'What happened?'

'After he did it? Why, I just walked out of his pen.'

With his shoulder-length hair, bright blue eyes, and tweed cap set at a rakish angle, Paul had terrific charisma. He explained that he began farming wild boar because he knew a great deal about pigs, but soon discovered that the two animals were markedly different.

'Take farrowing.' (He was sitting at his kitchen table at this point, sketching wild pigs on the margin of a newspaper, while his wife washed up in the backgound, looking exasperated at hearing this all over again.) He explained that an ordinary domestic sow reared her young by herself, and soon after birth each piglet chooses a nipple which it keeps to until it is weaned. But wild boar sows, although they give birth on their own, always team up with another sow a couple of days later.

'The two of them will lie belly to belly, and all their piglets will lie on top of them to keep warm. They share the upbringing of the litters, and they even cross-suckle.'

Also, Paul claimed that wild boars disliked 'pampering' – staying indoors and being stuffed with high-protein rations. He said they only really thrived if they lived as they would in the wild, in small groups of ten sows and a boar, making their own nests and eating natural foods.

The problem with this system – apart from the way they caught mange and lice off foxes and badgers – is that they never even approached being domesticated. It made catching them, and bringing them in for dosing, nose-ringing and weaning, perilous in the extreme.

He leapt to his feet, ushered me to his Land Rover, and drove me up a narrow path to the moor, explaining that he walked among his animals every day, feeding them potatoes or pig-nuts, and getting them used to his Cornish accent. That way they learned to trust him and didn't get too stressed when he had to restrain them. It sounded good, but the reality was unnerving, as I discovered when Paul helped me through a gate with a sign saying 'Warning: Dangerous Wild Animals'.

Greyish-black, with bristly jagged backs and small, evilly alert eyes, the wild boar were waiting beside a tunnelled-out spread of gorse, and the instant Paul tipped out a sack of food they charged up and began fighting each other for it, snapping and chomping their razor-sharp tusks.

The one thing I did know, from bitter experience, was that domestic sows were at their most dangerous when they had young. (When Henrye had had her first litter she turned overnight into a maniac. Charlie and I had to leap on to the roof of her pig hut halfway through feeding her the first day and hide there, shivering with terror, until she finally fell asleep and we could make a run for the fence.) Here, little stripy piglets were racing around, tripping over my feet in their eagerness to get at the pig-nuts. Paul told me breezily not to worry. According to him, you always knew if wild boar were about to attack because they came up and barked at you like dogs, with their bristles standing on end. Oh, and you couldn't possibly outrun them. They were simply too fast. They were so quick on their feet that out on the moor they caught and ate rabbits just for fun.

The only defence against a charging wild boar, apparently, is to keep absolutely still, because, like the Tyrannosaurus Rex in *Jurassic Park*, they have such bad eyesight that they can only see you clearly when you move. 'It takes some bravery to stand your ground when they're charging, mind,' Paul said, quite unnecessarily.

Paul caught the look on my face (I was just wondering why I had agreed to step into the pen in the first place. Was I mad? No. It was just that I had been conditioned over the years to do insane things because an entertaining man suggested them.) And, no doubt because he thought it would calm me down, he beckoned me over to have a feel of a wild boar pelt.

Reluctantly, I tiptoed over to where he was scratching the back of a large, bad-tempered-looking sow. Her outer hairs were coarse and stiff, but underneath was a soft, tangled down, clogged with twigs and bits of dirt.

'Excuse me,' I asked in a quavery voice. 'But has anyone in this country ever been killed by a wild boar?'

'No,' Paul said. And just as I was beginning to relax he added: 'But I do know a farmer who was out feeding them like this when a great big boar came up and bit half his buttock cheek off.'

When we were safely out of the enclosure, Paul, chuckling inordinately, told me about the hikers who had ignored the warning signs and bossily set off across an enclosure. (He heard thin, faint voices calling 'Help!' and found them backed against the fence, surrounded by a crowd of amused-looking sows.) Once, too, the hunt ran across his farm in full cry, and the fox and hounds jumped in with the boars: 'That was the best sight I've seen. The biggest male went in front and he had five sows either side of him in a V-shape, and all the youngsters went in the middle. They didn't actually kill any hounds, though they went after them, but the hunt was not happy.'

It was obvious that Worden was a clever salesman, and as I drove back I wondered whether he hadn't exaggerated the fearsomeness of his livestock for sound commercial reasons. As he said himself: 'My customers always say they don't mind eating wild boar because they are such ugly characters. I take care never to show them the piglets.'

When I got home I found Nat in his usual place, the chicken yard. He was sitting on the little wooden steps that led up to one of the hen-houses, a plastic doll's cup in one hand, filled with filthy water from the chicken-drinker, which he was sipping with epicurean delight. All around him the ducks and chickens were going about their business, grooming and sparring, completely unperturbed by his presence. He'd turned himself into an honorary bird by spending so much time there.

I carried him indoors to give him a clean, and found Charlie still at the kitchen table. He claimed he'd come up with an even better money-making scheme: one or other of us should write a book. When I protested that I'd already tried that, and it hadn't worked at all, because nobody bought it, he raised a hand to stop me.

'That's because we didn't realise how important marketing and publicity were,' he said.

John nodded. (He was still there, too. I hoped he'd been to work in the interim, because I'd been away a full six hours. I rather doubted it, though. He had the blurred look of someone who had eaten far too many basset-hound kidney-fat custard creams.) 'Give him a chance to explain,' he insisted.

'What we do,' Charlie said, smiling at the brilliance of his idea. 'Is write this book. It doesn't matter what it's about. It's the title that's important. We have to call it *The Smallest Little Whorehouse in Devon.*'

'I don't know anything about rural whorehouses,' I said. 'Though I'd be quite interested to find out. Are there any nearby?'

John shrugged non-committally. 'I've heard there may be one in Bridgwater.'

'Precisely,' Charlie said. 'You're interested. Who wouldn't be? And to publicise it – and this is the stroke of genius – we'll paint the words "The Smallest Little Whorehouse in Devon" on the side of our van, and fill it with prostitutes. Then we'll drive it round the stuffiest villages in the West Country, parking it up here and there until the locals kick up a fuss. Can you imagine the publicity? We'll be millionaires within a year.'

I thought rapidly. 'Won't Sam object to being collected from the station in a van labelled like that? And it might make my work for *The Times* a bit difficult.'

'I don't know why you always have to be so negative,' Charlie said teasingly. 'We'll never get anywhere if you keep objecting to perfectly good ideas.'

Chapter Thirteen

'Remember that Big is Beautiful, Resilience is Respectable, Softness is Suspicious and Mobility is Meaningful.' Advice on feeling a ram's testicles, given at a farmers' meeting about sheep-breeding by Dr K. C. Smith, FRCVS.

'The year before last,' Seymour said, making a pattern with his finger in the chocolate icing on his plate, 'I got 72.6p a kilo for my wool, and made £655.90p. This year I got 43.7p a kilo. Which means I made £394.80p, which only just paid for the shearing. My profit was nil. If the price falls any lower I'll start making a loss.'

'So,' Charlie answered, cramming a huge slice of chocolate cake into his mouth in one go, 'sheep farming has now joined the list of pointless things to do. A list headed by "trying to get a teenager to help around the house".' He was still sore from his latest tussle with Sam. They were always having ominous confrontations in the kitchen, where they'd shout, and then stare at each other threateningly – and Sam would end up by backing down and cleaning the floor in a mutinous fashion. (With one bucket of filthy water.)

'Do you realise,' Sam had said to me that morning, 'that all my conversations with Dad are now floor-related?'

Charlie got on far better with Kathy. They had a lovely, relaxed relationship where he'd tease her, and she'd sit on his lap – even though she was almost as big as he was – and say crossly: 'You're *so* rude, and *so* silly.' They were both equally mad about horses, too. Kathy had been riding since she was four, and had had a succession of deep relationships with different ponies and thoroughbreds, which Charlie always said was an excellent preparation for her later life with men. (Learning to love something larger, hairier and less intelligent than herself; having to clean up its dung, etc.) I thought this unlikely. How often, in a human love affair, did you have to decide that your loved one would be better off dead, and then watch them being shot? And even if nothing quite so dramatic happened, the inevitable was almost as painful. As you grew bigger, your dearest companion gradually dwindled by comparison, until it was far too small to accompany you anywhere and had to be traded in for another. As far as I knew, there was no parallel to this tragic situation in the whole of human romantic literature.

Charlie was happy now that Kathy was back for the holidays, but she wasn't. Because almost at once he went off to a French horse show, and she had to abandon her law books in order to help me run the farm. And, as always, she noticed things I was trying not to see. The farm looked even scruffier, and though my calves and poultry were happy and clean, the animals I needed Charlie's assistance to deal with were looking neglected.

I always felt like a dwarf in a giant's world – even the gates and shed latches were too high up, and too stiff, for me to open easily. And somehow, I had never progressed further than being an assistant to Charlie. It wasn't just me: any farmer's wife can tick off on her fingers the traditional male and female tasks: men throw bales and women stack them; men shear and women roll fleeces. Working indoors at a desk so much, too, meant that I was losing the will to struggle against this sexist barrier. And then there were those ever-present enemies: apathy and despair. Take shearing. I couldn't get the sheep in on my own, nor could I get them shorn. To do this I would have had to drive them to a shearer (and we didn't have a trailer – that had to be borrowed from a friend of Charlie's). Alternatively, I could have tried using the ancient, rusty, spring-loaded hand shears – but only Charlie's huge fingers could work those. And worse, attempting any of this would, most dangerously, have implied criticism of his methods. 'I've *told* you over and over that I'll do it, and I will. I'm just busy at the moment.'

The previous summer it had suddenly got suffocatingly hot, and the sheep, still unshorn, had started lying under the hedges and groaning sorrowfully. The fattest – and hottest – was a castrated ram called Moley. He should have been eaten years before, but had survived because he was a special pet of the children's and had learned to play football. (He butted the ball, and seemed to understand about goals.) When the sheep were finally gathered in one evening, Moley was kept in the shady stable and shorn last because Charlie felt it would be less strain on the poor animal's heart if he had time to recover from the round-up. By the time we finally got to him darkness had fallen, the air was deliciously cool again and the farm rang with the aggrieved cries of our lambs, confused because they could hear familiar voices, but only see horribly thin, bony silhouettes. Where were their comfy, fluffy mums?

As Charlie began clipping Moley, the ram gave deep breathy sighs and gasps. It was wonderful to see him gradually shake off his thick, stained, sweaty yellow wool, speckled all through with seeds and burrs. When it was finally over (and Charlie did it very skilfully, there were no cuts), Moley struggled on to his spindly legs, shook himself with relief – and fell down dead. He'd had a heart attack. Charlie knelt over him and tried every remedy he had ever seen on any hospital drama – massaging the heart, moving the front legs in and out. He even tried mouth to mouth resuscitation, but had to give up because his mouth wouldn't quite fit round Moley's snout. And besides, Moley's moustache tickled.

But this year, the sheep had been shorn early. They still looked uncomfortable, though. I'd tried to get Charlie to look at them before he left, but he'd given them a quick glance, insisted they were fine and rushed to be off, and I'd begun to doubt my judgement. Our sheep were mostly rejects from Seymour's flock, where, from time to time, Charlie worked as a lambing-assistant. He'd always come home with sheepy presents: orphans for me to mother, and old, but charming ewes that Seymour had judged too far gone to be profitable.

Helicopter was one of these. She'd gone on to give us five years of small, misshapen lambs (which she was very proud of). Her name came about because, although she loved these offspring, she found it hard to adjust the first time they drank from her, and would twirl her tail furiously. On our farm she immediately became the leader of the flock, and whenever they escaped on to the road we'd always find her lurching along in front, with her arthritic gait and long, bony, aristocratic-looking snout. The only thing that spoiled the grandeur of her appearance was that she suffered from an embarrassing personal problem known as 'dags', which meant that big bobbles of dried dung clung to the wool round her backside. We kept snipping these off, but they'd come back almost immediately, so wherever she went she was accompanied by a subdued clapping as they knocked together – as if being pursued by a small, but discerning audience.

And today, Helicopter was the only sheep that looked truly happy. She was sitting regally in the shade of a wild plum, sniffing the cool breeze that blew underneath it. The others were restless, and occasionally stamped their back legs and twitched their tails.

'Do you think they might have the beginnings of fly-strike?' I asked Kathy. 'I'm worried they may.'

'Well, let's get them in at once and see,' she said firmly. (She never had any problems doing what she felt was right, and I always felt more confident when she was around. She didn't even fear Charlie's anger. She frequently pinned up pictures of his horses in his workshop with 'Please give me some attention: I need brushing' written bossily underneath.) Physically, she was similar to her father, with the same well-defined cheekbones, wide mouth and flat glossy hair. Unlike Charlie, though, she *did* have an innate dress sense. She always looked like a model on a fashion shoot. Today, surrounded by dirty sheep and half-wrecked farm machinery, she could have come out of a special agricultural issue of *Vogue*. Her oatmeal jodhpurs showed off her long legs and the faded green jersey she wore (with its matching ribbon – she was always perfectly colour-coordinated) emphasised the whiteness of her skin.

She rousted Sam out of his bedroom and we all drove the sheep into the gated yard in front of the stable. They seemed panicky as they clattered in – except for Pongo, who ran up and stared cheekily at each of us in the hope of a snack – but as soon as Nat appeared with some chicken-corn they calmed down and began eating.

'You know,' Sam said, slipping out of the gate, 'you couldn't do a horror film with sheep in it. There'd never be enough tension and suspense. Within moments of any dramatic incident they'd all be happily looking round for food.' He was more like my side of the family, with his curly hair, deep brown eyes and olive skin. He had a playful character, was always searching for the comic angle and was mostly to be found playing on his computer in his bedroom, the cat draped across his shoulders. Now he shimmied back to the house with Nat; if at all possible, he absented himself from farm work.

I rugby-tackled the nearest sheep, and then Kathy held its head while I examined it. The very first ewe, which wasn't even looking uncomfortable, had maggots threading and winking in its wool. I had to scrub a disinfectant and water mixture into it with a brush, and then the fat, white, one-centimetre-long grubs rained down on to the concrete, where they writhed and inched about.

Some of the lambs looked truly dreadful, with raw red patches where the grubs were starting to eat their skin. These had to have soothing yellow cream rubbed in as well as a special chemical dripped down their backs to stop reinfection. I found it impossible to keep from shuddering, even though I had seen it all before, and I hadn't been that squeamish to start with.

'This is *so* horrible,' Kathy said, holding on grimly, but averting her head. 'I don't know how you can stand it.'

'At least we got it in time. And at least you were here to help me,' I said.

'I wish I *wasn't* here,' she answered crossly.

In between being caught and inspected, the remaining sheep sat around quite comfortably in the yard, legs folded. They'd licked up and mumbled all the grain, and were just cogitating to themselves and grinding their teeth when my lavender muscovy duck, Seagull, picked her way through them, making a watery hissing noise and bobbing her head backwards and forwards. When she saw the maggots she quickened her pace and began greedily shovelling them down her throat.

'Oh, no. This is even *more* disgusting,' Kathy said. 'How can she do that?'

'Well, it's interesting what ducks can eat,' I replied. But I thought it better not to tell Kathy the story I'd heard the previous week:

Interview with poultry keeper Jackie Stanley: 'I once had an old Aylesbury duck who used to stand by her food bowl quite motionlessly, like a statue, while sparrows hopped round her, feeding. And then she'd bring her head down, suddenly, and grab one, and stampede for the pond with it in her beak, where she'd swallow it back with mouthfuls of water. You wouldn't think a duck would eat a live bird, would you? But they do.'

'Charlie's home,' I said gloomily to TJ. 'And he's brought a disagreeable Frenchman back with him.' The list on her kitchen table today read: 'Catering turkey; school shoes!!!'

'Catering turkey?' I asked.

'Oh – they're marvellous,' TJ said. 'I've just discovered them at the supermarket. They have a terrifying label that says something like "this bird may lack the odd leg or be savagely slashed across the breast, but it is still perfectly wholesome to eat" – and they're dazzlingly cheap. And, of course, you have all the fun of wondering how on earth they got so bashed about. Josh thinks they fight each other in gladiatorial combat, but I incline to the view that catering turkeys are just tougher than other birds – a sort of poultry underclass, living on the edge.'

Nat had found a basket of coloured wools under the sofa and was weighing and squashing them in his tiny hands, and as I knelt down to take them away, she said, 'Don't worry – I got them for him from the jumble. I hoped he'd find them interesting.' She was even thinner. Her jaw was now clearly defined, and she even held herself differently, with more self-consciousness. You could suddenly see the teenager she'd once been. Perhaps she had something dangerously wrong with her, like diabetes?

'Have you seen a doctor lately?' I asked. 'I really think . . .'

'I'm fine.' As always she just smiled, and changed the subject. 'Tell me about this Frenchman.'

'He's the most dreadful person, rude, graceless, chauvinistic. He's staying for two weeks – can you imagine? And it's not just me that finds him hard to take: in Luxembourg he's known as "Mr Stinky". It's obvious why. He never washes, and any room he's in smells of cheese.'

'Why has Charlie asked him back, then?'

'Because he claims Mr Stinky is vital to his business. He has all sorts of useful contacts, apparently. But I've got this odd feeling that he's actually Charlie's revenge on me for having Nat.'

There. I'd said it. That was what was so wonderful about talking to TJ. I could say things to her that I'd never dare air anywhere else.

'It's that bad, is it?'

'Well, you know, I did have to persuade him.' Charlie hadn't really wanted another baby. I remembered breast-feeding Nat in bed one afternoon. I'd fallen asleep with him in my arms, when I woke suddenly to find Charlie staring at us with a look that was both hurt and jealous, as if he'd surprised me with a lover. And you could say that, by inviting a stranger into our house that I didn't like, he was mimicking what I'd done by having a baby.

175

'Marriage!' TJ was saying. 'I feel so trapped by mine. I can't see how it can possibly continue.' She stopped abruptly, put down her iron and covered her face with her hands. I got up, concerned, but when she took them away again she was smiling. 'Of course, it has to,' she said cheerfully, 'for the sake of the children. I'd do anything not to hurt them. I'll tell you what I feel like: as if I'm in a box, and I know there must be some way out, if I only look hard enough. And I do keep looking.'

'But marriage is about ups and downs, isn't it?' I said. 'You just have to wait for it to get better. I mean, at the moment Charlie is behaving as if he doesn't like me much, but he'll become loving again, I know. It's happened before, and he always does.' Privately, I thought that there was one way out of the box that TJ hadn't explored properly, and that was to get a job that used up all her creativity and intellect, and brought in some decent cash. It was a waste, just working in a supermarket.

My way out of the box had definitely been the column. It was a farm diversification that had finally freed us from financial worry. The only problem with it was that I was no longer a proper farmer's wife: I went out to work in a smart suit now, and I spent far less time with Charlie. But then, there were fringe benefits. For instance, because I was working for *The Times* I was invited on a press trip to promote Duchy organic foods. It included a tour of the crops at Highgrove, and a chat with Prince Charles, and, just before it began, we were asked to write a small description of ourselves. Hoping there was a chance of HRH reading this, I blathered on about how I was married to an inventor who designed horse-drawn machinery for use on organic farms. And later, when Prince Charles was advancing towards the waiting journalists, their faces lighting up and turning towards him, like flowers reacting to the sun, he touched me on the shoulder and said he wanted to see the machinery and I was to fix it up with his farm manager.

When we reached the gates that led to Highgrove we had to switch off the engines and sit, yawning, in our horseboxes, while a policeman with stiff joints got down on his knees and looked under them for bombs and guns. It seemed to me that it would have been ludicrously Machiavellian of Charlie to have run a shoestring business making machinery for horses for over twenty years – just in the hope that one day he might be able to use it to assassinate the Prince of Wales.

We were waved on, and drove into a big yard next to a stable, parking up beside a long open shed in the warm, early morning sun. There were four of us: me, Charlie, his business partner Don Townsend (in his sixties and recovering from cancer) and John Waterer, a horseman who was loaning two beautifully broken Shires for the demonstration, because ours weren't reliable enough.

We started unloading the machines and horses, and immediately the prince came round the corner, dressed casually in light trousers and shirt, and shook everyone's hand. He was very taken with Charlie at once, and the two of them went off to look at the hay meadow to be turned, Charlie rushing ahead in panic to open every gate.

The day had a dreamlike quality. Camilla Parker-Bowles appeared next, in pink, along with her daughter and Lady

Halifax. She began an animated conversation about horse-breeding with John Waterer, occasionally breaking off to shout at her dog, who kept running under the Shires' feet. She looked prettier, softer and slimmer than in her photographs, and after she'd walked back round the corner John and Don both said they quite fancied her.

Waiting out in the hayfield was the prince's farm manager, David Wilson, and his wife, the head gardener and his wife, and a host of under-gardeners. The cut hay, full of wild flowers, smelt especially good and there was some minor ribbing going on about the rare baby beech trees around the meadow. The prince said playfully, 'Whatever you do, *don't* cut down a beech tree,' and Charlie said, 'It's the Tower for me if I do, eh?' and the prince laughed. (Later, Charlie, who has met the Duke of Edinburgh at numerous horse shows, said that the prince was much nicer than his father, who always has to be the one making the funny remarks, and won't laugh at other people's witticisms.) HRH seemed to like risqué stuff, too, and was appreciative when David Wilson talked about a discussion he'd had with a German agricultural scientist, and how it had been complicated by the fact that whenever he mentioned his Ayrshire cattle the scientist fell about giggling. 'Ayrshire' sounds like the German for 'asshole'.

After watching the horses pulling the hay-turner from a distance in the shimmering heat, the prince climbed up to ride on the platform of the hitch-cart. I couldn't hear what he said then, but Charlie and John told me afterwards that he talked about how unhappy he'd been as a teenager, and discussed the 'bloody press' and the 'bloody government's plans to ban fox-hunting'. He described how the Canadian Eskimos were forbidden to hunt their native seals and now have just become drunks, with the seals being clubbed to death anyway by the government – and cited this as an example of the awfulness of government interference in traditional country sports. John said that the whole experience was given a comic twist because he kept shouting 'OK, Charlie?' and ordering him brusquely to hurry up and pay attention, and suddenly went raspberry with embarrassment, wondering if HRH had thought he was talking to him, and being grossly disrespectful.

The sun was getting hotter and more painful, and I sheltered my face with my hand, wondering if it would offend etiquette to put on the straw hat I'd brought with me. I was standing on the sidelines and talking to the head gardener. He said lugubri-ously that it was clear we'd been good and not told the press what we were doing that day, because if we had there would have been helicopters circling overhead. There was an official court photographer snapping away, and it was obvious that Prince Charles really disliked this; he winced every time the man lined up a shot. The head gardener kept glancing at his watch and saying: 'The prince always goes to church at this time, he'll have to leave soon.' But HRH decided to play with the horses instead.

After a while the machine stopped and the horses were teth-ered in the shade, where they happily ate the half-cured hay around their feet. The prince disappeared off to the house and reappeared with a tray of cans of soft drink and beer, which he handed round. It was odd how attentive he was to the moods of those around him; he kept glancing anxiously at other people's faces, as if trying to guess what they were thinking. When he and Charlie were having a teasing conversation, he suddenly turned round to see what my expression was. And another time, when I was wondering whether to help one of the under-gardeners pour his drink (he had cerebral palsy, and was having difficulty, and I did not know if it would be insulting to offer assistance), he stared at me, as if he'd read my mind. And was warning me not to do anything.

Later, I mentioned this to the farm manager's wife, Caroline, and she said that the prince was always like it. She'd been a beater on one of his shoots once, and one of the other beaters was an ancient agricultural retainer – a painfully shy Gloucestershire countryman with enormous dignity. And at the end of the day, when all the beaters were supposed to get a brace of pheasant, this chap hid back in the shadows. Prince Charles deliberately sought him out and gave him the first brace, as a mark of respect. 'That's typical of him,' Caroline said. 'He's also unusually sensitive and kind to children and teenagers.'

It was an odd sort of sensitivity, though because it had defi-nite limits. After two or three hours, I needed desperately to go to the loo, but I didn't dare ask if I could use the house. Nipping behind a bush in the immaculately perfect, heavily staffed gardens was out, too, for obvious reasons. And even exploring the wider landscape with a vague expression wasn't possible: we'd been told that HRH always has six detectives hidden somewhere nearby, shadowing his every move – so, presumably, any peeing would have been closely monitored by the SAS. I felt sure other people in the party were feeling the same pressing urgency; their expressions became more set as the morning went on. Don Townsend went a worryingly sickly yellow colour from the heat and stress, and it was a relief all round when we thanked the prince effusively for his time, and trundled off for an impromptu lunch at David Wilson's cottage on the estate. While she was putting a salad together his wife said that Prince Charles often wandered secretly round Highgrove on his own, and once he popped up suddenly beside her when she was walking the dogs. Another time, she came across him looking, thoughtfully, around her front garden. I wondered if she minded, and she said that, no, she was always delighted.

All the way home Charlie went on and on about how wonderful Prince Charles was, what a superb human being, etc., and when we got out of the lorry he couldn't wait to tell the children about his day.

'This is the hand that shook the hand of the future King of England,' he said, holding out his huge, pink fingers. (Actually it nearly wasn't, because when Charlie first met HRH his hand was all oily from unloading machines, and he felt uncomfortable about proffering it, but HRH seized it anyway.)

Kathy replied sourly, holding out *her* hand, 'And this is the hand that wiped Nat's bum for you while you were away.'

We'd been going to cut our hay the instant we got home, but it was raining and the crop had to wait, which was a nuisance as Charlie had arranged to go abroad in a week's time. All that week I kept praying the weather would dry up in time for Charlie to do the work, but it didn't. And then, twenty-four hours after he'd flown off to East Germany, the hot sun came out again.

Chapter Fourteen

Story told by a local engineer to illustrate the intriguing grimness of our recent agricultural past: 'In the 1940s, the first self-propelling combine harvesters came over from Canada. Back then, when a mechanic arrived to service a combine, farmers would ask him to hold out his hands. The threshing cylinder often jammed on damp English crops, and when you reached in to free it it tended to slice off your index finger. So anyone with a finger missing was an expert.'

There was still a blue haze over the fields, but it was obvious the day was going to be hot. The cut grass in the hayfield had bleached silver on the very top, but underneath it was pale green and smelt tobaccoey. Here and there, in among the fluffy heaps waiting to be shaken again, were heavy, slimy green lumps of unturned cut grass. There was a fault in the mechanism of the ancient tedder we were using, and it kept leaving these. They'd never dry properly unless they were individually pulled out with pitchforks.

I kicked one. Deep inside, in the wettest part, was a green frog the size of my fingernail. As I walked over to the water-trough with it I passed a ring of blackened shells. When the field had been cut by the local contractor a week ago it had been a whole pheasant's nest, on the point of hatching, each shell neatly sliced in half by the knife of the grass-cutter. I showed it to the contractor, and he said it often happened. Once the mother pheasant didn't flee in time and he cut her, too. Another time, when he was making silage, he killed a fawn. He was aware there was one about, because he kept seeing a red deer hind agitatedly flitting up and down beside the fence while he worked, but he never felt a bump. And it was only when he got off the tractor to eat his lunch in the shade that he found the fawn, lying as if asleep in a pool of darkening blood.

When I'd watched the frog swim safely into a fringe of weed on the side of the trough, I climbed the fence and walked down to where the horses were still asleep. They were lying flat out under the walnut tree, and I could hear Picasso snoring. Holbein heard me coming, and lifted his head, but Picasso didn't, and I managed to slip right on to his back and put my arms round his neck before he woke up. He felt warm and muscular, and smelt stalliony, his odour concentrated by sleep. It had a musky base-note – a bit like Charlie's armpits when he'd been working – and on top of that a bitter, manure-like tang. He snorted, and began to struggle upright, so I slipped off again, not wanting to bother him too much. It was always surprising to me, even after all these years, how late in the morning farm animals liked to sleep. Even now I could see the sheep laid out like huge pale mushrooms in the next-door field.

I was worried about the hay because Charlie should have been home to do it, days ago. He had gone off to East Germany, to run a heavy horse course for his friend Erich, and rung up the day he was due home to say that Erich's brother had died suddenly. Someone had to remain behind to look after the animals while the funeral arrangements were made, and he'd volunteered.

'But how are we going to make hay without you? Kathy isn't even here.'

'You'll manage. Get Sam to drive the tractor, and remember it won't do anything without Easy Start.'

'What's that?'

'It's an engine-starting fluid. The tractor has to be liberally basted in the beastly stuff or it won't move at all.'

And before I could complain about the difficulty of making hay with a bad-tempered teenager who hated farm work, and a restless toddler, Charlie launched into a description of the horrors of his living arrangements. 'Two new sheep arrived on the farm this morning, and when they drank some of the water we've been using for tea and coffee they keeled over dead. And I never know what I'm eating because the camp kitchen is right next to a dung heap, and my plate's always black with flies.'

The Easy Start can was empty. I drove round all the local garages trying to buy more and at last found a man in Honiton with some.

'You do know,' he said, frowning at me over the top of his

spectacles, 'that this should only be used most sparingly?' I nodded.

'If you use it too often,' he went on, clearly suspicious of my motives, 'it will gradually destroy an engine. You will end up having to use more and more. You don't want to go down that route, do you?'

He seemed reluctant to let me have even one can, and gripped it tightly with his fingers until I promised him, most gravely, that I would be responsible in my use of Easy Start, and never knowingly permit my tractor to become a substance-abusing junkie. And then I took a detour on the way home and bought a whole box of cans at another garage.

'I *loathe* farm work,' Sam said, climbing on to the tractor, and turning the ignition while I hosed the engine with starter fluid. 'Hate hate hate. I'm going to start a pressure group for farmers' sons called S.A.M.U.E.L: Sons Against Manual Unnecessarily Exhausting Labour. The most horrible bit about farm work is that it bears no resemblance to real work: you never get paid and you can't be sacked. You just have to go on and on doing it. And it's so vile. Who'd want to hold a piglet while it was cas-trated? Or drive a tractor for hours in the hot sun when they could be at the beach?'

'Well, if you like,' I said, 'I'll drive the tractor while you look after Nat and change his nappies.'

'I don't do nappies and potties,' he said haughtily, and clat-tered out to the field.

Nat and I busied ourselves with sorting out the barn, and then he played with a pile of earth in the purple shade under

the trees (and demanded drinks, sandwiches and fresh underwear at wearisomely frequent intervals) while I pulled at wet
knots of grass with a pitchfork. Some of the grass was well over
four feet long, and though it was satisfying seeing it fade and
dry so fast once it was spread out properly, the work was so
hard. Even under a straw hat my face soon went a boiled red,
and after a couple of hours I was close to collapse. Trailers laden
with bales kept rumbling up the road beside the farm, and I
rang the contractor to hurry him on with doing ours. He came
over late in the evening and smelt the hay disapprovingly.

'I wouldn't be able to look your husband in the eye if I baled
this. It isn't fit.'

'When will it be fit?'

'You spend another day out with the pitchfork, and get that
son of yours to turn it a dozen times and we'll see,' he said, with
the air of one conferring a huge favour.

When I rang Charlie for sympathy I thought I heard laughter
in the distance. He explained that he was cutting an environ-
mentally sound crop of hay full of dandelions and thistles. 'The
down blows around us like a blizzard all day, packing itself
tightly into every crevice of the cutting machinery and getting
into my eyes so I can't see. Which is bad, because wild pigs live
in the fields, and my horses keep falling into their tunnels.'

Our grass was so old and fibrous that as it dried it became like
wire, wrapping itself tiresomely round the central drive shaft of
the tractor. Every half-hour (or less) the machine would judder
to a halt, and Sam and I (with sizeable interference from a hot,
angry toddler) would have to saw the grass off with a selection

of bread knives. (Charlie had taken all the penknives off to Germany with him.) At lunchtime we made the mistake of parking the tractor up in a field the horses knew how to break into, and we returned to find they'd surrounded it, flipped up the engine cover and were licking Easy Start off with evident enjoyment. Worse, Picasso had wormed the instruction booklet out of the toolbox with his tongue and eaten about a third of it. And Holbein had made off with the seat cushion, and after covering it with slobber, stamped it into a cowpat. We did manage to get the tractor started again, but it almost immediately set fire to itself, in what had to be an Easy Start-induced fit of depression.

'The contractor says the hay still isn't fit, and we've got to spend another vile, boilingly hot day turning it and teasing knots out,' I said tearfully into the phone that evening, my nose covered in ultra-fashionable pale blue ski cream that my sister Caky, working at *Vogue* that week, had got free and sent down to cheer me up. A totally blue Nat, looking exactly like a Smurf, was riding on my back.

'You've got it easy,' Charlie laughed. 'Erich's got three bulls on his farm, and because the pens are crap, they keep breaking out and escaping, and I'm the only one with the nerve to put them back in. I have to get a pail of food, dangle it in front of them, run slightly faster than they do, and once they're in the pen, vault out before they can kill me.' Someone shouted at him in the distance and he yelled back, 'Keep it cold – I'll be there in a minute.'

'You will be home soon? ' I pleaded.

'I'm not sure. I can't let Erich down.'

The next afternoon the contractor big-baled the hay. As he left the field he didn't tie the gate with a special Egremont anti-horse knot, and the horses and cows did a victory gallop round the bales, before tearing the first one apart. That evening I listened unsympathetically as Charlie described Erich's eighty-strong herd of horned Salers cattle, and the trick they had of breaking into fields of tiny bales, spearing them, and rushing around with them on their heads.

'And then we have to re-bale them the next day,' he added. 'Which means I can't come home for a while yet.'

When he finally did return his skin was scorched by the sun, his hair bleached almost blond, his clothes torn and dirty and he had a mass of bruises up one leg, where a team of horses had bolted and dragged him across a field. And he frowned when he finished searching for his bag in the coach boot and turned round to see me. He had an air of melancholy and distress.

'What's wrong?' I asked.

'Nothing.'

He didn't want to talk about his experiences in Germany to me, though I heard him giggling to his friends about them on the telephone. He had a distinctive way of using it: he always tucked the mouthpiece right under his chin, so he had to bellow to be heard the other end. It made it almost impossible not to eavesdrop on his conversations.

I couldn't find him when the children had gone to bed, and

eventually discovered him sitting in the garden at the collapsing picnic table, gazing up at the stars. He said he was worried about his overdraft, and the way it was a struggle to even pay the interest. The money from Germany had hardly made an impact on it.

Above us, aeroplanes twinkled across the dark sky, and a cow on heat in the next field bellowed angrily for sex.

'I feel stifled here, in England,' he said. 'I'm sick of doing repairs for local farmers – they never pay enough, and I'm always welding up rusty garbage that would be better off in a skip. I'd rather live abroad, on a farm where we could be properly self-sufficient and do everything with horses again.'

'What about the children?' I said. 'I know Sam's about to start university but he and Kathy will still need us nearby – and besides, all my work is here.' I wasn't any good at arguing – I never felt I had the right, somehow, to express a firm opinion that someone else disagreed with. So I didn't say that my idea of torture would be starting again on a derelict farm in Eastern Europe, with no friends, no family close by, and hordes of wild pigs to fight off. Besides, I dreaded living in any country where I couldn't speak the language well enough to understand complex jokes and catch the subtle nuances of gossip.

'And I think we should mortgage the house immediately,' Charlie added. 'Then we could pay off all the money I owe. It's stupid to be sitting on such a big asset and not draw cash from it.' I kept quiet, but there was even less chance I was going to agree to that. How would we pay a mortgage if we were already making so little money we kept sinking into debt? But I'd have to counter the suggestion the only way I knew how: stubbornly, and with no confrontation whatsoever.

Confrontation didn't work with Charlie. I'd tried it once. Five years earlier, encouraged by my sister Caky, I'd screwed up all my nerve and told him I thought he ought to try to earn at least £150 a week. Because otherwise we ended up owing money to countless small, local businesses and being unable to repay it, and that was dishonest.

'I am *not* getting some crappy job just because you and your sister want me to,' he said fiercely. 'Dishonest! How do you think that makes me feel, when I'm struggling to get the machinery company on its feet?' He stormed out, and did not return until the very early hours of the next morning, when he bedded down in the spare room. His clothes were soaking from the knees down, and I suspected he'd driven to Bettiscombe and walked over the valley and up to the wishing stone. After a number of days he gradually became less hostile, and unthawed enough to forgive me for speaking my mind. But I'd learned my lesson: this time, like a housewifely Resistance fighter who specialises in lulling the invader into apathy with soft cushions and stodgy cake, I slipped next to him on the bench and put my hand in his. 'Isn't it time we went to bed?' I asked.

Nat started school at last. He wasn't altogether sure about it, and after dropping him off I'd walk uneasily home through the lanes, my coat catching in the high, brambly hedges and my latest article humming in my head. The Calf Processing Aid Scheme, which used to pay farmers £70 a head for their unwanted bull dairy calves, had ended back in July. And there was a story going round that a farmer in Tiverton, desperate to get rid of his four worthless calves, had tied them up to his front gate with a notice saying 'Free to a good home'. When he came back a couple of hours later there were a dozen there.

Most people shot their bull calves in the head now, the instant they were born, and it seemed such a waste. I remembered all the calves I'd reared with deep affection – except for the Horrendoes. But then, they were a special case. Usually we would buy in a scared, milky-looking creature with a trembling wet mouth, and I'd spend day after day trying to coax it to drink from a bucket. This was much harder than you'd think. The calf, used to a nipple and longing for its mother, would recoil from the pail of milk as if it was red hot, and I had to spend hours crouching in the straw, gently pushing its nose into the milk and simultaneously opening its lips with my fingers. It would bite with sharp little teeth, and leap backwards with horror, and sometimes butt me so hard in the face that I wept. And I could never lose my patience or my will to win. (If I did I ended up creeping into the local farmers' store and buying a special red rubber object for the calf to drink with. It was such a rude shape that it was an embarrassment to be seen holding it in public.)

The Horrendoes had loved their milk, even stolen milk from other, weaker calves in their pen, and, feeling annoyed that they weren't getting as much to drink as they wanted, they improvised. Soon they were addicted to a certain sexual practice. You could see why it happened: it was very similar to suckling from their mothers, and, best of all, both of them could do it at the same time. But it troubled me and my kids (who gave them the name). More worryingly, it fascinated male visitors. A whole group of Charlie's friends began calling round, just to watch the Horrendoes at their suckling. Sometimes they would wonder aloud if there was any commercial advantage in an animal that liked that sort of thing – and at that point I'd flee for the farmhouse. When the Horrendoes lost weight we separated them and, luckily, they forgot the whole business when they grew up.

Surely there was something better to do with newborn calves than just killing and burying them? I searched for a farmer who was managing to make money out of rearing these rejects, and found Peter Foster, at Magdalen Farm in Chard. He was producing a type of veal – pink, not pure white, and known as 'baby beef'. And instead of struggling to get his calves to drink from buckets, he got cows to adopt them, gradually introducing the two in a covered yard. When each cow had bonded with at least a couple of calves he'd let them out to pasture. They looked very pretty there, out in the rain-drenched autumn fields, because the cows were all red and white, and the calves smoky blue, cream, brown, red, black and white – every breed there was. Some cows were lovingly grooming just one pampered-looking baby, while others were feeding four at once.

'That's Roo,' Peter said, pointing to a bony matron with a throng of calves gathered round her flanks. 'She lets anyone suckle. If all else fails, and a calf won't drink, we call Roo in. She's always got at least six calves round her, and you tend to think "Hang on, that doesn't add up. She's only got four teats." '

Roo was unusual, though. Although the other cows seemed

to enjoy having extra calves, and let them drink, they did make a distinction between their own calves and the adopted ones. They even had varying feelings for the adoptees. Some inspired such deep affection that the cows fought over them. And some left everyone cold. 'Usually, when you wean a calf, the cow cries for it for twenty-four hours. It is a bit sad when you take one of these foster calves away and no one sheds a tear.'

While we were leaning on a gate, watching calves skipping about in the long grass, a big red cow waddled up for a pat, wearing a spiked metal plaque on her nose.

'This is Fat Helly,' Peter said. 'We've had to put those spikes on her nose because otherwise she drinks the other cows' milk.' Apparently, the flaw in his system was that it only worked if he had easy-going cows, accustomed to letting relative strangers feast on their dugs – and this tolerance made them vulnerable to other particularly clever and predatory animals. It wasn't just Fat Helly who stole milk. Some of the full-grown bullocks in an adjoining field liked to try their luck, too.

It stopped raining as I walked along, and the reflection of the gunmetal sky in the wet road made the fallen leaves look as if they were floating on the surface of a river.

Behind me, footsteps hammered on the road, and I turned to see a neighbour, Lily, running towards me. She stopped, out of breath.

'I shouted, but you didn't hear. I wanted to know what you thought about TJ.'

'What about her?' I asked. 'Is she ill?'

Lily looked astonished. 'You mean you really don't know? You haven't heard? I thought you two were close.'

'We are. What's happened?'

'She's left her husband and she's run off with one of the managers at the supermarket. Apparently, they've been carrying on for months.'

I leaned against the wet hedge, stunned. 'It can't be true.'

'It bloody is. Her husband's in a shocking state.'

'But she'd never do that. She'd never break up her family. And besides, she'd have told me. I only saw her last week.'

'I don't know how she could bring herself to do it — but she did.' Lily sounded disgusted. 'Those poor kids.' She stamped off back to her house through the puddles. It started to rain again, and I wandered home in a daze. I felt a mixture of feelings. I was appalled that TJ hadn't been able to tell me about herself, when I'd told her every problem, every painful thought in my head. Had I been so egotistical that I hadn't left her the space to discuss her own problems? And I also felt bereaved. She hadn't left an address or telephone number for me, so for a long time there was no way I could get in touch with her. I missed her dreadfully.

The emotions I didn't feel were hatred or disgust, because I knew her marriage had been difficult. But the other villagers took an altogether harsher, more old-fashioned view. They were outraged by the very idea of adultery and desertion, and over the next few months there was a huge outpouring of sympathy for TJ's husband. But surely, I thought, as I went out into the chicken-yard each morning and tried to stop my muscovy drake from making rude overtures to the cockerel (and, even, sometimes, the cat) – when a relationship went wrong it was never just one person's fault?

Chapter Fifteen

Country tip — How to tell if a bull is about to charge: according to Leslie Preston, expert on Welsh Black Cattle and champion breeder of bulls, a bull (or cow) always gives plenty of warning before it charges. It nods its head slowly, paws the ground or bellows, and most unequivocal of all, its eyes change colour. 'A cow's eye is all dark, you do not see the white. And adrenaline makes them go grey-blue and cloudy. You can see this from fifteen yards off.'

Cries and bangs came from the yard where Charlie was working Picasso. I always felt edgy when any horse-training was going on. It was like living with someone who had an abusive partner: Charlie would come limping in, with a black eye, and immediately launch into a long eulogy of whichever horse had done it to him: 'The finest little stallion in the world.'

Picasso was in a cart today, something he wasn't altogether sure about. From the kitchen window I could see that his huge, dark fringed eyes looked nervous, and he was sweating, not heavily, but just enough to make his chestnut coat stick down in flakes, as if it was part of an oil painting.

'Back!' Charlie shouted. 'Back, back, back!' trying to make Picasso reverse into the shafts of the cart. The cart was tipped forward, so the ends of the shafts rested on the ground, and each time Picasso tried to do as he was told, he'd accidentally stamp on them or kick them, and startle. He was doing his best to understand the task – there was an earnest, thoughtful look in his eyes – but you could sense he was finding it hard not to panic, too. He was a smallish, compact Ardennes, with a neat black mane and tail and a white blaze on his nose, and he always had an air of anxiety, which made me warm to him. And he must have felt under pressure, because he had recently developed sweet-itch – a skin rash that made his shoulders, and backside, look as if they belonged to a moth-eaten stuffed bear. A healer was going to call, later, and have a go at treating it.

There was an extra-loud bang. Picasso trod on a shaft and plunged forwards. 'Whoa!' Charlie called. He caught the horse by the halter, and after stroking its muzzle with a strange look on his face, teeth slightly bared in imitation of Picasso's expression, he began pushing it back, steadily, between those two tricky bits of wood. I turned around and sat down at the kitchen table again, relieved. I realised I'd been listening to the tone of Charlie's voice, flinching as I waited for him to become angry. Just as sometimes, at home, he became overbearing and unreasonable – where he had always, previously, been so sweet-natured and gentle – so, occasionally now, with the horses, his patience would wear thin. It was as if his character was changing, becoming more inflexible and less light-hearted. And as for me, I was now spending so much time indoors, writing at the kitchen table, that I was even beginning to lose my nerve around the animals. Charlie had scolded me only this morning for being too jumpy and anxious as I cleaned out the stable. Maybe the best I could do now was just watch the countryside through a window.

'Off back around,' Charlie called, and there was a jingle from the yard as Picasso, harnessed up and in the cart now, tried to make sense of this complicated command. There was a bang as he got it wrong and the corner of the cart slammed into a wall.

Charlie clicked his tongue and called out, 'Walk on.' I could see he was planning to drive Picasso out of the little stable-yard gate and into the bigger front yard, where he'd have to weave round the van, an ancient, rotting grass-cutter, a seed-drill and two half-dismantled scrap cars. One of Picasso's ears was back, and one forward, as if he, too, was doubtful about this challenge.

The cart rumbled into the gate with a splintery sound and Picasso seemed to lose heart. He was sweating more profusely, now: his sides were black with it. 'Walk on!' Charlie urged, and the horse kept stubbornly still. 'If I say you'll walk on, you'll f***ing well Walk On!' Charlie yelled furiously, smashing a stick on the front of the cart. Picasso rocketed forward, whistled through the gate, and thundered between the van and the cutter. At that moment a little sports car roared past on the main road, tootling its horn most cheerily, and Picasso quickened his pace until he was almost bolting. The cart bounced off one of the scrap cars, hit the seed-drill and ricocheted off the side of the house in a little snowstorm of pebble-dash. I couldn't see what was happening any more after that, because they'd gone out of range of the window, but I could hear stones and gravel flying, Charlie crying 'Whoa! Ho!', and then a crackling roar from the other side of the house. I grabbed Nat and ran out.

Charlie was picking himself off the drive when I turned the corner, and Picasso was half buried in the hedge, his sides bellowsing in and out. 'Good boy,' Charlie said softly, walking towards him. One leg of his trousers had almost completely torn off along the bloomer-line. I saw him gently examine Picasso for scratches and cuts. 'That's enough for one day. What a hot and bothered little chap you are!'

Nat struggled out of my arms and ran over to hug him round the leg.

'Is Picasso all right?' I asked, and Charlie said 'Fine', in a flat voice, without looking round.

He'd been very strange lately. It had all started at the beginning of November, when he went up to the Scottish Highlands to deliver a cart to a young farming couple. When he got back he spent hours in the office, on the computer and the telephone, and was furious if anyone went in and interrupted him. And then last week the cart had broken, and he'd felt morally obliged to go back to Scotland and mend it. He'd only been home a day and was so cold and distant. He even refused to cuddle me at night and slept at the extreme other side of the bed with his back turned. I couldn't think what I'd done to annoy him so badly.

It was a relief when my friend Sarah arrived to collect me and Nat in her car. She was one of my new, toddler-group friends, an unmarried mother with two small sons, and we were always going on outings together. Today, because it was so close to Christmas, we were going to take a ride on one of the South Devon Steam Railway's 'Santa Specials'. Nat was jiggling about with excitement at the thought of meeting Santa, and when it was his turn to go up the carriages into the red-papered grotto he wasn't disappointed.

'Hello, my lover!' Santa said, in the broadest Devon, pulling Nat on to his lap and giving him a toy. He was a wonderfully authentic Santa – not only white-bearded and stout, but with an unusual air of command. I found out later that he was a warden from Exeter jail and all the helpers were his charges. When we were back in our fuzzy maroon and cream seats, and enveloped in the train's coaly, steamy smell, enjoying the sound of its whistle, prisoners, dressed as nursery-rhyme characters like Old King Cole and Dr Foster, handed out mince pies and mulled wine.

As we drove home I told Sarah about the mysterious, slightly spooky side of horses, which was my favourite bit. In the beginning, Charlie had wanted to breed from his Ardennes. He particularly wanted to be present when a foal was born, because he'd heard that when the little animal first comes out it has a magical pad on its tongue. In a carthorse this is about the size of a man's palm and half an inch thick, and looks like a piece of liver. It is called the hippomanie, and the foal swallows it with its first breath, but if you are quick enough you can reach into its mouth and grab it. And, carefully dried, it is supposed to calm the wildest stallion. Whenever we went to any big heavy horse event there was always some pleased-looking old gentleman in the crowd with a wizened hippomanie tucked into the breast pocket of his tweed jacket. I once asked our vet about it, and he said there was no magic involved. 'It's just demon sex. The smell of a mare quietens stallions.'

But our horses were very secretive and swift when they foaled, and Charlie had never managed to get hold of a hippomanie. And gradually, year by year, he'd given up on the whole idea of breeding. This was because we never, ever had a live filly foal. Often a pregnant mare Charlie had sold would have a filly on someone else's farm, but the few fillies we had on ours were invariably born dead. When Charlie found the last one, it had been lying stiff and creamy-coloured the other side of the gate into the walnut-tree field, and he'd sworn never to keep a mare again.

Our bad luck with fillies was so mysterious that I asked a Yorkshire horseman friend of Charlie's, Geoffrey Morton, about it. He said that Charlie ought to pay more heed to ancient superstition, and propitiate evil spirits by spreading his horse afterbirths on hawthorn bushes. Geoffrey always did this, and he had far more than his fair share of fillies. But Charlie just said 'Bollocks!' when I mentioned it.

Still, he was superstitious enough to hire a whisperer to treat Picasso.

She'd arrived when I got back. The cart was parked outside the stable, Picasso was in his stall and the sheep were clustered round the gate, gazing in at the visitors and giving conversational baas.

'*The Silence of the Lambs*, indeed,' Charlie snorted, smiling at the whisperer. 'As if lambs ever *are* silent. Next they'll be making a film called *The Abstemiousness of Rats,* or *The Delicacy of Rutting Stallions*.'

The whisperer was called Jodi Canti, and also did hands-on healing and reiki. She was a slender, nervy-looking woman with short red hair, and she explained that each morning she shut herself away with a silver pendulum and communicated with distant horses and dogs, asking them questions about their problems. 'Recently, I did some work at 11 a.m. on a stallion,' she said, as she slipped into the stable and approached Picasso. 'I rang his owner when I'd finished and she asked me what time of day I had done it because she'd got really worried about him. She'd never ever known him to lie down during the day, yet that morning, at 11 a.m. she'd seen him lying quietly in the field. She reckoned he must have been listening to me.'

Feeling a bit sceptical, I asked Jodi what it was like when a horse talked, and she told me it varied. Sometimes she got a feeling – of fear or sadness. Occasionally she would receive a picture: once she suddenly visualised an iron bar coming down on the back of a horse she was treating. And other times she would simply hear a voice in her head. 'I had been treating a little pony with head-shaking problems, and I had managed to clear them up. A thirteen-year-old boy rides him, and his mum rang me and said the pony had recently competed in an event, and had done his cross-country and show-jumping perfectly, but been a prat when it came to the dressage. So I asked the pony, and I heard a voice say: "I find dressage boring." '

Jodi had brought a healer friend with her called Barbara Harvey, and while Jodi laid her hands gently on Picasso in the stable, I sat next to Barbara on the edge of the damaged cart and she told me she practised in London, on both humans and animals. Meanwhile, Picasso was visibly relaxing under Jodi's gentle massage, and, catching me peering round the door, she whispered that he would probably slump down on the floor and have a good sleep when she had gone. Charlie frowned at me, and pushed me back out again.

I went back to my seat next to Barbara, ashamed of what she might be thinking, after seeing my husband be so unfriendly. But she didn't appear to have noticed. Instead she described how she'd seen many pets sympathetically develop the same illnesses as their owners. She'd even come to the conclusion that animals got sick – and even died – if they found themselves caught up in a disastrous human relationship. She said she thought they probably did this to be helpful. 'The most extreme example that I ever came across was a French couple I knew. The man was absolutely besotted with his cat. And out of the blue she died. Then she came to him in a dream and said: "Now you can begin to love your wife the way you loved me." '

Tears prickled my eyes. Was Picasso's skin disease connected to the way Charlie was behaving?

Part 3

Chapter Sixteen

All women with children should be given the absolute right to duck out of five Christmases. There would be no guilt involved. They would just have to tear off one of the five little bunk-off slips provided by the government (in a booklet not unlike the Child Benefit one), and say: 'I'm awfully sorry, but this is one of my bunk-off Christmases. I won't be buying any presents this year or doing any cooking or cleaning. I can go to parties and have a good time, of course, but I'm simply not allowed to take on any responsibilities. Think of me as if I was a fourteen-year-old boy. That's roughly the level of input I will be making into Christmas this year.'

I felt so happy after writing this in my diary. As if it would ever be possible! Christmas 1999 did not start that well, but then, farm Christmases have a peculiar, masochistic flavour to them anyway. This is because animals do not understand that it is supposed to be a time when humans have long, leisurely meals and lie about in front of fires and televisions. Often the weather is troublesome, too.

That year the pipes froze up the night before Christmas Eve, and as I was putting the finishing touches to a roast lunch, Charlie opened the back door into the kitchen and began rolling muddy churns in with a self-righteous air. He stacked them by the sink and started filling them with a short length of hosepipe. The door was left open so that a frigid blast of air – and a number of inquisitive chickens – could come in.

'Do you think you could do that later?' I asked, pausing in my potato mashing to flick off a blob of mud that had travelled there from the churns.

'No,' Charlie said shortly, increasing the pressure on the hose. When the churns were full he rolled them across the yard and manoeuvred them through the gate to the cowsheds. Peering out of the kitchen window at him, I thought it seemed a great deal of heavy work, just to get water that short distance. And, after twenty minutes, during which the kitchen got pretty thoroughly carpeted in dungy straw, the same thought seemed to occur to him, too. So he fixed a longer hose to the tap, and opened the kitchen window so it could snake out into the yard. We had a rather trying meal as a result, sitting round the table in overcoats, scarves and hats while the ill-fitting hose, attached to the highest possible pressure of water, squirted us like a lawn sprinkler. The icy breeze that came in through the window made the gravy congeal on the plates, too. Still, at least we were allowed to stay indoors. More usually, just as we were (1) watching the gripping conclusion to a thriller, or (2) sitting down to an elaborate meal, Charlie would rush in to tell us one of the cows was out in the wrong field, and all hands were needed to get it back in the right one. We never needed to be told which cow it was. It was invariably one of 'the Horrendoes', now huge bullocks, and expert escapologists.

On Christmas Eve it was the turn of the yellowy-brown Horrendoe with Jersey blood to escape. This was a creature that was both acrobatic (possibly even double-jointed) and fiendishly cunning. After a brief scuffle in which both of the older children tried to stay indoors by pretending they could not find the right-sized wellington boots, or had flu, we emerged into the yard. It was cold, and there was a substance falling which was mid-way between rain and hail: wet enough to penetrate clothing and trickle down the back of your neck, but solid enough to sting your cheeks and hands. Charlie ordered us into position, and we began trying to round up the Horrendoe, but it was hopeless. Sam and I cornered him over by the gate, but all that happened was that a roguish gleam came into the Horrendoe's eye, and he sprang vertically into the air, whizzed over the gate, and galloped across a further, more distant field, flicking up his tail with excitement. When we cornered him in that one he ploughed cheerily through a bramble bush and escaped into one even further off.

Cows are quite unlike other farm animals: chasing them does not appear to tire them at all. On the contrary, it energises them. After three and a half hours of being hunted across country, their eyes sparkle, they snort with excitement and they are doing complex balletic jumps just for the fun of it. Also, unlike human beings, they have no qualms about tackling barbed wire or thickets of blackthorn.

Finally, we managed to chase the Horrendoe into a place that would do for the time being. It was not the field we had wanted to get him into. (In fact, it was the one he had first been sighted in.) But by then we were too cold to care. As I pulled my boots off outside the kitchen porch I saw the Horrendoe watching me wistfully from a gateway. He was probably wondering why all the fun had suddenly stopped.

Still, the rest of Christmas started all right: we made love on Christmas Eve, and there was a lot of teasing the next morning when the presents were given out because Kathy had given Charlie a German phrasebook (so he could buy four different types of sausage on his next trip abroad). The best part of it was a rude section giving the correct German for 'Where can I buy condoms?' and 'Would you like to go to bed with me?'

My favourite part of Christmas always began after lunch was over, when everyone lay about, uncomfortably full, and I knew I wouldn't have to do any cleaning (no point, as the house was full of toys and torn paper) or cooking for days. The children watched TV in front of the fire but Charlie retreated to the kitchen and sat at the kitchen table, working his way steadily through the bottle of whisky he'd been given. And when I joined him he started telling me what a terrible wife I'd been, and how he was going to leave, and go off somewhere wild and unspoiled, like East Germany or the Highlands. He wanted to take his favourite stallion, Picasso, with him, too. My main flaws as a spouse were that:

1) I had not been to enough ploughing matches,
2) I had not been sufficiently enthusiastic about his heavy horse machinery, or

3) The motorbike he had made from scrap metal.

I wept. It was true that I had not liked watching ploughing matches, and I had secretly found the intricacies of hitch cart (and motorbike) design horrifically dull. I had just switched off my brain whenever he talked about them (though still smiling and nodding politely). I had been feeling, for a long time, that I was deficient as a farmer's wife. I was too scared of inflicting pain to tackle jobs like injecting or castrating, and still not capable – even after all these years – of harnessing up a cart-horse and working it on my own. So when he began to attack me, starting every sentence with 'I know it's unpleasant to say this, but . . .', I felt he was justified. My irredeemably townie nature was being laid bare. I'd been found out. I was a failure. But as I mopped up my tears with the tea-towel, I couldn't help thinking, too, that his plans to go off into the wilds with his horse were preposterous. So did the older children the next morning. Kathy even said teasingly that she planned to set off for Outer Mongolia with one of the ducks as a travelling companion.

'Is there another woman?' I asked, a little later.

'No. Of course not,' Charlie said, frowning at me for even thinking such a thing. He had always, over the years, insisted that he was completely faithful.

Despite his strange mood, we decided to go ahead with a planned lunch party on New Year's Eve. After all, it was the turn of the century. The guests arrived and ate roast lamb, and Charlie took them out on his trials bike in the mud. (The sub-postmaster got so wet he had to eat tea in his underpants.) And when it started to get dark, Charlie took most of them home in the horse and cart.

It was a cool, damp night and there was excitement in the air. Music floated faintly across from the Honiton area where a huge party was getting under way, and over by the barn I could hear the plaintive whistle of a Little Owl. A bat swooped low over my head as I struggled, with a typical Egremont torch (wonky switch, dying batteries), to round up the ducks and stuff them through the pop-hole in the chicken-house. The old drake refused to go in and I had to chase him into a brambly corner of the poultry yard and grab him. He felt like a badly wrapped parcel smeared with Brylcreem and hissed crossly at me. When he was in I lifted the lid of the hen-house and looked at the birds lined up on their perches or cuddled into the nest-boxes. (The cockerel always slept above the drake's head, so he could get his own back for numerous daily indignities by crapping on him in the night.) I loved their warm perfume: it was a bit like the smell of sleeping children – with a hint of pissed-on mattress.

As I walked back to the farmhouse I heard Charlie talking loudly. It surprised me, because I thought all the guests had gone home. Perhaps someone else had arrived. I wandered over to the stable to see who it was, and as I rounded a corner the still night air carried his words more clearly.

'I just want to put my arms round you and hold you.' There was a pause, and then he added fiercely: 'That's the last party I'll ever give with *her*.'

I ran round the other side of the house and stared at him

from the gate by the back door, where I knew I couldn't be seen. He was sitting on a bale of straw, illuminated by a shaft of light from the open stable door, and talking into the mobile phone I had given him for Christmas. He rustled as he shifted position. 'I've just been taking everyone home in the horse and cart, and coming back alone down the road I kept thinking: "I want to be with you." ' I slipped into the house and stood there, numb. It couldn't be true. It just couldn't. It felt completely unreal, as if I was listening to a radio play, or watching a film. I went upstairs and started running a bath for Nat, and while water thundered into the tub, and Nat played with Lego on the landing, I stole into Kathy's room, which overlooked the stable yard, and listened at the open window. Charlie was confiding that he had a very good feeling about their relationship, and referred to the woman on the other end of the telephone by name. I switched off the taps and ran downstairs to the study, where I searched through the battered exercise book where he wrote down his orders to find the name of the young couple in Scotland he had delivered the cart to. It was not a young couple. Just a single woman. The same name I'd just heard him say softly down the telephone.

I had to get away and think, so I bathed Nat swiftly, and dressed him, and packed a bag. When I took him downstairs I found Charlie had finished his conversation and was lying on the sofa in the kitchen. He looked at me coldly. There was almost a reptilian cast to his eyes, I thought, as if they belonged to some ill-natured old monitor-lizard. I told him I was off to spend New Year's Eve with my mother and he did not even ask why.

When I arrived at my mother's she was hosting a party. Her neighbours were drinking champagne, cracking open fortune-cookies and eating smoked salmon, and as midnight approached they lit a fire and danced round it. Church bells rang, and on all the hillsides, as far as the eye could see, other bonfires flickered. I felt like a ghost through all this: as if it was going on on the other side of a lit window, and I was completely excluded. Very early in the morning we went to bed and, because the house was full of guests, Nat and I crammed into my mother's pink boudoir, which she shared with her whippet, Ben, and a grey tabby cat (which generally spent its nights hidden inside the duvet cover). Nat lay asleep between us, and my mother gripped my hand tightly as I told her, through a thick fug of tears and phlegm, what had happened. 'Don't take him back,' she said, which was an odd comment for her to make. She had always been so forgiving to my father, and in the past I had heard her being dismissive of women who reacted badly to infidelity. (The way to save a marriage, I knew, was to stay calm, say nothing, tell no one, wait for the man to come to his senses, and when he did, be as friendly as possible and avoid making him feel guilty.) Besides, she disapproved of divorce and loved Charlie. I do not remember much else of what she said, it was one of those endless, soothing feminine conversations, a bit like being stroked over and over again, and eventually I drifted off to sleep.

I woke with a start. Something hard and wet had landed on my face. I lashed out, and there was the sound of a whippet cannoning into a laundry basket. It was Ben. Feeling thirsty, he had trotted off for a drink of toilet water, and then leapt back into bed, forgetting I was there. He seemed rather intellectually challenged, because he did the same thing twice more before his woolly brain grasped that it was not a sound strategy. Then he took to howling, and galloping downstairs after imaginary burglars. In the brief interludes when he was not doing this, or slaking his thirst in the lavatory, my mother, who is an insomniac, would fumble about with light switches and spectacles, and listen to the World Service. Half asleep, I wondered whether I could apply for a prize somewhere, for the most trying centenary night, ever. (Afterwards, of course, I realised that I was only one of many thousands of wives who had discovered about their husband's infidelity on brand-new mobile phones over the holiday. Mobiles were that year's most popular gift; and Christmas has always been a time when marriages founder. My situation was far from unique or original.)

When I got home, Charlie looked as if he hadn't moved, because he was lying on the sofa again, thinking. I told him quietly that I knew he had been having an affair and he was not at all abashed. In fact, he got up at once and telephoned his girlfriend. Later, I asked him if he had slept with anyone else during our marriage and he said he had. He refused to give any details, though.

The shock of his disloyalty was dreadful. I couldn't believe it, and yet I felt utterly smashed by it, too. It made my whole life appear fake, as if up until now I had been living in a childish, painted world full of toys and now it had been torn away. Perhaps I had been stupidly trusting, and I should have realised what was going on, but whenever I'd been suspicious of any situation (and it hadn't happened that often) I had always accepted his innocent explanation.

The older children came back from staying with friends and the days and nights collapsed into a blur, when we were all tired and distraught, and meals were plates of hurriedly assembled sandwiches. Kathy and Sam reacted differently to the crisis. Sam hid in his bedroom, taking in all the elderly old fan heaters and turning them on, so it was toasty warm. He also had a portable TV in there, and when I went in to see him it was almost possible to forget what was going on in the rest of the house. He didn't want to discuss it; he just watched TV and played with Nat, who chanted nursery rhymes over and over to himself, and wet his trousers pretty well constantly.

Kathy talked to Charlie and pleaded with him to give up the other woman and stay. As night closed in she'd go into the study, or the bedroom where he now slept alone (I slept with Nat, or rather, lay in his bed, clutching him sleeplessly), and start discussing it all, in a low murmur that I could hear through the walls. They had reasonable, quiet conversations that would sometimes break into high, emotional keening. She had always been good at winning arguments – it was one of the reasons she wanted to be a lawyer; even Charlie couldn't best her.

'You don't understand,' he kept reiterating. 'I have never been able to trust anyone, not since I was sent away to boarding school by Gaffer and Ma.'

I crept into the room. 'But you could have trusted me,' I said. 'I would never have let you down.'

When he turned to Kathy and said pitifully: 'Going away to that school was like being sent to prison for something I hadn't done,' she replied, 'So now you are going to leave, and deprive Nat of his father, just the same. How do you think that will make anything better?'

He couldn't answer; he wept.

'If you desert your family now,' she went on remorselessly, 'how are you going to feel when someone else takes me to the altar on his arm, and Nat ends up calling another man "Daddy"?'

Another night I was trying to write my latest article, which was almost impossible. Just stringing sentences together was nearly beyond me. At 2 a.m. as I was scribbling gibberish on a bit of paper, Charlie came in and sat down heavily.

'You don't know how hard it was to be faithful, and how tempted I was,' he said, putting his head in his hands.

'Yes I do,' I insisted. 'I've been tempted as well. But do you think I would ever hesitate if I had to choose between my personal fulfilment and my children's happiness?' He looked at me oddly. His expression was unfamiliar, and I only realised later that it was a mixture of pity and distaste. We had completely different values – and I'd never been aware of it before.

He was quite determined to leave us. This new woman was the love of his life, and what he'd once felt for me didn't even come close. Kathy and I went on trying to persuade him to stay, and sometimes he would appear to waver, but then he would go off and telephone his girlfriend and be icy again.

'You don't need me, anyway,' he said one morning, as our bedroom filled with ghostly dawn light.

'Yes I do,' I answered. 'You are my best friend, my rock, you are the moon in our children's constellation of stars.' He turned away, repelled by the kitsch imagery. But there was no other way of putting it. It was what I felt. His voice was sad. 'I hope you will still think well of me when I have gone.'

I had always been an obsessive reader of magazine quizzes on marriage, and ours invariably scored highly because we communicated well, found each other amusing and had sex often. Those quizzes were wrong.

Real signs that your marriage is in serious danger, and infidelity may be going on out of sight:

1) Your husband's friends change. He is no longer interested in socialising with happily-marrieds and gradually begins to spend his time, instead, with single men or womanisers.

2) Any power you have over him (for instance, to get him to do the washing-up, remember anniversaries, help with DIY) gradually ebbs away, giving you an odd feeling, like putting your foot on a stair that isn't there any more.

3) Your husband has phases of talking endlessly about a particular woman. He is not necessarily complimentary about her – I remember a long period when Charlie extensively discussed the blonde hair on Sofe's chin, and the way it glinted horribly in the sunlight. At the time I thought this strange – but now I think it must have had a special significance.

4) Occasionally, a woman will become a close friend – and then, for no discernible reason, she will disengage from you, and try to avoid those long, deep conversations or cosy shopping trips. It is done quite delicately and kindly, but it leaves you bewildered, because she is still attached to the family, and dropping round all the time.

5) Although he has no reason at all to be jealous, your husband is highly suspicious of your behaviour. He reads your diaries, rummages through your bags, and if you ever ring him to tell him an old boyfriend has dropped in unexpectedly for tea he is home in a flash, and looms menacingly over the poor man till he leaves. This seems peculiar at the time, because *you* aren't worried when he goes off to buy horses with a female friend, or spends the day giving heavy horse tuition to a lady farmer. But he's judging you by his standards. He knows that it's perfectly possible to leap into bed with someone a couple of hours (or maybe less – how would I know?) after meeting them for the very first time.

6) From time to time you are plagued by mysterious small infections and itches in intimate places, and give the cat a hard time about his flea problem.

7) Poltergeists move into the house.

This last may sound far-fetched, but it isn't. I discovered there was a reason why the house had been haunted after we collected the Bettiscombe furniture. As soon as Charlie was gone, all the sounds stopped; even the stairs no longer creaked at night. When I wrote about this, a member of the Society for Psychical Research, Mary Rose Barrington, got in touch to say that poltergeists thrived on tension and often popped up when a marriage was in trouble. They specially liked households where no one shouted, but there was just a simmering, resentful silence.

For four days and nights – up until 5 January, when Charlie left in his lorry – the light bulbs in the house fizzled and popped until we were mostly living in darkness. I did not bother replacing them until a couple of weeks later and then I discovered that the fittings had melted inside. (As had some of the electric fires in the house. The clocks and watches all stopped working too, and even to this day they only function erratically.)

He had promised to stay until all the farm animals were sold, but in the end I lost my patience. On the penultimate day he told me it was best if we did not consult solicitors: 'I will never be able to give you any money for the kids. But you can stay in the house until you find someone else, and then we will sell it and divide the proceeds.' The next morning I caught him on the telephone secretly discussing divorce proceedings with a solicitor. I shouted at him to go, and threw all his clothes in the back of his pick-up, and while Kathy wept in the office he stuffed papers into a briefcase, leapt into the lorry – and went.

Chapter Seventeen

'Whatever else you do DON'T take him back. It can never be the same. He has destroyed that special something that exists in every marriage, even poorish ones, by openly disowning you and walking out.'
Advice from *Times* reader William P. Boyd

Charlie might have gone, but the farm animals hadn't. And it had never struck me before that when a farmer bolts from his marriage it is not just his wife and children who are thrown into confusion, but his animals, too. The first on the farm to feel the change were the horses. Picasso was collected by Charlie two weeks later, along with nearly all the machinery, and went off to Scotland where I often thought of him, standing on some remote, windswept hill, forging an uneasy alliance with a black Highland bull. Meanwhile, the other stallion, Holbein, was sold locally. Though he went to a kind home, his new owners were bent on gelding him – and he probably soon regretted Charlie's departure as much as I did.

The only farm equipment Charlie left behind was a wheelbarrow and a pitchfork, so the other livestock gradually began to realise that the farm had passed into less competent hands. Since he hated hauling bales, Charlie had big-baled all the hay and silage, but if you happen to be small and slight – as I am – unrolling a big bale and feeding it (in a wheelbarrow) is a slow process. It always reminded me of *The Borrowers*, where the tiny but resourceful family has to tackle nightmare challenges, like cutting into giant truckle cheeses. I'd scramble up on the bale and attempt to unroll it by running backwards and forwards on top. And then I'd have to tear off a mattress-sized piece, hump it on to the wheelbarrow and charge at the mud round the barn, running as far as I could before the wheel blodged solid with mud. When it did I would be surrounded by a jostling herd of ravenous cattle – and, beyond them, little knots of miserable-looking sheep.

It was not long before the sheep had had enough of my dodgy stewardship. They fled through the hedges into the next-door farm and the only solution was to sell them. The ewes were loaded up and despatched, but for a few days the ram remained, along with a sheep that was too rickety to be sold – Helicopter. Although she was not the most physically attractive animal I had ever seen, I had always admired Helicopter's dignity and character. The ram did not, though. In a bizarre parody of earlier scenes at the farmhouse, he decided that he simply was not interested in such an ancient, if loyal, companion, and set off across the fields in search of something more appealing.

It would have been easier if the cows could have gone, too, but, sadly, another minuscule flaw in Charlie's make-up was his unwillingness to do paperwork. As a result he forgot, until the day before he left, to apply for cow passports. Nowadays, if a cow does not have a passport it enters into a Kafkaesque limbo where it does not officially exist. It cannot be sold, nor can it be killed in an abattoir and eaten. It just hangs about, making a thorough nuisance of itself: escaping into other people's gardens, bellowing noisily and eating frequent, heavy meals. A week after Charlie left, in an uncharacteristically light-hearted mood, I rang the British Cattle Movement Service to enquire if I was allowed to stab the cows to death (with a pitchfork) and bury them. But I was told that I needed to apply for a permit if I wanted to do this, too.

The only creature on the farm that was thrilled with the new regime was the cat. He and Charlie never truly got on. Their whole relationship was a low-key struggle for mastery of the farmhouse (and the sofa) – a struggle that Charlie always won, by the low stratagem of taping up the cat flap. Soon after he disappeared in his lorry the cat bit all the tape off, and joyfully took possession of the house, where he ate a pizza before going upstairs to pass out on the marital bed. He soon doubled in size, and when I looked closely at his black, hairy face, he seemed to be smiling.

Life was very grim. I felt as if I was living in an underworld – a dark, cheerless place where I was completely alone, and the person who had always been there to console me in bad times had fled. All my life I had thought of Charlie as a kind person – much more soft-hearted and compassionate than me – but that had changed. It is hard to describe how painful and bewildering it is when your very best friend, the person who knows you better than your own mother does – suddenly and most abruptly turns against you. Because Charlie was not just indifferent. He now seemed to actively dislike me, and worse, think me unworthy even of compassion. It was as if he had decided that I wasn't really suffering. I was acting; feeling so little pain that it didn't need to be taken into account.

This was brought home to me very sharply the day before he left. From the moment he told me that he had never loved me the way he loved the new woman I had been unable to stop crying. I had no choice: one minute I would be holding my own with dignity, the next I would be hit by a tidal wave of emotion. And on this particular evening I was washing up. I was weeping silently, so no one would know. I heard Charlie come in and sit on the coolest Aga lid (which had a buttock-shaped dent in it because everyone sat there). He stared at me. It was the detached curiosity a scientist might have had for a pickled specimen. I turned my head away, ashamed, and after a while he got up and went outside. He telephoned his girlfriend from the yard, a few feet away from the kitchen window, and I heard him say cheerfully, 'She's crying a bit now, but it's nothing much.' It hadn't occurred to him at all that he ought to comfort me.

I found this so distressing that, late one night, I rang TJ for advice.

She answered warily. Her voice was very quiet, as if she was trying not to wake someone close by. And when I asked her if she could give me some insight into Charlie's state of mind it felt as if my words had dropped into a pool of still water at the bottom of a well.

'If he is anything like I was,' she said after a long pause, 'he will be thinking "At last! I'm going to get the fun and happiness I deserve. This is 'me time'." He is feeling a bit guilty, but he is stamping on that feeling, and he is convinced that *he is the only one who is suffering*. He isn't aware of your feelings at all. It will only repel him if you cry, so try not to.'

It wasn't just me that Charlie had turned against. It was our whole life together. 'You don't understand,' he said at one point. 'I'm fond of the children, but I didn't want to have them. And I don't want to sit down to eat at a table with them all around me.' I gazed at him, beyond words. Was he saying he didn't want to be a father any more? And if so, why didn't he? The only possible explanation was that he wanted to undo the past and be young again. And that just wasn't possible.

The older children were as badly affected as Nat, but in a different way. While he regressed back to being a baby, needing constant cuddling, Sam became numb and distant with shock – especially as Charlie had left without talking to him, or even saying goodbye. And Kathy was outraged that her father could put a woman he hardly knew above the needs of his own children. 'What am I supposed to do?' she cried. 'I've admired him all my life for being a good father and faithful husband – and now he's just, just . . . a scumbag.'

The wind whistled round the house, making the timbers creak like an old galleon at sea, and after hours of talking she decided to take action. She e-mailed all his family and friends to tell them that he'd left. That done, she began moving furniture. 'You can't sleep in this bedroom again the way it is. Too many bad memories,' she declared. She pushed cupboards about and moved the bed into a corner. Then she dusted her hands off and went into the spare room. 'Dad tortured us by having people like Mr Stinky to stay,' she said. 'Let's not have a spare room any more.'

So Sam and I hauled the bed downstairs and threw it into the yard, where it slowly sogged up with rain, and the spare room became an office. It was a very kind thought, but who needs two offices? Maybe it could be Nat's office.

Then Sam decided to make some changes. 'Dad never let us listen to anything except the blues,' he said. 'So let's get you an extra-loud CD player and some music.' When I demurred he insisted. 'You've never spent enough money on yourself.' He installed it for me, and soon Spanish jazz rang out over the farm, making it sound like student digs. The only bit of Charlie's lifestyle they both desperately wanted to keep was his sock drawer. 'I always loved helping myself to Dad's socks,' Sam said wistfully. So I bought some terrible socks and filled it up again. These were just brief moments of liveliness, and then they both went back to college – Kathy to take her finals. 'Why couldn't he have waited till June? How am I going to get the grades I need now?'

Soon it was just me and Nat, cuddling up in the double bed, while ice formed leafy patterns on the insides of the windows, draughts rippled the carpets and, somewhere in the darkness outside, the wind ripped corrugated sheets ruthlessly off the barn roof. I became insanely, pointlessly obsessed with the other woman. I knew nothing about her except the details Charlie had given me: she was a thirty-four-year-old separated farmer with 600 acres; she was horsey, German, tall and had short hair.

'Is she pretty?'

'Not a pretty face – a lovely face.'

Down the back of a filing cabinet I found a scrumpled photo of an extremely stout, hideously ugly woman with yellow hair, crouching in a dirndl beside a field of vegetables. This, I decided, must be her. The only other things I had that gave a clue to her character were a music tape and some e-mails. The e-mails made me feel bleak, because it was clear from them that Charlie was reinventing the past. He seemed to believe now that he hadn't really loved me even when we married.

I found the tape in the player in Charlie's lorry on one of his brief visits back to the farm to collect more agricultural machinery. It was hand-compiled, and had female handwriting on the side. So I pulled it out and substituted a tape Charlie had given me for Christmas as a joke: *Elvis Sings 27 Yuletide Hits*. After he'd left I giggled to myself at the thought of him turning on the player and hearing the King belt out 'Rudolf the Red-Nosed Reindeer'. The mystery woman's tape mostly contained jaunty songs on the theme of dumping an unsatisfactory partner. But there was a folk-ballad in there that I grew deeply attached to. Called 'My Damsel Heart', it was a syrupy confection by Sally Oldfield about a love affair with a distant, romantic, unattainable horseman. I found it consoling to listen to, because it was clear that this unknown woman loved Charlie for exactly the same reasons that I had. Every night, when Nat had fallen asleep, I'd get up and play it over and over again, walking round the kitchen table. I'd walk until midnight, sleep for an hour and then walk until dawn. I did not feel the slightest bit tired (or hungry). I wished I could have walked across country, but I couldn't leave Nat. Later, the woman running the local second-hand shop told me that she walked round and round her smallholding after her marriage ended, always in the middle of the night. It got so her dog would whimper with dismay and scuttle under the dresser whenever he saw her putting on her coat at 2 a.m.

Everyone in the village soon knew what had happened. And though Charlie had never been the slightest bit violent he immediately metamorphosed in local minds into a hulking brute, capable of almost any dastardly act.

'He isn't giving you any trouble, is he?' a farming acquaintance asked one morning, stopping his tractor and rolling up his sleeves to reveal vast, rippling muscles, at my service if any hand-to-hand combat might be required. My female friends were subtler: they left anonymous pies and crumbles on the doorstep (much to the delight of the drake, which generally found them before I did).

One of the toughest challenges I faced was keeping my column going. I couldn't afford to stop, because I needed the money too much. Doing any work at all was very difficult, though, because my mind was so crowded with thoughts about Charlie. Nat clung to me desperately, too, like a little monkey, vomiting in terror. 'I don't feel *safe* now Daddy's gone.'

He slept under my desk while I wrote in the upstairs office – and I thought it unwise to leave him with anyone else for even a few hours while I did interviews. So, first, I persuaded the village postman, Marty Richards, to drop in and let me ask him about his job. Olive-skinned, with a dark moustache and a kind, inquisitive look in his eyes, like a friendly robin, he described the horrid sensation he had had one morning, when he opened a letter box in the next-door parish and something flabby fell into his hand. It was one finger of a rubber washing-up glove, which had been snipped off, filled with loose change, and glued to the corner of an envelope instead of a stamp. 'That's a very rural thing to do,' he said.

The mainstay of our community, in between delivering post he drops in shopping, carries money to the bank, changes light bulbs and continually moves furniture. One day he'll be asked to drag a wardrobe across a hall, and as likely as not have to haul it back twenty-four hours later, when the owner changes their mind. And he explained that he was always being asked for advice: farmers on the edge of his round will ask him whether he's heard anything doubtful about the young man their daughter is courting, and angry wives will complain to him about their husbands. (And then the husband, waiting at a gate further down the road, will put his side of the story – so Marty has to be diplomatic.)

'But I never guessed your marriage was in trouble, not once,' he said, putting his head on one side, and giving me a sympathetic look. 'It was a surprise to all of us.'

A few days after I'd written about Marty, a farmer two fields away asked me if I could do something about the plight of the pig industry. He told me that he and all his friends were holding a vigil on a traffic island in Parliament Square, and had taken a pig down there. So I packed a bag, got a friend in to mind the animals and took Nat to stay with my sister Caky in her houseboat beside Battersea Bridge.

When I arrived I found the pig, a Large White (called Winnie after the statue of Sir Winston that her pen nestled under), being looked after by four farmers at a time on a twelve-hour rota. And as I scratched her back I wondered how on earth they had managed to get away with keeping her there. Ian Campbell of the National Pig Association explained that they talked one extra-sympathetic police sergeant into allowing a farming demonstration, and then casually slipped a pig in. 'There was an initial reaction of the "You really *can't* leave a pig here" sort,' he laughed. 'But the longer Winnie stays the more she becomes a fixture.'

Living in London was very good for the pig because, as Campbell explained, she was an eight-month-old barrener who was about to be slaughtered because she had shown no sign of being fertile. 'Sometimes, when a gilt won't come on heat, farmers drive her in a vehicle over bumpy fields, or introduce her to an especially attractive boar, but in Winnie's case just being in Parliament Square did the trick.'

One night, when she was obviously ready, Winnie was discreetly artificially inseminated, watched only by the Westminster CCTV cameras. As a result pig fertility became a popular topic with visitors to the traffic island. And one of the farmers had a particularly interesting conversation with a lady peer, the Countess of Mar, about her Saddleback pigs. Apparently, she and her husband were about to go on holiday when one of their sows came on heat. Mar inseminated the creature during the day, and then decided to give the procedure another go at 2 a.m., just before she left. So she and her husband went to the sow's pen, where it was sleeping soundly. Her husband, meaning to be helpful, kicked the sow to wake it, only to be smacked round the head with the AI catheter.

'Why did you do that?' he asked in an aggrieved tone.

'Because you don't understand pigs – or women,' Mar replied.

Of course, it wasn't all jollity and rude stories: anyone who turned up to play with Winnie was left in no doubt about the shocking state of the pig industry. This was due to the already low price, along with recent legislation banning stall-and-tether systems. The new equipment (which meant pigs like Winnie would no longer have to spend their pregnancy chained in a pen) had been expensive to install. Yet when British farmers tried to recoup their costs in the market place they were undercut by a flood of cheap imported meat from countries that still kept their pigs tethered. And now, to make matters even worse, they had to pay a surcharge of £5.26 each time they had a pig slaughtered, to cover the cost of disposing of the offal.

The situation was so bad that many of the farmers on the

vigil were not only facing bankruptcy but mental breakdown, too. But even so, they managed to find humour in the situation. Arthur Fidler, for instance, a farmer-worker from East Anglia, was approached by three ladies of the night during his evening stint. 'They came across and asked us if we were looking for business. I took one look at them and said I would rather get in the sty and sleep with the pig. They weren't at all amused.'

Rod Tuck, from Norfolk, and his companions tried to enlighten a tramp about conditions in the pig industry when he approached them for money. 'We explained that if we *had* any money we wouldn't be having a vigil in Parliament Square. The dosser replied crossly: "Well, this job isn't what it used to be, either. It now takes me two hours to earn £6." One of my friends replied: "Still sounds better than keeping pigs." At that the dosser scarpered. I think he thought he was about to be tapped up for a quid.'

Nat and I came back chastened. It suddenly seemed as if we weren't that badly off after all. At least we had somewhere warm to sleep, and no debts. And the passports for the cows finally came through, which meant that the animals could go at last. As if they sensed our situation had eased, all sorts of people started dropping in unexpectedly. The policeman turned up and spent a whole day fitting locks to my windows, the Jehovah's Witnesses (hopeful of a sudden conversion) called twice a week, and I got plenty of kindly advice.

'I reckon what went wrong with your marriage,' one of my nearest neighbours said, sitting down comfortably in front of the Aga with a biscuit, 'was that you just can't trust horsey people. They are always at it.'

'You shouldn't have let him go abroad by himself,' another said, lifting the lid of the teapot and peering inside to see if another cup could be squeezed out. 'Asking for trouble, that was.'

Other men called in to see if they could help with any heavy jobs and wandered round, poking about in the farm's capacious sheds. These had leaky roofs and were full of rusting iron-mongery. Some bits had once been part of a motorbike, others belonged to tractors and ploughs. Charlie had left them all ran-domly jumbled up and half-beached in pools of oil. My male visitors would gaze at this vista with their mouths open.

'What a terrible fool the man was,' they would say at last, fin-gering part of an ancient grease-nipple. 'How could he bear to leave all this behind?'

Less welcome were the total strangers in frayed raincoats tied with baler-twine who knocked on the door late at night to say they had heard in a distant pub that I was selling up, and could they buy the farm cheap? Sometimes they had Afghan coats and pointy woollen hats, were female and bedraggled, and just wanted to buy an acre, to keep a few hens on. I was always polite to them, although I was upset that everyone for miles around seemed to see the farm as an asset ripe for pillaging. I gradually got less well disposed to another contingent, though: other women's husbands hoping to get lucky. They would turn up for a perfectly legitimate reason, stay so long I had to offer them tea and then casually drop into the conversation the fact that they no longer had any sort of sexual relationship with their wives, but were more like brother and sister. I do not know why they thought this would thrill me. As far as I was concerned, if a married man wanted to tell me how rubbish his wife was he could do it while standing under the leaky drain-pipe in the yard. (Preferably when it was raining.)

One night, at ten, I was playing 'My Damsel Heart' at especially high volume, because that way the tinkling bells in the orchestral section made the hairs on the back of my neck stand up. I was lying on the Aga wrapped in a rug, as I'd got so thin the house seemed even colder than usual. And Nat – wearing an outsize ski suit from a jumble sale (in which he couldn't walk, but only flump with a strange caterpillar motion) – was sitting under the table rummaging through a broken box of make-up and painting his toenails very carefully with foundation. (We had given up on different bedtimes. We both fell into bed fully clothed at about eleven. Sometimes we both wore bobble-hats, scarves and overcoats, and we always lapped ourselves about with hot-water-bottles.)

I'd just been on the phone to Kathy and Sam, discussing what I ought to do next. I'd filed for divorce, and was hoping that I might be able to go on living in the house – but if not, they suggested that I should buy a flat in London. That way they could both live with me when they finished their degrees, and help look after Nat, and I could perhaps get a job in an office, and maybe – as Kathy pointed out – after a very long time I could find a nice, wealthy intellectual to go out to operas with.

But continuing to live in the countryside was appealing, too.

The locals had been so kind recently – especially to the children. The older ones used to complain bitterly about being forced to spend their entire childhood – from toddler group to A levels – with the same small band of village children (which, of course, included their enemies as well as friends). But they'd been touched by the way everyone had been so thoughtful since Charlie had left. It had made them feel as if the village was a huge, extended family.

I was still wondering whether it would be best to move to London when there was a knock at the back door. I opened it warily. It was somebody pleasant for a change, an old friend of Charlie's, a heavy-horseman who lived a few miles away. I had always thought of him as 'Mr Wooster' because he was eccentric, rich and had an upper-class voice. He was wearing a loud tweed jacket and a tie with horseshoes on it, looking as if he had stepped out of a 1930s drama, and he winced rather at the music.

Saying he wanted to consult Charlie about the horse society they both belonged to, he sat on the sofa. (This seriously annoyed the cat, who now regarded it as his private territory.) When I told Wooster that Charlie had left me, he looked astounded. I got out the cake-tin – still full of Christmas cake everyone had been too upset to eat – and he devoured a quarter of it, before telling me, quite tearfully, that *his* wife was leaving *him*. Indeed, as he spoke (he said) she was packing trunks and slapping labels on to furniture. It seemed the most extraordinary coincidence.

He wrote me a cheering letter, and rang a few times, and after a while we began going on little trips together with our sons (his was a very quiet, sweet-natured teenager), spending whole days at the zoo, or fishing for crabs off a jetty. It puzzled me that a man should choose to do this, and actually show enjoyment while it was going on: Charlie had hated family days out and only agreed to go on them once a year, when it was my birth-day. And most of all we talked endlessly. I would babble on about the awful things Charlie had said and done, and Wooster would tell me how deeply he loved and missed his wife (which was rather annoying, really, as I was getting a bit tired of men telling me, in enormous detail, how much they adored other women). Often, Wooster would sob brokenly. He wept even more than I did, and I was the weepiest I had ever been. Even I was ashamed of how much I cried.

It was disconcerting listening to him because, in so many ways, I identified with his wife. For instance, she had objected to the amount of dogs he kept, and the noise they made at night.

'Why, how many do you have?'

He paused to count them on his fingers – there were the four attack dogs chained up by his stables, the different kinds of ter-riers . . . : 'Twenty-three,' he said, finally.

'It does sound like *quite* a lot,' I said, trying to be fair to both sides.

In fact, I was rapidly discovering one of the pleasures of being a divorcing person: swapping grim stories about absent spouses. It was not just that it was comforting being able to tell anec-dotes with enormous bias. (And be believed.) It was as much fun, as a wife who had been found severely wanting, hearing

236

about the transgressions of another female. So many times, as Wooster described what his wife had done and I gasped 'No!' in horror, I would be thinking to myself, with a strange, guilty thrill: 'I did that, too!'

Chapter Eighteen

Every day, do something that you know would really annoy your husband. I started smoking and used nothing but his priceless Meissen plates to stub the cigarettes out on. I also taped over all his Clint Eastwood films and rugby international matches. It made me feel so much better. Advice from anonymous *Times* reader, February 2000

'What do you think that is?' Wooster asked one day. He was sitting in his parlour, an elegantly proportioned room where every conceivable surface was covered in wood-ash and half-eaten plates of food. Over by the old-fashioned cast-metal range a rabbit was living (rather morosely) behind a fender, and there was a jackdaw hopping about in a cage by the window. Packs of dogs raced in and out, fighting and growling under the tables, and two doves fluttered around the next-door kitchen, where they were attempting to roost on the plate rack.

A strange, masculine logic dominated the place: there were rows of wellington boots soaking in the bath, and if you had a cup of tea you could choose between whitening it with ice-cream, lamb milk-powder or tinned rice pudding. (Ordinary milk was not an option: Wooster kept forgetting to buy any.)

There were ferrets in the porch and geese hissing on the path. (Later, there was a fist-sized gosling that ruffled its down and lowered its snub beak in challenge.) And that was quite apart from the farm, where there were cows, pigs, sheep, chickens and ridiculous amounts of horses. Each time he went anywhere Wooster was late because he had so much pet-feeding to do first, and he generally took the odd one or two with him. A one-eared Jack Russell seemed to live permanently in the cab of his Land Rover, feeding on the upholstery.

His house had an unforgettable perfume, a blend of horses, dogs, harness and wood smoke, and I breathed it in happily, thinking it was a million times better than anything you ever smelt in a town, as I looked in the direction he was pointing. Crawling unsteadily across the floor was a plump little creature the size of a kitten. Its eyes were tight shut, so it was obviously very young, and it was covered in soft, charcoal-coloured fur. It had a pointy tail, and a snub, V-shaped head with a deep wrinkle across the nose.

I picked it up to cuddle it and it mewled. I wanted to see if it had webs between its toes, because I thought it might be a baby otter, but it didn't. When I gave up guessing Wooster told me it was a fox cub his terriers had dug up. Originally there had been three – the others had been torn apart before he could reach them. He'd found a doll-sized feeding bottle and bought some proprietory puppy food, and he was going to hand-rear it.

As he explained this he took it from me and sat it on his knee, and it wriggled as it sucked, giving high, singing whimpers of appreciation. Afterwards he upended it and rubbed it with an old bit of towel.

'You have to encourage it to pee by doing this,' he said.

'How do you know?' I asked, and he explained that he had kept about half a dozen in the past. The first escaped soon after reaching adolescence and set up home, rather tactlessly, in a children's petting zoo a mile up the road, where it helped itself, every day, to a selection of pedigree rabbits and rare-breed poultry. Whenever he met the petting farm people Wooster used to look innocently sympathetic as they complained about their fox problems. But the game was up when it was finally trapped.

'You know that fox that has been causing all the trouble up here?' they said in an icy phone call. 'Well, we've just caught it and it is wearing a little tartan collar with your name and address on.'

Another pet fox bit through its tether and leapt over the garden wall just as a hunt met nearby. Because Wooster had never dared let it roam free (in case it got shot) it did not know the surrounding countryside at all, and when the hounds caught its scent it did not behave like an ordinary fox. Apparently, hunted foxes always double back on themselves and go to ground. But, to the hunt's astonishment, this one didn't. Instead it ran in a dead straight line for eight miles, until it reached a council estate, and then it hid. The hounds milled around, causing outrage as they uprooted bean poles, knocked over lines of washing and poured in and out of kitchens, but the fox had completely disappeared. No one ever worked out where it had come from, though the local Master of Hounds had a shrewd idea and kept bringing the subject up, teasingly, when he went drinking with Wooster.

Unlike Charlie, Wooster didn't object to hunting at all. He had a robust, no-nonsense attitude to it, and so did his friends. To him it was just part of everyday rural life, like shooting and fishing. (Which Charlie had not approved of, either.) It was peculiar discovering this parallel universe that had been going on all the time I'd been living in the country, and that I had never had anything to do with before. I could see now that Charlie had set such narrowly defined limits to his experience. He'd even chosen his friends most carefully: lovable rogues – grave-diggers, scrapmen, poachers, dealers – and charismatic farmers, their faces as arresting as those in an ancient sepia photograph. He'd always avoided and disliked anyone county or upper class – unless they were the Prince of Wales, or enjoyably eccentric.

In doing this he had shown an inverse snobbery typical of those who romanticise the countryside. But then, rural life is riven with class and money divisions of all kinds. The old agricultural families detest the young professional incomers who want to take over the parish councils. (The classic way they show this is in the judging at local shows, where they fail masterpieces of townie baking on specious grounds, like: 'a gateau never has decorated sides'. Or, more insulting still, by awarding third prize to the only entry in a section.) The council estate families resent the small, independent farmers, the nouveau-riche agribusiness millionaires try to patronise the yuppies and the county set cause resentment by acting as if the countryside is a feudal kingdom. (Which, to some extent, it still is.)

It was so disconcerting when I first turned and looked properly at those elements of country life that Charlie had encouraged me to steadfastly ignore. For instance, Wooster's hunting friends did not fit the 'rich upper-class bastard' stereotype at all. Like Roger and his glamorous blonde wife Sue, who ran a Dyno-Rod franchise and spent their working lives cleaning out drains. Every spare moment of their free time was spent hunting, and they honestly could not see anything wrong with it. Roger, who serviced the innards of a large local abattoir, believed that no matter how well run a slaughterhouse was, there was something a little inhumane about killing a thousand animals a day in one spot.

'Personally, if I had to be killed I'd far rather be hunted like a fox. And have someone say, "I'll count to a hundred and you can run." Wouldn't you?'

And his wife explained that foxes rarely died pleasantly in the wild. 'They are like characters in *EastEnders*. They always have something gruesome happen to them. They starve to death, get mange, or are run over.' When I asked timidly why a fox had to be involved in hunting at all, and couldn't she just go drag-hunting and chase paper, or an aniseed trail, instead, she was even more forthright. She explained that the route on a drag-hunt was dull because it had been worked out by a human being. 'The difference between fox-hunting and drag-hunting is like . . . well, like the difference between masturbation and making love. Both are pleasurable in their own way, but one is a foregone conclusion – and the other is exciting and unpredictable.' I said I didn't think town people would ever really sympathise with this point of view. Though her frankness might help them understand it.

'We don't want sympathy or understanding,' she answered firmly. 'We just want to be left alone to get on with things, without townie interference.'

My older children were startled to discover about Wooster.

'Really, Mum,' Kathy said. 'If Dad had been lost at sea people would be outraged at how fast you've found someone else.'

If Charlie had met with an accident I probably would have mourned for years. But this was different. I wasn't my normal self, and talking to other women who had been through the same thing was disturbing. One told me she had just climbed into bed, turned her face to the wall and given up. She neglected her children, lost her job and did nothing but lie there, month after month, pining for her ex and thinking about him non-stop. I didn't want to be like that. I wanted to do something, fast, to stop the pain and humiliation – or at least take the edge off it. Sleeping with another man was an obvious solution, a kind of revenge. The trouble was, I had been faithful to Charlie for so long that I doubted that I would ever be able to have sex with anyone else. I thought I would come up against an invisible barrier, like the force field that protects the crew of the *Starship Enterprise*.

Another deserted wife had said to me reassuringly on the phone, 'I hope you are going to pin up a poster in your bedroom that says "I am *not* crap in bed" – because husbands always tell you that, just as a little extra insult, as they're leaving.' And it's certainly a question that hangs over you when your husband has fled. When local men dropped in afterwards, I could often sense them struggling to work the conversation round, as tactfully as they could, to the subject of whether some grim frigidity on my part was the reason for the split. (I suppose it was a backhanded compliment: it showed they couldn't see any other obvious reason for him to leave.)

Secretly, I was sure it *was* the real reason. When I first met Charlie he had the gift – common to most rural men – of being able to find the 'tickle spot' on any farm animal. He knew exactly where to scratch a Shire horse to make its lips tremble and its jaws champ in ecstasy (the inner thigh) or how to make a full-sized pig buckle at the knees and roll on its back, exposing rolls of wobbly fat in joyful surrender. But while watching this and laughing, I would also think – sadly – 'why can't I enjoy it like that?' I assumed this was my fault, and felt sorry for him, having to spend his life with a woman who wasn't fully awakened. I'd grown used to thinking of myself as cold and unsatisfactory, and felt menaced by the world outside my marriage, full of louche, exotic women who were good at all the things I wasn't. It was the fear of being ticked off and criticised by this sort of person (in the guise of a doctor) that had stopped me ever suggesting to Charlie that we tried sex therapy. In retrospect, though, he probably wouldn't have agreed. He loathed being told how to behave by authority figures.

Wooster was much shorter than Charlie, and more energetic, with tanned skin. He had lovely white teeth, too, smelt delicious and slightly flowery when he had just bathed, and talked in an oddly seductive way, as if savouring every word. The hardest thing to adjust to, though, was the way he made me feel so different. Over the years I had become frumpy and overweight, my appearance not made any better by the jumble-sale clothes I always wore to save money. But in the first few weeks of Charlie leaving I lost nearly two stone – and then I was with Wooster, who saw me as a *trophy*. This amazed me. I couldn't get over the bizarre novelty of it. He actually gave me flowers, thought I was *beautiful*, said so often, and enjoyed walking into places with me on his arm. I started standing up straighter, taking more care with my appearance and buying first-hand clothes. This was possible because, for some puzzling reason, I suddenly had spare cash. The telephone bills were vastly less, and there were no vets or feed merchants to pay. And a dairy farmer up the road asked if he could use the farmland and pay me for the privilege. 'Farming and being with Charlie,' my sister Caky declared, 'was like keeping a racehorse.' She had a point.

Bit by bit I became obsessed by Wooster. He was so kind and thoughtful, and yet never touched me at all, except for a brief peck on the cheek at the end of each date. Early on, he took me out to lunch with one of his oldest friends, and this man took me aside afterwards and warned me to take care, Wooster had a fearsome reputation as a womaniser. But I couldn't believe it. He didn't act like one at all, and he had told me, over and over, that he had always been faithful to his wife.

Finally, I couldn't wait any longer. I kissed him passionately and we fell into bed. It was astonishing. I wanted to do and try everything, I felt as if I was swimming in a new, and yet utterly sympathetic element. It was so much fun, too. When you have been married for years, and the erotic side has gone flat, every gesture, every touch has a sad history attached to it, a memory of yourself (or your partner) murmuring: 'No!' Or flinching, or turning away.

In a new relationship all that is swept away and forgotten. Wooster didn't know I was supposed to be frigid. He was delighted with me. And as for me, I didn't know that such feelings could exist, or that I was capable of having them. I felt such powerful desire. It was like being a teenager again, only better. Before I was married my boyfriends had had such young, perfect, smooth bodies; I found Wooster's far more erotic because, with its scars and flaws, it was more personal and individual. I'd gaze at him while he slept and marvel at how lucky I was. When he described some near-accident on his tractor my eyes would fill with tears at the very thought of him being hurt. I even kept a shirt of his and slept with it when he couldn't be with me. And there was a painful sweetness to all this because he wasn't sure we had a future. He kept insisting that he was still in love with his wife and might never feel anything like that for me. This uncertainty of his made my feelings even sharper and fiercer.

At first he and I only made love very late at night, when Nat was already deeply asleep in my bed, because Wooster was still lambing and he couldn't spare much time from his farm. It meant, at least, that Nat had no painful psychological adjustments to make. At about 2 a.m. I'd hear a rumble as a familiar Land Rover turned into the drive. I'd rush downstairs to find Wooster on the doorstep in his wellingtons and lambing overalls. These were so stiff with grease and mud that when he took them off in the porch they keeled over and fell into a kneeling position, like a headless person brought low by a ludicrously powerful bolt of desire. He'd always have a couple of bottles of lamb milk, complete with teats, in his pockets, and when he was about to leave I'd have to warm them in a saucepan so the very first thing he could do on arriving home was feed his orphan lambs.

Sometimes Nat and I would visit Wooster's lambing sheds in the day, to assuage our homesickness for farm animals, because all we had left now was empty sheds and barns full of dung and stale hay, and fields where the incessant rain was gradually smoothing out hoof-prints. And we would often go to horse shows with him. Doing this was almost as unsettling as the sex because I discovered *that I could actually enjoy heavy horse events.* The early morning would be spent companionably polishing harness to the radio, and then we'd drive off together, Wooster holding my hand from time to time and Nat cuddling a plastic bucket with Foxy inside. I'd help Wooster brush and harness up his horses, and then, while he was working them, he would look up frequently and catch my eye and smile at me, finding me no matter where I was in the crowd. And at lunchtimes he would eat on the grass beside us before amusing Nat by taking his terriers off to explore suspicious-looking holes in the hedge, and whistling them back up again.

One of the oddities of my position was that I could not possibly have had a love affair with anyone Nat disliked. I was with him night and day, seven days a week (except for school hours). But he took to Wooster at once, enjoying chatting to him at length. Besides, Wooster's farm was full of delights. There was a small, old, fat pony to learn to ride on, baskets of new puppies, and if you sat quietly on the patio outside his house, you could watch farm rats the size of guinea pigs shinning up a bird-feeder and nibbling peanuts.

On the rare occasions when Wooster stayed the whole night the jackdaws would wake him in the morning. And he'd talk sleepily about his childhood, and how, even now, his first action on waking, before he even opened his eyes, was to relish the relief he felt at not being in his narrow bed at boarding school. (Like Charlie, he had been sent away aged seven, and never got over it.) There used to be a huge rookery next to his parents' house, centuries old, with about a thousand birds in it, and when he was eight he overheard a countryman say that you could never get rid of an established rookery – the birds always came back whatever you did. So Wooster – with the boundless energy and optimism of a small boy – determined to prove him wrong. He and his best friend got hold of a couple of airguns one summer holiday and kept going to the rookery and firing off shots at the birds. They used subtle tactics like walking

underneath the rookery with a group of friends, and then getting the others to leave, so the birds (which cannot count much
beyond three) thought everyone had left and fatally relaxed.
They only killed about twenty rooks in all, over a period of
three months, but the birds obviously had a discussion about it
and decided that they just could not stand to raise their chicks
anywhere near Wooster and his beastly little friend. They all left
in a wheeling flock one day and never, ever returned.

Some mornings I would go straight off to see a rural character
after spending the night with Wooster, and I always knew, then,
that the interview would work, because I was so relaxed and
happy. There had been a very black time, just before Charlie left,
when something in my face and manner completely repelled
strangers. They'd recoil in horror when they saw me, say they
were too busy to talk and divulge nothing of interest whatever.
(I could never work out what it was. And I'd always look in a
mirror after the interview, just out of curiosity.)

'I wish I didn't have to see to my animals, and could come
with you,' Wooster said wistfully one spring morning, when I
was off to see a bat-warden. 'I could do with a day playing with
bats.'

I felt I'd never had enough quality time with bats, either.
They flitted above the farm, but the only time I ever saw one
close enough was when the cat caught them. Once I managed
to snatch a baby pipistrelle off him before he ate it and it immediately gripped tightly to the front of my jersey, like a small,
brown, furiously angry brooch. It jabbered inaudibly there,

occasionally swivelling its face and baring its teeth at me, for a whole day, until it summoned up the nerve to leap off and flutter into the evening sky.

When I rang the bell of Rowena Varley's cottage in Cornwall I had a moment of panic, because she looked so conventional: smart and tweedy, like the headmistress of a private school. Surely someone like that wouldn't be entertainingly eccentric? I needn't have worried. After making me tea in a bone china cup she led me into her front room, which was crammed with little wooden boxes of bats (along with a laundry basket smelling horribly of cheesy feet, where some noctules – our largest native species – lived).

She explained that her job was mostly about mediating between humans and bats. 'A lady doing B&B got in touch recently because she had a cloth lampshade with tassels on it in one of her bedrooms and it was the ideal place for a lesser horseshoe to hang upside down in the day. When thirty of them started doing it at once, her guests complained.'

While I wondered how anyone could be so mean-spirited, she went on to describe some of the other dismal things that happen to bats. She's always searching for them in the inner recesses of wood-burning stoves, or unpeeling them from the extra-large flypapers used in milking parlours. She's even discovered the best way of doing this: you grease the little mammal thoroughly with cheap margarine until it flops off, then wash it in baby shampoo and warm water.

With similar care, she's worked out that the best bat food consists of mealworms bought by post from a firm in Sheffield, and fed for a few weeks with a wholesome diet of brown bread and vegetables. Her youngest bats get them squeezed out and offered on the tip of a No. 1 paintbrush; the older ones eat them whole. Only, quite often they fumble and lose them, and then the mealworms wander off into the house. 'I find them in my cupboards and wardrobes,' Rowena said helplessly. 'And of course if I *don't* find them they turn into beetles, which are even more troublesome.'

She picked up some of her pet bats to show them to me, and when they jabbered soundlessly in her neatly manicured fingers she turned on the bat monitor beside her, tuned it, and suddenly the room was alive with grumpy squeaking and twittering.

'What wonderful animals to have as pets,' I sighed.

'I don't approve of anyone keeping a bat as a pet,' she said severely. 'I always return them to the wild if I can.' She explained that she was helped in this by the fact that bat mothers – unlike most other mammals – will accept their young even if they have been handled and fed by humans and smell all wrong. 'A vicar near St Mawes found a natterer's baby early one morning on the bookshelves at the back of his church. It was badly dehydrated and only two days old. I collected it and fed it goat's milk and water at three-hour intervals, bringing it back to the church in the evening, just as dusk was falling. We waited and waited, and finally we found the natterer's colony up near the altar, where there were some cracks in the plaster. I held out my hand with the baby in it, and a mother flew out of the shadows. So I put the baby on a hassock, and the mother came down, landed on it with her wings outstretched, and they both disappeared off together, the baby clinging tightly to her fur. It was wonderful: worth all the hard work.'

It was obvious that Wooster was never going to let his fox return as easily to the wild. He had a book in his parlour which advised never, ever playing with, or cuddling a cub, and maintained that you should rear it with another baby fox if at all possible, so the two of them would always retain their fear of humans. Then they could be safely released into a wood as soon as they could manage hard food. Although Wooster had read this section over and over he couldn't bring himself to do what it advised. The cub was too adorable.

After a few weeks its snout was bigger and faintly russet, and it became very playful. It fought its hot-water bottle, and nibbled Wooster's fingers with its sharp little teeth. It ate so much that its stomach was all swollen with milk and dog food, and when it was lying on its back, being massaged with a towel, it looked exactly like a tubby little grey werewolf – with a look of untameable wildness to its toothy grin. Wooster would put it down on the floor and say, 'You watch! He'll come back to this spot in a minute.' And it would set off, crawling with a wobbly, kitten-like gait, its body too stout for its legs, its fat pointy tail sticking up ridiculously, and gradually circle back to our hands. Wooster explained that you couldn't ever leave a pet fox cub alone with a laden tea-table.

'While you are in the room with them they will lie quietly, curled up on a chair, but the moment you go out of the door,

whoosh, they are up there eating everything, the cake, the milk
– even the sugar.'

The other problem about them was their attitude to excre-
ment. Foxes enjoy soiling what they eat. 'They do it in the wild,
too. If they find an old dead sheep out in the fields, they'll mess
and pee in the carcass. Then they'll come back the next night
and feed from it again. You wouldn't think any animal would
want to do that, but a fox does.'

These Rabelaisian personal habits made carrying Foxy
around in your pocket (as Wooster liked to do) a mixed pleasure. If the little creature poked his head out and saw something
he didn't like – an extra-large dog, for instance, or an unfamiliar
human – he messed himself. If he was travelling in the car with
Wooster, and started tussling with the earless terrier to while
away the time (they were best friends), and the play got a tad
too rough and he got nipped – he'd mess himself. Wooster was
always having to park up near rivers and wearily mop diarrhoea
off the inside of his Land Rover.

Chapter Nineteen

'In the case of some women, orgasms take quite a lot of time. Before signing on with such a partner, make sure you are willing to lay aside, say, the month of June, with sandwiches having to be brought in.'
Bruce Jay Friedman, quoted in *Sex: the Most Fun You Can Have Without Laughing* by William Cole and Louis Phillips

Foxy was old enough to be left behind with a bowl of dog food the evening Wooster, Nat and I went off to a gypsy party together. We had to leave when it was still light and my poultry were indignantly refusing to go to bed. Wooster told me to change my trousers and drape the ones I had been wearing over the hen-house door.

'Foxes and badgers don't like the smell of fresh human,' he explained. He added that it also deterred predators if you simply peed beside the hen-house. (But the effect only lasted for about eight hours, so I wasn't to get over-confident.)

We were late getting to the party. The rough driveway was already jammed with cars and trucks and beside it was a scattering of muddy-looking tents. We weren't going to stay in a tent, but in the open back of the Land Rover, which Wooster felt he had made marginally more rainproof by piling old wooden signs on to the roof and weighing them down with a selection of rusty pots and kettles. I liked the ridiculous logic of this. He was always putting rubbish to odd uses: his farm was crammed with saved-up bits of machinery and wood, all of which he had firm, carefully mapped plans for. Now he blew up a dusty rubber mattress and laid it out carefully in the back, clearing bits of harness and old ploughshares out of the way. He spread out the quilts and knelt back to admire the effect. 'Right,' he said, pronouncing the 'r' as if there was a 'w' in there somewhere. Then he assembled his costume.

Wearing the correct outfit for every possible occasion was important to Wooster. It wasn't just a matter of wearing a suit occasionally – though he did have a couple, for whenever he walked the few hundred yards to his parents' house to attend one of their smart cocktail parties. It was more about having exactly the right rural accessories to blend in, as if his whole life was one vast, ongoing fancy-dress party. (For instance, when he worked with any sort of combustion engine, he put on a soft Trilby with a cog-wheel nestling in the brim, and point-to-points merited a tweed jacket, flat cap and special clean green wellies.) Now he clapped a wide leather hat on his head (which made his nose look as if it had been sharpened), pulled on an oily leather waistcoat, and carefully knotted a black string tie round his neck. Then he nodded to himself gravely, and took my hand. Indoors, in a bungalow, a group of people were playing violins, banjos, flutes and guitars. Some were small, wiry and sandy; some were hippies; and a few had the black hair and fierce faces of old-fashioned Romanies. And they were all wearing variants on Wooster's dress, too. Perhaps the countryside was an ongoing fancy-dress party and I had just never noticed it before.

The music was irresistible: fast and melancholy, and it was rather like watching a jazz session; the musicians would nod at each other, and then one or other would launch into a haunting solo, violin bow moving so fast it blurred. I wanted to go on listening for ever, but every hour or so it would stop, so we could eat mutton stew, drink rough cider and talk about subjects like hunting with lurchers.

Nat bedded down happily in the quilts at midnight, and at 3 a.m. I thought it wisest to join him as, no matter what time he went to bed, he was always up by seven. I left Wooster sitting in a circle of men round a bonfire, singing rude folk songs. Each tune sounded exactly the same: a wavery, drunken monotone, and there was a particular refrain about a gypsy girl that kept recurring:

Before the age of thirty-one
A thousand men had come and gone.

Wooster's tenor voice droning those words wove itself insistently in and out of my dreams. And at half past six he woke me to ask if I knew where the sausages were. He was thinking of making breakfast for all his new friends. I sat up, enraged.

'You are *not* frying sausages,' I declared. 'You are either driving me and Nat straight home – or coming to bed this instant.'

He looked startled, because I never usually protested, however strange his behaviour was. I felt terrible: more tired than I had ever been in my life before, and I had a headache from the cider. It was raining, and water was slowly seeping into the quilts, and I felt sticky and dirty – a major inconvenience for someone as keen on washing as I am. Just to cap everything off nicely Nat woke up and started jumping on top of me.

After a while Nat bounced out of the open end of the Land Rover and found a couple of small children out there. I could hear him talking excitedly in the distance. And Wooster started cuddling me. He grew more passionate. I responded – and suddenly it happened: he found my tickle spot. I felt like a prize bull I'd once seen being scratched, which had started by being haughty and aloof, then pushed its stout buttocks a little closer to the farmer's finger, then arched its neck and widened its nostrils. After a few more minutes it had snorted convulsively. A sort of internal volcanic eruption seemed to be happening: its eyes half closed as successive ripples of ecstasy began sweeping across its vast, charcoal-furred body. You almost felt sorry for it as, trembling, and weakly fighting the unfamiliar – but too powerful – feeling, it had very gradually and slowly buckled and sagged at the knees. Finally, it ended on its side in the mud, stunned, uncomprehending and humbled. But dazed with happiness. Why had it taken nearly half a century for the same to happen to me? It was a bit late, really, because Wooster was already losing interest.

This was partly because I had written about him in my column a couple of weeks back. I'd remarked, in passing, that I was going out with a farmer. And that, after living for years on scruffy, badly maintained holdings, I found myself strangely awed 'by the sight of a fence that actually keeps in livestock, *or a well-hung gate*'. I had sniggered to myself wickedly when I wrote about the gate, but I thought it would somehow slip by. It's easy to forget that — at least in rural areas — whenever you write anything dodgy it is always read by the person who will be most annoyed by it. Close relations, neighbours, the vicar, the family doctor . . . and, in this case, Wooster's mother. She was a slender woman with an upright carriage and fearsomely neat white hair, who bore a strong resemblance to Charlie's mother (and had an equally powerful influence over her son), and she was outraged. Wooster started out being pleased, and then got a little weary when everyone he'd ever met came up and sniggered at him in pubs all over the West Country. At one point I wondered, guiltily, if the phrase would end up being engraved on his tombstone.

But it wasn't just my indiscretion that ditched me. I had forgotten that when you aren't married to someone you are supposed to play it cool and be mysterious. I was far too keen. I gazed at him entranced, I cooked huge roast dinners for him, I agreed to his every suggestion, I was as kind and helpful as I could possibly be. And I would come home from seeing him, lay my head on the kitchen table and howl with pain at his increasing coldness. The affair — which had started out by being the best possible distraction from the horror of being left by Charlie — now just added to it. When I wept I was crying over the two of them.

I understood that Wooster didn't want to get married again at once; he wanted to try lots of different women and play the field. But I longed to feel safe and loved, and be back in a happy partnership. And I was crazy about him. I couldn't imagine a life in which I didn't see him all the time. I had to, though.

Suddenly, I had far too much time at weekends and no farm or pet fox to help out with any more. So I started going to 'apple days' with Nat. These are seasonal festivals, invented by the charity Common Ground to save orchards and publicise local varieties of apple. And one, at Landscove, near Totnes, sounded especially appealing to us, because if you took a scarecrow with you, you got in free. (Though, to get there, you had to travel on a steam train and then a coach.)

We wandered round the farm sheds looking for clothes to make a scarecrow out of, and found some overalls and boots that Charlie had left behind. When we had made a head out of an old pillow-case, and everything was properly stitched up and stuffed, both Nat and I sat back, shocked. Although they were Charlie's clothes, we had managed to make a scarecrow that looked exactly like Wooster. Along with his powerful, slightly eccentric appearance, it had a penetrating smell of mould and a tiresome habit of shedding straw.

We'd assumed that the station platform at Buckfastleigh would be full of happy families, each with their own scarecrow companion, but no. We were the only ones. *The only people in the entire West Country taking a scarecrow to the apple day.* We were stared at in amazement. Small children pointed, and grown-ups made jocular remarks on the lines of 'I don't think much of your boyfriend, love.'

The train was full so Nat and I had to sit, with considerable reluctance, on the scarecrow's knee. And I found I could only keep my balance by putting my arm around its neck, which made me feel even sillier. We were pariahs: even the ticket collector was too embarrassed to look us in the eye. He mumbled and addressed our feet instead, avoiding the scarecrow's huge muddy ones, which were oozing straw.

The seats in the coach were unusually narrow, so here the scarecrow sat heavily on top of us, and by the time we reached Landscove Nat and I were longing to be rid of its pungent, tickly company. The village green was bedecked with arty-looking scarecrows, so we dumped ours roughly in a corner, and when we went back to check on it later we discovered a wag had moved it to a bench, and positioned it so it was rapturously embracing a more traditional scarecrow, with a red spotted necktie.

Looking round at this event, I realised there was a human being in the same outfit, a man with leather gaiters, corduroys and sideburns, who was lecturing the crowd in thick rural tones. He looked very like all Charlie's (and Wooster's) older horsey friends, and spoke the way they did. But there was some indefinable element that was wrong about him, too. When he stopped for a coffee, I went up and talked to him and he dropped the burr and revealed that he was a retired history teacher called Clive Fairweather, and he liked impersonating a Norfolk farmer from the 1870s at weekends.

Just around the edge of a marquee was a trio of medieval musicians eating crisps, and it got me thinking about the appeal of country events. Mostly, nowadays, these are nearly always organised by retired incomers, and they conjure up an enticing, but unreal version of country life. Three main periods of English history are always represented. The first is 'Merrie England', a version of the Middle Ages in which folk played silly musical instruments while sporting tights and waving pig bladders. Then there is a period that might loosely be termed 'Mr Darcy and the Age of Gracious Living'. It is the countryside you see in period dramas on TV, full of sprigged muslin dresses, sprung horse-drawn carriages and sulky men in over-loose fawn trews. And then there is the recent agricultural past, a time when engaging – but dim-witted – characters roamed the hedgerows, playing folk music, stooking corn and quaffing cider.

At every event I went to with Nat that autumn, these three eras were assumed to have run concurrently, so that, for instance, at Cockington's apple day we approached Cockington Court by trotting through rolling parkland in a horse-drawn Victoria. And as we did so, we passed a wandering Elizabethan minstrel, mournfully tooting on a three-holed flute, and a gang of morris dancers – much the worse for cider.

The scarecrow sat slumped beside our back door for months, where he was strangely comforting. It was not just me that missed Wooster desperately; Nat did too. What he mourned most were the feel of a little hairy dog as it wriggled in his arms, the musty darkness of a bush by a yard gate and the shine on the top of a balding head. He was so sad that I realised I had to be very careful what I did next.

'You shouldn't go out with anyone else,' my daughter Kathy said. 'It hurts Nat too much. All my friends with divorced parents say that it was dreadful getting fond of their mothers' boyfriends, and then losing them.' She was right, but I couldn't imagine going without male company for the next ten years. Besides, Charlie was so far away – over 800 miles – that Nat only saw him infrequently, for a couple of hours at a time. I felt he needed a constant father-figure in his life just as much as I needed a lover.

Wooster dropped in to describe his new girlfriend (very tall, blonde, eighteen years old) and tell me the latest about Foxy. The full-grown cub had been tethered out on the lawn the last time I'd seen him, leaping into the air to snap at pet doves and tunnelling down to catch moles. He'd even started stalking the resident chickens, lying with his eyes half shut on a coiled up length of chain, and trying to lull them into venturing too close. But the previous week he had gnawed through his collar and escaped into the woods, stopping briefly in his flight to eat the pair of ducks I had given Wooster as a parting gift.

'What you need now,' Wooster said, cheerfully ploughing his way through a ginger and sultana cake, 'is someone young and strapping.' I winced, because Wooster himself was four years younger than I was.

I was back to surviving on my own. The first time I unblocked the loo or wobbled up the tall ladder and worked out how to replace the rusted-up bulb in the yard light I felt a tremendous (if quite disproportionate) sense of achievement. But on farms there are worse challenges to face. While Charlie had still been around, one of my bantams had been in the habit of wandering chattily into the stables, laying in the hayracks and pecking bits of fallen grain from among the horses' feet. One morning she got stepped on and I heard her screaming in terror and pain. I didn't know what to do, because Charlie wasn't there, and he always despatched everything on the farm. I was afraid of wringing its neck wrongly and inflicting more pain. While I panicked and wept with the little crushed hen in my hands, the policeman, who had called in hoping for coffee, pushed me aside and quickly delivered the *coup de grâce*. But now I was on my own with a full poultry yard I knew I had to face the inevitable, and learn how to kill.

So I enrolled on a survival course in the woods near my village. You were supposed to stay all night, but I couldn't do that because children under twelve were excluded, and I couldn't leave Nat. So I arrived at dawn as the others – a group of male teachers – climbed out of the underbrush looking miserably damp and unshaven and started roasting earthworms on a shovel in front of the fire. They were doing this because the ex-Royal Marine who ran the course, Jonny Crockett, had told them it was a fine, high-protein breakfast. It turned out everyone else had small children, too, including Jonny, who confided that he slept far better on a pile of bracken in the woods than he ever did in a house containing his two-year-old.

After breakfast we were shown how to make snares out of

picture wire and bits of stick and hide them in the hedge; and Jonny told us, very seriously, which wild creatures (apart, of course, from the obvious rabbits) to catch. Badger tasted good – like ham, he claimed – but was so vile-tempered it was best left strictly alone. 'It is like being attacked by a 42-lb shaving-brush with non-retractable claws.' And if we were desperate, we could eat rats, provided we cut off their breasts, and boiled just these, 'very heavily', before consumption. There was an unreal element to this enthrallingly grim information, because we all knew perfectly well that if we got desperate by that afternoon we would not really have to climb a pine tree and throttle a dozing pheasant. All we'd have to do was saunter down to the shop fifteen minutes away and buy a Mars bar.

Then came the moment I had been waiting for: Jonny produced two large white hens and asked for a volunteer, and I put my hand up. 'Hold the chicken by its legs,' he said, inverting one of the poor creatures so it squawked. 'And then, with its head pointing away from you, pull steadily and swiftly downwards – like this.' The bird flapped and was still. I took my bird from him, and it dangled mournfully from my hand, its round white head facing away from me. I felt sorry for it but, even so, I took a deep breath, grasped the head – and tugged. There was a squelchy, cartilagey feel as its neck dislocated. But it was simple and quick. And afterwards we ate the birds round the fire.

The instant I got back I ran up the road to tell my friend Lynn what I'd done, and offer to kill any of her chickens when necessary. 'Oh, I already know how to do it,' she said, answering the door with a recipe book in her hand. 'I got a smallholder a few doors up to show me. But I must warn you, it has had a most peculiar effect on my marriage. My husband looks at me quite differently now – and I swear he is better behaved.'

If I could solve the chicken problem so easily, couldn't I do the same for my love-life? I was beginning to believe that there was always an answer to any difficulty. You just had to think hard, and be prepared to spend money and change your behaviour. For instance, there were problems getting the children back to university, because Charlie always used to drive them. So I bought a car for Sam (who could drive) and told him he was now in charge of ferrying all the studenty stuff backwards and forwards. It was simple, really.

Earlier, while I'd still been married, I had researched an article for *Country Living* magazine for the start of a campaign they were running, called 'The Farmer Wants a Wife'. The article was about rural dating agencies, and I talked to the matchmakers running them and learned – among other curiosities – that no one ever wants to meet unusually short men with heavy facial hair, or women over the magic age of forty-five. The matchmaker I warmed to most was Polly Langford, who ran the curiously named 'Just Woodland Friends'. Besides being the cheapest agency, it allowed customers to select their own partners from a list (closely resembling an estate agent's particulars) which arrived every month. This suddenly seemed an attractive idea to me, because I was three years over the forty-five-year age limit. And, after all, what did I have to lose? At the very worst I would have a few amusingly embarrassing incidents to describe for my column.

And besides, I had grown to like rural men so much. They were so practical. They always carried spanners and penknives around with them and could fix anything that went wrong in an instant. They weren't squeamish, either – years of coping with horrific pig, sheep and cow obstetrics meant that few things a woman did could appal them. I loved the way they combined enormous muscular strength (and beautiful bodies) with great gentleness. I liked the way they prided themselves on being decent and honourable – and weren't obsessed with material things. And because farms have rapidly changed, in only fifty years or so, from highly social places to isolated ones – if a farmer is alone, it is probably not his fault.

Maybe, though, I had been going for the wrong sort of farmer. Charlie and Wooster were rather similar. They had both lived on big country estates owned by their parents, been obsessed by antiquated farming methods and scarred by public school. There were bound to be less complicated, more affectionate men somewhere out there.

So I sat down and wrote a little paragraph about myself. Unfortunately, it kept coming out so that I sounded either mad or clinically depressed. And in the end the only good bit was the section where I was extremely vague about how old I was. Then I told my sisters about the plan (they instantly christened the agency 'Feathered Friends'), and waited. No one rang me. (And, in fact, no one ever did. I obviously got the formula *so* wrong.) Finally I started ringing farmers up myself, and had a few flirtatious conversations with men I was never tempted to meet.

I went Christmas shopping one evening with Nat. Exeter was full of twinkling coloured lights, and a delicious perfume of sugar and fried banana drifted from the pancake stall. After we'd had a couple of turns on the fairground rides in the Guildhall I noticed a caravan tucked away in a corner which promised gypsy fortune-telling. I hesitated and looked down at my hands. I hadn't worn my wedding ring for a year and the finger it had been on had plumped up: the little dent that used to be there was gone. I didn't think a fortune-teller could tell I'd once been married.

I stepped into the caravan with Nat, and we both sat down at the picnic table inside. The gypsy was a slender, grey-haired man, who didn't look the slightest bit Romany. He was more like a post-office clerk. He took my money swiftly and said in a great rush: 'You are very psychic. This will get stronger as you get older, and you must always trust to your intuition. I can see someone standing behind you who has just passed over and is no longer in the flesh. I don't know who it is, but they are now helping and guiding you.'

I had to stifle a smile. I'd recently gone to a psychic fayre in the little market town of Axminster (largely, it must be said, to mock) and been struck by the way that almost every member of the audience had been told that a spirit guide was sitting helpfully behind them. Later, for a small fee, a different person had offered to paint portraits of these guides. Two things struck me about this:

1) It was a brilliant money-making wheeze. No one was ever going to look at their spirit-guide portrait and say,

'Nonsense! It doesn't look anything like that!'

2) Nearly all the guides were dead American Indians or, more rarely, Tibetan monks with oddly shaped heads. Why should these dignified folk choose to spend eternity shadowing the inhabitants of obscure West Country towns?

The gypsy had seized my hand and was scribbling on it with biro. 'I'm very sorry,' he said, 'but your marriage is not going to last. It's either just ended or it's about to.'

'It's ended,' I said, startled.

'Ah.' He looked more closely at my palm. 'Your husband was a split personality, a Jekyll and Hyde, and you haven't seen the last of him yet.' He sat back, my hand still in his. 'You'll find a new man soon, a little younger than you, a real . . .' – he searched for the right words – '. . . a real man's man, who will always treat you like a queen.' As I got up to go he added: 'And this Christmas is the last you will spend in your house. You will never eat Christmas dinner there again.'

Chapter Twenty

Holsworthy Local Weather Forecast: Temperatures will be on the chilly side at first in a light northerly breeze, but thickening cloud will bring a warmer air stream and we should see temperatures rising to around five hundred degrees Celsius to the north of the town. The thickening cloud will bring localised downpours of hair, skin, and flesh particles . . . However, there will be some brighter spots here and there where dioxin, carbon monoxide, sulphur dioxide and phosgene will be released.
Black humour by Alan Beat, smallholder near Holsworthy

A shudder ran through my village at the end of February 2001. Foot and mouth disease had been discovered at Cheale Meats in Essex, traced back to Northumberland, and then popped up in north Devon, in sheep owned by a dealer named Willie Cleave. Farms were suddenly no longer on the postman's round, skittle matches and dances stopped dead, and there were terrified discussions in the post office.

As disasters always make me want to panic-buy food, I bicycled up the road to Lashbrook Farm in Talaton to get sausages from John Carter. A large, jolly man with a bright pink face, green corduroy breeches, checked shirt, and feet that seemed a fraction too small for his nimble body, he was sitting in his tiny shop in the farm drive reading a tome called *Managing Pig Health and the Treatment of Disease*. And he remarked cheerily: 'Did you know that the virus from one pustule on a pig's nose can blow thirty-six miles over flat countryside?' He had to interrupt our conversation to serve all the other anxious folk who were queuing up to stockpile bacon and joints of pork.

Beyond the shop were acres of outdoor pigs on stubble. Matronly saddleback sows were staring threateningly at the crows stealing their feed, while parties of little piglets skipped gaily about in the sunshine between snow flurries. And over it all hung an odd noise. Somewhere between clicking and sucking, it sounded like loose change being stirred in hundreds of wet trouser pockets. This was the sows chewing small stones as if they were gum.

John confided that there was no way he could realistically stop the virus getting to his pigs – and if it did he would lose not only thirty-five years of careful breeding, but everything he owned. Unfortunately, in 2000 he was under such terrible financial pressure that he decided to cancel the foot and mouth insurance he had been keeping up for thirty-three years. It cost £567 annually and seemed an expensive luxury.

'I thought I was the only fool to have made such a mistake,' he smiled. 'But it turns out most of my friends did the same.'

'How can you be so cheerful about it?' I asked.

He explained it was just the way he was made and, besides, 'After going through the last three years, when I thought I was going to go out of business at any moment, I have learned to be more philosophical.' He needed to be: when all the food in his shop was sold he would have no source of income whatsoever unless the government allowed him to take more pigs to the abattoir. He already relied on the goodwill of his bank manager in order to feed his five hundred sows and two thousand piglets. My mouth dropped open. I hadn't realised that even farmers miles from the infected sites faced ruin because their businesses were at a standstill and debts mounting. The trouble with foot and mouth this time, as opposed to previous outbreaks, was that it was about to hit an industry already in financial crisis. But then, when I talked to Jack Caley, who farms at Aldbrough, near Hull, he said the worst thing about the disease was always the emotional pressure it put on farmers. He was twelve when it hit his family farm just after the war. 'We had a dreadful wet harvest, and we had been shut away on the farm for months when father's Friesian herd got it. The ministry vet back then had the power of God, and he said the animals had to be slaughtered in the big barn, up against a pile of fertiliser. The blood from the slaughter would have ruined the fertiliser – which was still rationed, of course – and this tipped father over the edge. He was a real gentleman. He did not have a temper, but when the vet would not agree to them being killed anywhere else my father fetched his gun and said "the first animal you shoot in that barn, I'll shoot you". He meant it, too. Tears were streaming down his face. He was beside himself.' Jack's father never truly recovered from that incident. He could never afford a pedigree herd again and died young. But it was something Jack said as an aside that astonished me most: back then the infected meat was taken away to be sold in butcher's shops, and he remembered his mother being furious because she was only given a little pile of offal to feed her family with. Although, of course, the disease does not harm humans, no one nowadays would willingly eat liver or steak riddled with foot and mouth.

I was sitting at my kitchen table, surrounded by piles of notes and empty cups of tea, trying to make an article out of these and other bits of information, when the policeman turned up. He explained that he hadn't visited for a while because he had been doing extra overtime, guarding the gates of infected farms.

Always a fan of gruesome detail, he settled back more comfortably in his chair before telling me how he had watched MAFF officials climbing over piles of carcasses awaiting cremation, spraying them with disinfectant to keep down the smell and flies. Because the bodies were decomposing so fast, they kept exploding with a loud pop as they were stepped on. And early in the mornings, when he relieved others on the gates, he'd often find animal limbs scattered across farmyards because badgers, foxes and feral dogs had been worrying at the piles of corpses in the night.

'Once,' he said, biting into a bourbon biscuit, 'a magpie flew right over my head *with an eyeball in its beak*. And that's not to mention the rats. How do they reckon they're going to keep the disease under control when that sort of thing is happening?'

His most memorable story, though, was one that had been told to him by a MAFF man in a white paper suit on one of the grimmest mornings, when pieces of burned flesh and hair the size of a child's hand were floating across the fields in a pall of smoke. On the farm the MAFF man had just left, there had been a flock of sheep, and back at Christmas the farmer and his wife had given an orphan lamb to each of their little sons, to rear up on the bottle as pets. The boys grew to love these creatures, so they were distraught when foot and mouth disease was found in the flock. And after all the sheep were killed the slaughtermen did a tally and discovered two lambs were missing. There was a big search of the whole farm, while the boys stood by, white-faced, and in the end the lambs were found hidden in a wardrobe in their bedroom.

'The MAFF official told me that all his colleagues, and even all the slaughtermen, were in tears that day,' the policeman said. He hesitated and swallowed. 'It was because of what they'd seen those little boys go through.'

E-mail to Caky: 'Have just spent all day at the Fleet Air Arm Museum with a feathered friend and it was surprisingly enjoyable. He is younger than Wooster (only forty-three), and even his woolly sweater was attractive. (Farmers always wear unimaginably horrid ones: the reindeer sweater Mr Darcy wears in Bridget Jones *is nothing to the sights I've seen.) His thirteen-year-old son was with him, and was kind to Nat, and we roved round the museum, which is full of odd tableaux of small, thin mannequins with Beatle haircuts standing around in engine rooms while a voice-over relays dismally facetious air force conversations. Things wrong with the feathered friend: very shy, didn't seem as witty as Charlie, wearing spotless white trousers. Things right: he's been divorced four years, and like me had an affair immediately afterwards.'*

'Why are we here?' Nat asked.

'Because I thought you'd like to see some helicopters – and because I'm meeting a friend here.'

'What do they look like?'

'I'm not absolutely sure, but I know he's called Ian.'

The Fleet Air Arm Museum had just opened, and I was looking around anxiously, craning my neck as I paid for the tickets. Then, over by the barrier, I saw a tall, dark man, and my first instinct was to feel frightened. He was too good-looking and young for me. Then I was through the barrier, and we were shaking hands. Nat had an Action Man doll in his hand, that he carried with him everywhere, and Ian looked like a tormented version of the doll, with his dark hair, hazel eyes and wide, full mouth. But if I felt an immediate attraction, I was also aware of resisting it. I was sure there must be a catch somewhere.

I'd picked Ian out of that month's feathered friend particulars because he described himself as a keen morris dancer with a collection of canoes. It conjured up such an intriguing image that I just had to meet him. And though I instantly liked him, I was wary of being hurt again. I kept ticking off pros and cons. He was exactly my type, but then on our second date I'd seen the tied cottage where he lived (he managed a cereal farm on Salisbury Plain) – and been taken aback by it. It contained an anxious-to-please spaniel, which, though thoroughly likeable, had a powerful odour. ('One of those houses,' as Charlie used to say rudely, 'that smells like a dog's bottom.') The kitchen was stuffed with farm paperwork Ian hadn't yet got round to doing, and dirty dishes he would wash when he next had a spare minute, and in the hall, in a grey-brown miasma of dog-dust, was one of his canoes (ginger plastic). If you managed to squeeze past it to get upstairs you found three bedrooms and a bathroom like a stage-set for a particularly sinister Victorian murder. It was all beautifully warm, though, because Ian had installed his own central heating: pipes wandered vaguely up the walls and shot off at odd angles round corners.

One Sunday a few weeks after our first meeting I went there for lunch and afterwards left the children playing on a computer while we went for a brief walk across the water-meadows. It was a crisp, cold day, and as we wandered over little wooden bridges and squished through grass where the water lay in pale blue puddles I saw a movement in the distance. It was reddish, and flickered through a stand of trees.

'It's a roe deer,' Ian said, and then he paused. 'A doe. I think she's injured.'

We got closer. The field bordered the busy A36, and the animal must have been hit by a car. She struggled across the open grass two hundred yards ahead of us, her front left leg dragging painfully, the shoulder a wet patch of blood, and then she slipped into the strongly flowing brown river, and drifted downstream towards a little island.

'Can you wait and watch her for me?' Ian whispered. 'I want to get my rifle.'

'Are you sure that's the best thing to do?'

'There's no way she can recover from that injury, and it's cruel to leave her to suffer.' He ran back long-leggedly across the field, and I waited, pressing my gloved hands together to keep the circulation going. I could see the deer's frosty breath floating up as she lay in the eddy beside the island. After a long while she carefully dragged herself out on to the dry. I was behind a tree, and I didn't move, but she obviously knew I was there. She stared directly at me with her dark eyes. Cars whooshed by in the far distance, and swans fluttered on a further meadow while the water went on rippling smoothly beside the deer. Then, perhaps half a mile away, children in a garden shrieked – I could see their bright knitted clothes as they ran about – and the deer startled at the noise and dragged herself into the shadow of a little thicket. She was moving slower than before and seemed unable to pull herself upright now.

It was lonelier when I couldn't see her. I crouched down, with my back against the tree, and waited, feeling colder and colder, and wondering what I was doing there. The situation felt so alien: I remembered Charlie's dislike of guns, and the awful stories he'd told me of things screaming and flailing in agony, and running off, riddled with shot, to die slowly of lead poisoning. It was one of the many times when, instead of being furiously angry at him for leaving me, or painfully confused by his reasons for doing it, I simply missed him. I wished I could talk to him about my problems and hear his point of view. It seemed so wrong that all these strange adventures were happening to me and he knew nothing at all about them.

Ian reappeared on a tractor. He stopped a hundred yards away and hurried towards me. I pointed to where the deer was and he approached her warily. She hadn't moved far: she was crouching like a shadow in the underbrush, and she half rose in terror as he took aim. Then there was a muffled bang, and she fell dead at once. Ian put his gun down. He walked over to her and knelt down, laying his hand flat against her breast. Then he bowed his head, as if in prayer, and stayed there for well over a minute.

Later, when she was strung up on a beam in his garage by her back legs and he was eviscerating and skinning her into a deep bucket, I said: 'Did you pray over her just now?'

'No. I don't believe in God. It was more of a pagan gesture: a thank you to her for giving up her life so we can eat. American Indians and Aborigines always do it – it would feel disrespectful not to.' He looked at me intently, waiting for my response. He was always listening, extremely closely, to whatever I said; it was most disconcerting. I'd hardly spoken at all when I was with Wooster. I just smiled while he talked and he praised me for my 'mysteriousness'. But Ian seemed to want to know what I was really like. Also, even though he was untidy he was intensely practical. His two teenaged sons lived with him, and he was always washing clothes and cooking huge meals of stew and mashed potato. These were served up on a table where a tabby cat sat cosily on a soiled cushion, opening her eyes wide whenever a serving dish was popped down near to her nose.

Perhaps because foot and mouth was so terrifying, all sorts of ridiculous stories circulated in the farming community. The random outbreaks that would suddenly occur well outside the infected zone were put down, by many, to extra-marital affairs: farmers and MAFF workers nipping off to see lovers and forgetting to disinfect properly. It seemed much more plausible – and less alarming – than wind-blown infection. And a neighbour who worked as a public rights-of-way officer told me a number of true anecdotes about the silly behaviour of ramblers and tourists in the West Country. A typical one was of a walker who was stopped by a ranger and asked not to use a particular path because it had been closed to limit infection. 'But foot and mouth doesn't affect me,' she said indignantly. 'I'm a vegetarian.'

Another rang the office of her local authority and demanded that a rights-of-way officer explain to her dog why it could not take its usual walk. A few seconds later the officer was astonished to hear a dog panting on the other end of the telephone.

'The thing about relationships,' my son Sam said, 'is that there's always a crucial moment early on, where one person gets power over the other. The winner has a great time and the loser just gets to wait around for phone calls that never come. This is known as "the trouser fight", as in who gets to wear the trousers. You have to win the trouser fight.'

I'd had some useful romantic advice from my children since Charlie left. Kathy had been appalled by my relationship with Wooster. 'Honestly, Mum. Haven't you ever heard of playing it cool?' And when I thought about it, there definitely was an evening when I lost the trouser fight with Wooster. I'd arrived, bathed and perfumed, full of longing, to stay the night with him – and found him slumped gloomily in front of the television, in dirty clothes, his farm work unfinished. So I borrowed boots and oilskins and followed him round for an hour, holding the torch and helping him bed down horses and cows, and check on sick sheep. (Although I was a bit surprised he hadn't done all this earlier, as he'd promised. It was a very rare, eagerly antici-pated treat for us to be alone together; Kathy was babysitting.) And then when we finally got back to the house, and I tried to kiss him, he pushed me away, saying there was a phone call he had to make. It was very clear, from the first words of this, that it wasn't urgent. After listening to five minutes of joky small talk, I snatched up my bag and coat and ran outside, meaning to storm home in a rage. But I just couldn't do it. I gripped on to the little gate at the end of the pathway, listening to a dog scratching itself thoroughly on the porch, and a vixen shrieking far away in the woods, and realised that I couldn't bear to risk never making love to Wooster again. So I went back inside and meekly waited for the phone call to end, and our relationship went downhill from that moment.

With Ian it was a remark. He told me he thought I could be sixteen from the neck down.

'What about my head?' I asked.

'Well, I suppose it's averagely attractive,' he replied.

I wasn't having it. I took violent offence. He explained that he had only said exactly what he felt. I tended to frown, which rather spoiled my appearance. Besides, he considered it vital to be honest about his feelings – even if they were unwelcome.

'Wouldn't you have preferred it if Charlie'd always told you exactly what he was thinking – instead of keeping it secret?' He had a point, but so did I. What good was a boyfriend who insulted you? I told him if he didn't retract that remark wholly and utterly, and come up with something more complimentary I wasn't ever going out with him again. I meant it, too. I knew, now, how quickly a relationship could go sour, and how painful it was being with someone who treated you unkindly. It was better to be single. But it was thoroughly peculiar, finding myself so adamant where I had always, previously, been so soft. It worked, though. He apologised. And a few days later he told me he was starting to fall in love with me.

'This is where I first saw a cow limping,' Pete Walters said, taking me out to his deserted, spotlessly clean cattle yard, where a robin was poised on a gate, warming its wings in the sunshine. I'd met Pete at a church service for farmers, and when he said his entire farm had been culled, I asked if I could talk to him about it. He was a burly man, tanned very brown, with a shaven head and large moist eyes, and though he described himself as hard he came across as gentle and emotional. But this was probably because, as he explained, he had been altered for ever by what had happened to his animals. It was the morning of 18 March when he noticed one of his cows had a blister on its hoof. Like many others, Pete had heard that foot and mouth was quite a mild disease – akin to flu – so he was shaken by what happened that evening, when he was feeding his cows their last meal before the planned slaughter the next day. One began bellowing, and gave birth, and when the calf came out on to the floor it behaved like no newborn Walters had ever seen before. It writhed and twisted, giving formless cries. It was obviously in terrible pain: he rang up the vet in a panic, and then despatched it swiftly with his shotgun. He hadn't realised that the disease could be that virulent.

He said he didn't remember much about the next day, when everything else was killed, except that he had a favourite ram called Basil, who always used to run to him, big ears flapping, whenever he called its name. And he asked the two vets who were directing the slaughter if he could have a moment alone with Basil before the end. He sat down in the barn with the ram, and stroked its ears and talked to it very softly and reassuringly, and then he got up and left − and the rest was just a blur. Two weeks went by which he just couldn't remember at all, although he was told afterwards that he was on the telephone for most of it − to all sorts of unlikely folk: feed reps, even people at the bank. He awoke from this dreamlike state to find that he was a passionate activist, and began to devote himself to saving his neighbours' animals from contiguous cull.

We had wandered back to his kitchen and were sitting in a sea of friendly sheepdogs, their tails waving excitedly, while he explained this, and his wife, who was cutting sandwiches beside the sink, cut in. She explained that at that time, if you went out on to the nearest high spot in the quiet of the afternoon, you'd hear a sinister, highly distinctive noise in the distance. 'Click click. Click click. It was the sound of a captive bolt killing all our neighbours' stock. I hope I never hear that again,' she said.

Walters was outraged by the behaviour of those in authority. 'The way they hid the numbers of animals killed! Everything was put down on a ministry website, and when my farm came up I noticed they had put that 125 animals had been destroyed. So I rang them and said "How come it says 125, when I have got a bonfire on my farm with more than 700 animals burning on it?" They never changed the number.'

He is also convinced that foot and mouth got on to his farm through an unhygienic ministry vet. 'He had dirty fingernails and he didn't wear gloves. And, unlike the other vets who came and did regular checks, he didn't stand at a distance. He insisted on getting into every pen where they were lambing and calving. Much later, Liverpool University Medical School rang me because they were investigating the spread of the disease. They said 80 per cent of the farmers they spoke to were sure it had been spread by vets.'

What was he planning to do in the future? He knew exactly. He was going to restock as soon as he could, and go to the Suffolk breeder he'd bought Basil from and buy two more rams. 'Then I'll have two Basils on the farm,' he said. 'I'm not giving up. Why, if I did I'd be letting the bastards win, wouldn't I?'

'There are definite rules to going out with a farmer,' my friend Sarah said. 'And it's all completely different to how Bridget Jones behaves.'

'Well, not completely,' I disagreed. 'What about all those tender meetings in the snow? Because, you have to agree, nearly all romances with farmers start in winter or early spring, when there isn't so much to do.'

'Some things *are* different,' she insisted woozily, a bit the worse for wear after a gin and champagne cocktail. I'd discovered the joys of alcohol after Charlie left, which meant female pals kept dropping round to try out my new cocktail cabinet. 'Food isn't important to Mr Darcy. He doesn't care that she can't cook. What farmer would ever be like that?'

It is true that cooking matters to rural men. In fact, some even prefer older women because of their superior expertise with pastry. There are three things you must be able to make if you want to date a farmer:

1) A full English breakfast. (Remember to hide the wrappers if you have used Danish bacon.)
2) A roast with every imaginable trimming.
3) Some sort of gateau (preferably chocolate) so he can put it in his lunchbox and show it off to his pals, much as an urban bloke might pass around a glamorous photo.

One of the defining moments in a relationship with a farmer comes, not when you go on a mini-break with him, but when he asks you to help him look after his animals. I remember my excitement when Wooster first invited me along to tuberculosis-test his cows. I spent hours choosing just the right costume that mixed sexiness with practicality and when I made notes in his record book I used my best handwriting. I only messed up when I was asked to drive the second batch of cows out of the field, and found myself looking right into the moody, bulging eyes of a fully grown bull. I gave a squeak and leapt the fence, and I could see I got a black mark for cowardice. It was easier with Ian: I only had to mind his dog while he went off to a tractor event. And since farmers, though kind and fair, tend to be a little strict with their dogs, I could make the little spaniel blissfully happy just by sitting him in front of a roaring fire and letting him help himself to those dog-treats that resemble fig rolls.

'How can you find out if you really fancy someone or not – if you aren't sure?' I asked Sarah.

'Haven't you tried kissing him?' she asked, astonished.

Chapter Twenty-One

'When the gorse is out of blossom, kissing's out of season.' Dartmoor saying. (The gorse is always in blossom.)

It was 3 a.m. and pitch dark when the car stopped. I felt fuzzy and disorientated, and a little anxious about Nat, who was sleeping back at the house with the other, older children. All around, crowds streamed past, dark figures against the charcoal sky.

I slid out of the car and we began walking across the rough ground, stumbling over rabbit holes. I gripped tightly on to Ian's hand, but it wouldn't have mattered if I had let go. I would have been able to find him again: his legs were jingling so loudly. Really, I just wanted to hold his hand. Since that first kiss, I hadn't been able to stop touching him. I'd never felt such a violent passion for anyone else in my whole life. And it wasn't just a physical thing. He was so kind to me, too. He was the first man

I had ever met who would drive through the night on impulse to see me. I loved it when the telephone rang suddenly at midnight and I'd struggle up from sleep to hear his voice say, 'Well, aren't you going to open the front door and let me in?' Huge bouquets of flowers arrived, and every time he turned up at the farm he would mend something that, even with my new-found survival skills, I hadn't been able to fix.

But there was the odd doubt still in my mind. The sky around me had lightened now, the beginning of midsummer morning. We had reached the path leading to Stonehenge, and I could just about see Ian and his friends in their pure white outfits, bells tied to their knees with ribbons.

Although I'd initially wanted to meet Ian precisely because he was a morris dancer, I'd had many twinges of unease since. Morris dancing has such an astoundingly bad image. It is considered weird without any redeeming feature: dull, unmanly and – even worse – not the slightest bit amusing. Although I had to admit that whenever Ian talked about his group of dancers his stories gave a different impression. He liked to describe how, several years earlier, they went to a festival at Flers in Normandy and only discovered at the very last minute that they'd forgotten their hazel sticks. So, since they were in a hurry, they just went to the nearest *boulangerie* and bought some stale baguettes instead. This astonished their French hosts, who hadn't been expecting the storm of breadcrumbs that was unleashed when the traditional stick dance began.

As we got closer to Stonehenge the musicians in the group tuned up and began playing. There was a bodhran (a type of drum), a serpent, a flute, a guitar, and a button-box accordion, and soon they were pumping out tunes that oozed rural charm. We could almost have been back in Hardy's Wessex as we strode along, if it hadn't been for the revellers passed out on the edge of the path. They were in an advanced state of intoxication, and strongly objected to morris men.

'Bollocks!' they roared, as our beribboned capes appeared through the mist. 'F★★★ off!' Or, more inventively, and spoken in tones of withering sarcasm: 'Are you trying to scare the fairies?' I was quite frightened by the level of aggression, but the dancers shrugged it off. It was normal: in the past they'd often had beer and sausage rolls thrown at them, and been roundly jeered. For some odd reason the British detest their folk-dancing traditions with passion.

Next to the stones, the atmosphere was even worse. It was exceedingly *herbal*, too, and one dancer sighed, as we entered the thick fug of illegal substances enveloping the monoliths: 'That's my passive smoking done for the year.' A hippy with dreadlocks like snakes on his head deftly snatched away one of the morris handkerchiefs to a roar of approval from the crowd. And as the men lined up for their first dance two women with bright pink hair and strangely unfocused eyes ran in among them and started groping them roughly. The dancers ignored all this and began again, and when I saw Ian waiting patiently for the correct beat, his hankies raised above his head and one toe pointed, surrounded by that baying, hostile crowd, a sentimental tear came into my eye. He was mad, maybe even certifiably silly – but very brave.

The mood by the stones changed, though, when Ian's friends began the Upton-upon-Severn stick dance. This is very fast, and involves lots of sweating and jumping, and the vigorous clashing of heavy sticks, and as it progressed the hippies in the crowd were impressed despite themselves, and stopped booing. Then the music started for a dance that I recognised: 'Old Woman Tossed Up'. This is a fertility rite, and is always entertaining to watch, because an unsuspecting woman is plucked from the crowd, and introduced to each of the dancers in turn in a very gentle, courtly fashion. The men skip about, and while she watches from the sidelines, vaguely pleased to have been chosen, one of the dancers creeps up behind her and throws her into the air. The look of surprise on her face always makes the crowd laugh – and after this she is enthusiastically kissed by each of the men, and blushes scarlet with embarrassment and pleasure. Little does she know that there is a hidden coda: almost every woman drawn into this dance finds herself pregnant within the year. 'It's true,' the group's historian, Bob Hill, told me. 'In fact, the publican at the Angel in Heytesbury has banned us from doing it to any of his barmaids again, because we got three of them pregnant one after the other.'

I was just wondering who they were going to pick when Ian seized me by the hand and dragged me into the ring. The sun was coming up by then, a great red ball – some lunatic in a hang-glider was gliding in front of it – and drums were drowning out the lively beat of the accordion. It all happened very fast. I heard the crowd cheer, and then I felt as if I was whizzing through a washing-machine cycle. I was buffeted, ruffled, stunned, kissed and dropped just outside the ring.

'Magic mushroom?' a genial man in a horned cap asked, proffering a tray, as I sat down, dazed, in the grass. I shook my head. I desperately hoped I wasn't going to get pregnant again.

'Romance when you're a single mum. There's a subject.' It was my divorce party. I'd given quite a lot of parties since Charlie left. The most miserable was the Non-Valentine's party (all the food red or pink, smoked salmon, red-pepper tart, strawberry cake – and pink champagne), where I got together with all the other women in the village who had been let down by men. It was a desultory occasion, spoiled because the liveliest woman invited couldn't come: she'd just started a fling with the fish man, who sold haddock door to door from a little white van. The divorce one was more cheerful. It seemed a fine way of celebrating the arrival of a small, but significant piece of paper, and it ended with a whole group of us sitting round a table, chatting.

'Children are fine judges of character,' Lily said, putting her arm around her seven-year-old, who'd darted in for a slice of pizza. When he'd gone she explained how, long before she began to feel anxious about her latest relationship, he had taken her aside and told her, very seriously, that she should finish it at once. 'That man is no good for you, Mum.'

I remembered asking Nat about Ian very early on, anxious that he might have hated him. (Nat was in the middle of a violent tantrum at the time, because I wouldn't buy him a toy in a gift shop, but he broke off his yelling long enough to answer my question quite seriously.) There is nothing quite like having an early date with someone and getting an instant, positive assessment from an onlooker who has spent most of it bouncing inconspicuously on a nearby trampoline.

Of course, there are parts of any relationship that have to be kept hidden from children at all costs, and my friend Sarah had a useful tip about this. She recommended that anyone with smallish boys invest in old *Thunderbirds* videos, because not only are they unusually enthralling, but each episode lasts fifty minutes, which gives you a decent amount of time to get up to no good in a tucked-away broom-cupboard.

I laughed a bit too heartily at this, because my erotic life was very odd, what with Ian living with two teenagers and me being accompanied at all times by Nat. In fact, what it reminded me of most was being a teenager myself: all the subterfuge, and hiding, and assignations in unlikely places. We were constantly having to squeeze behind boilers, and lock ourselves into bathrooms, or buy expensive electronic gadgets so that everyone under the age of nineteen was plugged into a PlayStation and effectively in cryogenic suspension for the evening. Not only had sex suddenly turned into a burning need, like a raging thirst that could never be quenched, but it took so damn long. The minute you'd finished it, you wanted to start all over again. A hobby that used up this much time took some concealing, I can tell you. The only factor on our side was that no one *under* the age of nineteen could possibly imagine that sex was the reason why their parent was invariably to be found fiddling with the boiler.

'And don't you find,' Lily said, 'that once your boyfriend

moves in you become so popular in the mornings! All your kids are in your bed from 7 a.m. onwards, jumping up and down and play-fighting with your man!'

Ian, who always worried about my column for me, suggested that we should all go out rabbiting with his friend Bill, a retired gamekeeper. We started off by eating large quantities of cake in Bill's house: a very cosy place, where only a few, favoured dogs were allowed in the lounge, and the rest gazed mournfully in at us from the garden. An Alsatian kept trying to squeeze itself in through the top of the lowest window with a lot of toenail scrabbling, and being rebuked by Bill's twenty-year-old daughter, Louise. She was one of those extremely formidable rural women: covered in tattooes, expert at horse-breaking, not averse to the odd bout of fisticuffs. It turned out that she was having a brief holiday from cleaning up foot-and-mouth-infected farms on the Welsh Borders, and while we drank our coffee – and somewhere out of sight the ferrets were brushed and popped into special carved wooden carriers – she told us all about it.

'Do you know what a bobcat is?' she asked. I didn't, but Ian explained to me that it was a small digger. 'To start with,' she said, getting up to push the Alsatian's nose out of the gap in the window, so the dog fell back with a thump and a disappointed yelp into the garden, 'the rule was that only contractors with driving licences were to use bobcats. But so many of the contractors were eighteen-year-old kids off the dole who didn't know how to drive that it got changed so you could use one if you had a bit of common sense. Bobcats are dangerous in the wrong hands – they shoot all over the place.' There were hundreds of accidents. She'd seen operators tip bobcats over and slowly and inexorably bury themselves in the mud, or press the wrong levers and jump sideways on to cars – and of course MAFF had to pay the bill.

There was a farcical element to the picture she painted of the clean-up. Apparently, all these teenage contractors kept defying the rules, and were always stripping off their paper suits in order to sunbathe, and being discovered in distant fields, blissfully asleep. And this could be quite dangerous, because a classic problem on the farms Louise supervised, which had been stocked with sheep, was infected wool. Little rags of it were everywhere, lining hedges, stuck on barbed wire, trimming every bit of machinery or wall that the sheep had ever scratched themselves against. MAFF had decreed that it all had to be destroyed with blow-torches. 'But the teenagers kept setting fire to everything. So then they said there had to be a bloke with water following the one with the blow-torch. But they still ended up torching the hedges because the bloke with the water kept going off and sunbathing.'

As if irresponsible teenagers weren't enough to cope with, there were insanely perfectionist vets, too. When a farm was being cleaned a vet was supposed to decide what needed to be done, and then return to check that his orders had been followed. Only, because of the confusion, the same vet rarely returned, and they all had different standards. 'One told us we had to pressure-wash the roof of a corrugated barn. And another came along to check the work and said: "Hang on. How is a cow supposed to have crapped up there?" '

Her most haunting story, though, was of a thoroughly bad farmer. (I normally never wrote about these – though almost every village has one. Farming has a bad enough press already.) As the Alsatian put his head down and tried to charge the window – all he accomplished was a muffled bang that left him looking dazed – she described one farm that was a particular mess. 'The owner was a chap in his fifties, who wandered about all day with a shotgun in one hand and a can of Special Brew in the other, and had been the bane of his neighbours' lives for years. His animals were always dying of neglect and he'd been reported over and over to the RSPCA. MAFF didn't just have to clean all his sheds and barns, but his fields, too, because they were so full of rusty machinery and animal bones. It all had to be buried – at one point there were forty contractors there. Because the place was so muddy they had to lay a stone drive before they could get machinery in. And after months of work this evil chap had a lovely clean, levelled farm, and all the locals felt it wasn't fair. They kept saying, "Can't we have new drives, too?" '

The farm we were rabbiting on certainly hadn't had a clean-up recently. It was criss-crossed with deep tracks, each an awkward mix of liquid mud and loose rubble. There was a rusty old VW beetle half-submerged in a little stream below us as we scrambled over a bank with our ferret-boxes and bags, and on the horizon sheep, blurred by rain and hobbling on their elbows and knees because their feet hadn't been trimmed, watched us with suspicion.

Each time we found a warren under the twisted roots of a grown-out hedge Bill would walk round it carefully, placing little purse-nets over the rabbit holes. Then a writhing ferret would be popped down. The first one was not wearing a radio-collar, so when it failed to reappear (and no rabbits ran out, either) the men had to resort to ancient methods of detection. They lay down on the grass, pressing their ears tight to the ground, and listened. And they pushed their arms down likely looking holes and felt around, with faraway looks on their faces. When that didn't work, Bill, a small, leathery man dressed in faded camouflage, who wore his tweed cap as if it was an SAS beret, would sigh, get out a big rusty shovel and dig. He did this so often that I began to think 'rabbiting with ferrets' was quite the wrong description for what we were doing. 'Shovelling for ferrets' would have been more accurate.

Then Bill put down his shovel, felt about in the latest hole and called out excitedly: 'I can feel the ferret!'

'No you can't,' Ian said from the other side of the bank, where he'd been exploring a burrow of his own. 'That's my hand you've got hold of.'

Bill pulled out his arm and blushed. To cover his confusion, he told us about the time he put his hand down a rabbit hole and a rat bit it. Apparently, lots of different creatures live with rabbits: weasels, badgers, foxes, even owls. Rabbits seemed to be much more mysterious creatures than I'd imagined. For instance, there was one thing Bill had seen a rabbit do that he had never fully understood. One morning he was clearing a rabbit-infested garden when he came across a wild duck that had just hatched out a clutch of sixteen chicks. 'I opened the gate so she could take them down to a brook, and ten minutes later heard her quacking. When I caught up with her she had only two duck-lings left and a rabbit was *fighting her*. It was jabbing at her with its front feet like a professional boxer. I've thought and thought about it since and the only explanation I can come up with is that the other fourteen ducklings must have fallen down its burrow and annoyed it. But I'm willing to be corrected.'

When the ferret had finally been caught we went off to another warren and stuffed it down there. And, of course, it van-ished again. As the shovel came into play again, there was a short, testy monologue from Bill about why this kept happen-ing. It was because Nat and Bill's grandson were giggling and running about in the distance. The noise and vibration made the rabbits reluctant to leap into the nets.

While this was probably true, it seemed illogical to me that the rabbits would not have been equally outraged by the smell of Bill's roll-ups and the keening of his dogs. Bill had brought along a shivering whippet and a terrier like a large bristly sausage, and they both whimpered incessantly while staring at the rabbit holes. So while we waited for a different ferret to per-form a skilful (and, alas, wholly invisible) hunting manoeuvre underground I tried to think up some country sporting rules, and only managed one:

Country Sporty Rule No. 1

1) *The noise made by women and children is always bad, and that made by men and dogs good. Dogs may be shouted at crossly all day (in fact, they nearly always are). But at the end their owners will congratulate them — and each other (with tears in their eyes) — on how exquisitely the dogs have behaved, and what a joy it is to watch them working.*

Still, on the plus side, Nat seemed to get a great deal from these rural activities. He admired the kind of masculinity that came into play: hardy, mildly militaristic, able to do ingenious things with sharp knives and rolls of string. When a geriatric, suicidal rabbit finally hurled itself into one of the nets Bill grabbed it and killed it swiftly. Then he called the two little boys over and showed them how it had to be pouched: the steaming pink and mauve guts spilling out into a specially shovelled hole. And one of the back legs split so the other could fit neatly into it. Nat watched all this, grave and round-eyed, and then asked if he could carry the rabbit when we set off home. Looking back at him I could tell he was consciously trying to copy Bill's stiff, bow-legged walk.

In fact, it was a shock to me how much he needed a fatherly influence in his life. Depriving him of this was like denying him air. Sometimes, when we had all spent the day together, and Ian had been specially attentive to his own sons, I would find Nat weeping quietly into his towel in the bathroom, just out of desperate longing for his own father. Phone calls and letters simply weren't enough.

Chapter Twenty-Two

A spell to rid yourself of obsessive thoughts about a loved one: find a small pot, and, every day, write down a sad thought about your love on a piece of paper and put it in the pot. When the moon is waning, sit down at midnight with the pot and a dark blue candle. Read out each bit of paper to yourself and burn it in the flame of the candle, catching the ashes in the pot. Then smash the pot and bury the pieces at the furthest corner of your property. Cassandra Latham, witch at St Buryan, Cornwall

We hadn't seen Charlie for months. He had unlimited access to Nat but he would only very occasionally call in on his way back from visiting his business partner in Dorset, and stay just long enough to pick up a few bits of equipment and drink a cup of tea while Nat sat on his knee. I'd hover in the background, getting out cakes that no one ate and trying not to be upset by the way that all the affection that used to be in Charlie's eyes and voice had gone.

He'd try and find out from me what the older children were doing, because he missed them desperately and longed to see them again. But they refused to do this because they were still so angry about him leaving. They'd also made me promise not to give him any information about them, so, feeling uncomfortable – because it was cruel – I'd be politely vague. Sometimes I'd try to get him to talk about the break-up, because I was still tormented by its suddenness. But these conversations never made anything clearer, and were always brief, because he would leave soon after they began.

'You know you said, back in January, that as far as you were concerned our marriage had been over for years?' I'd said, the last time I saw him.

'Yes?' He looked up from the workshop where he was kneeling down and rummaging through an oily cardboard box full of springs. There was a spark of alarm in his eyes.

'Well, if it was over, why didn't you tell me that it was?'

'Because I thought it might get better.' He spoke as if wearily explaining the obvious to a moron. Then he abruptly stuffed the whole box in his car and left. What did that mean?

E-mail from Annabel: 'I don't think it is at all wise for you to go up to Scotland. It will be far too traumatic. If it was me there is no way I would even look at that woman, let alone speak to her.'

It was Nat's leg that started me thinking about going up to Scotland. He broke it playing on a scooter in a friend's garden, and, after a horrible two days in hospital having it set, was in a wheelchair for nearly three months. Throughout all this he had longed to see his father – but Charlie was too busy with hay-making and harvest, and Scotland was too far away. The only thing that had really consoled Nat was that his elder brother came home to help look after him, and the two of us bought him a small, remote control Sports Utility Vehicle. It was Sam's idea. He thought it would make Nat feel less powerless, and Nat spent hours sitting under a shady bush in the yard in his chair, driving it about. My chickens and ducks were out there too, mobbing him whenever he threw them bread, and because he was with them so constantly he noticed something I had missed.

Our little Buff Pekin cockerel, with his honey-coloured body and feathery legs that made him look as if he was stumping around in custom-made bell-bottomed trousers, was a bully. When no humans were around, except for an unseen spy under the bush, this cockerel, called Wooster because Wooster had given him to Nat as a present, would torment an old Maran hen. It was a sustained campaign of abuse. He crept up behind her and jabbed her with his beak when she was trying to eat, he drove her away when she tried to stretch out her legs and sun-bathe on the edge of the path with the other poultry, and he raped her over and over again. She ended up spending most of her time crouching dismally in the shade, and her days – and probably her nights, too – were haunted by anxiety. Her comb was even fading to bluish-pink, because she got so little food and drink. (I'd noticed this, but put it down to old age.)

Nat couldn't drive Wooster off the hen himself, so he used the Sports Utility Vehicle. Each time Wooster eyed up the hen with evil intent, and began to sidle towards her, the SUV would crackle remorselessly out of the undergrowth and chase him away. It circled the poultry yard constantly, keeping him in its sights, and you could almost see the cockerel getting twitchy and paranoid. After a few weeks of this he was as jumpy as the hen had been, kept glancing fearfully into the darker parts of the garden and decided that the hen had a powerful (if strange) protector and was best left strictly alone.

When I wrote about Wooster, I triggered a rush of similar stories. Mrs Jo Welch told me that when her cockerel got too unkind to his harem she would wrap him up gently in those big, loose rubber bands that come free with the post, and leave him to stew for a while. And Roger Morsley Smith passed on a gripping tale about an army major pal of his, Ronald Whitworth, a man of 'irreproachable integrity'.

'In the 1960s Ronald had to visit a farmyard with an acquaintance from Vienna. Ronald warned the man that the farmyard contained a big, ferocious cockerel that attacked strangers and pecked them, and as they reached the place Ronald saw the bird charging, and shouted "Run!" To his surprise the man stood his ground, uttering low noises as the bird approached. He then bent down, picked the bird up and it lay contentedly in his arms, making quiet sounds of delight.

'The man explained that his father had been killed in the First World War. His mother had found a job in the Civil Service, but had no one to mind him, then aged only two years old. Times were hard, and in desperation she resorted to a most unusual measure. She confined him in a playpen with some bedding, putting in a broody hen for company. This worked surprisingly well. He played with the hen, and at lunchtime his mother was able to come back to check all was well. Such an upbringing naturally resulted in a special affinity with poultry.'

The bullying-cockerel stories didn't stop there. A few weeks later I was in the post office when my friend Lynn came in complaining about her Light Sussex cockerel. Named 'Gullitt' after the former Newcastle United manager, he had become such a keen serial rapist and general all-round pest that her hens kept burrowing under the hedges on either side of her garden and fleeing to nearby poultry yards. And, of course, when Gullitt followed them there he annoyed the neighbours, who didn't want their poultry harassed either. Besides, everyone in the area had had quite enough of Gullitt's boastful, round-the-clock crowing. Lynn was planning to kill him, but the sub-postmaster persuaded her to change her mind.

'Why don't you try pheasant-spectacles instead?' he suggested. 'I've got some at home, left over from when I was a gamekeeper, and we used them to stop feather-pecking.'

He came round the next day and fitted them on Gullitt. They looked like tiny red plastic sunglasses, only instead of hooked ear-pieces they were kept in place by a bar through the nostrils. To Lynn's relief, Gullitt didn't appear to feel pain as they were put on. He seemed far more miffed by the indignity of being picked up and held tightly.

I called round later, when Gullitt was back to patrolling his yard, and from a distance you couldn't really tell that there was anything different about him at all, because the specs were exactly the same colour as his rosy comb and wattles. When I got closer, though, there was something arresting about his appearance because the specs so closely resembled a pair of designer shades. They only restricted part of his vision: he could still see quite well peripherally, and he was still following his wives about, but now there was a charming, courtly uncertainty to his behaviour. Even his crow was subdued and apologetic, as if he was clearing his throat in order to stammer out a declaration of love.

'Whenever I walk past him now,' Lynn explained, 'he twitches his head, startled, as if thinking: "Did someone go past?" It's the same with his hens. He goes: "Is that a hen?" And they can easily dodge out of his way now. I know it's sort of sad, but at least he gets to go on living.'

When Nat was finally up on crutches I booked airline tickets to Glasgow. I thought it would help him to see where his father lived, and appreciate how far away it was. And also, I have to admit that I hoped it would be good for me, too. I hated the way my mind just kept running over and over the divorce, without coming to any useful conclusion.

I wasn't quite brave enough to go to Scotland alone, though. I asked Ian to come with me, and he said that of course he would. So we hired a car from Glasgow airport and set off through the Highlands. At last we came to the Corran ferry, and crossed over on to the Ardnamurchan peninsula. Here the road became narrow and twisty, with acres of grey loch on one side, and a steep slope covered in forest on the other. Every so often there would be a sheep in the road, blocking the traffic. A clean, fluffy, well-kept sort with a black face, that placed itself cosily right in the middle, like a pet dog, and refused to move until you got out of the car and shooed it to one side. It was so disconcerting making this journey and knowing that Charlie had done the same only two years earlier, and fallen in love at the end of it. And it was exactly the sort of wild landscape I knew he adored. When we stopped for lunch at a little pub we were ushered into a musty, maroon-papered parlour where a log fire burned in a grate, and fed floury venison stew while, round a corner, a succession of deliverymen flirted with the landlady. It reminded me so much of Cécile Blaise's heavy horse farm in France, and as we drove on I imagined that the place we were going to would be like that, only more so, a tumbledown paradise containing everything that Charlie loved most. There'd be old carts and machinery peacefully rotting in the yard, and indoors more pet pigs, chickens and lambs than we'd ever had in the West Country. A place where he was surrounded by hordes of friends. And where no one ever ate goat's cheese. Charlie had an especial loathing for this. He complained about the 'bierdos' – weird men with beards and sandals – (or, alternatively, women with moustaches) who made it. And the way it tasted like the rudest part of a billy goat. I shared his opinion, of course, but after he left, just as a gesture of defiance, I tried eating the stuff, and after a while I grew quite fond of it.

After four hours' driving we found ourselves on a bleak hillside, rough grass sweeping down to a silent, waveless sea. I knew the farm was very near now, and felt cold with panic. What did I look like? Horrible, probably, because I was tired and dirty from the journey. While Ian and Nat got out to pee in the rocks I glanced into the vanity mirror on the sun-shield, and saw that I had four thin black hairs sprouting from my chin. Aaargh! Superfluous hair! Charlie hated that more than anything. I got rid of them quickly and couldn't bear to look at myself any more. Everything about me was fifteen years older than this other woman, that was for sure.

Ian hugged me and told me not to worry, I looked fine, and we drove on down the narrow little track. A post van had stopped just ahead of us, at a gateway marked by a pink dustbin, and the driver was talking to Charlie. He straightened up, looking older and more fatigued than I remembered, and we bumped down ahead of him to the farm.

It was awesomely tidy for a six-hundred-acre enterprise where beef and sheep were raised. There were dogs, but they were barking explosively in outdoor wire cages, and there was no sign of any machinery, just an immaculately swept yard and plenty of scrubbed-looking barns with freshly tiled roofs. As we got out of the car Charlie's girlfriend came out of the house and stood watching us cautiously, from a distance. She, too, was nothing like I'd imagined. She was tall and slender, with reddish-blonde hair cut rather mannishly. No make-up. And despite the awkwardness of the situation, she had an air of being totally in control. Something about the determined tilt of her chin told you that here was a woman accustomed to getting her own way. Her face was oddly familiar, too. She looked like . . . like . . . Charlie's mother and sisters. There was a distinct family resemblance. The same blonde skin and fine bone structure.

We went indoors for coffee, and the kitchen astonished me more than anything. It was brand new: newly laid tiles, stripped pine, red Aga. It was all pink, too, Charlie's least favourite colour, and it sparkled from a thousand points, as if someone had just that minute stopped shining it with a damp cloth. (Another activity Charlie abominated. He even called one of his friends' wives 'Mrs J-Cloth' because she would never stop buffing.) And there were no pets in it at all. It was so puzzling. If he had always wanted to live like this why had he so steadfastly refused to tidy up and repair the West Country farms we'd lived in? And if he was helplessly attracted to women who looked like members of his own family why had he ever had anything to do with me?

It was clear, too, even in a brief glimpse, that he had quite a different kind of relationship with his girlfriend from the one he'd had with me. Another friend of his had rung me after visiting them and said wonderingly, 'He's a lot quieter now. When he was with you he was always so full of it.' They were obviously very close, but Charlie looked more anxious than I remembered. But that could just have been the effect of seeing me. She flirted a little with Ian, and though in repose her face was almost plain, when she was animated it became very attractive: a lovely wide, white smile and bright turquoise eyes that matched the single earring she wore. I didn't dislike her; I just felt numb.

When we collected Nat the next day – having spent the night in a nearby hotel – the yard was full of naughty-looking gingery goats with bells on their collars. And while I piled Nat's bags and coats in the car I asked her about them:

'Do you milk them?'

'Yes, we do.'

'What happens to the milk?'

'We feed it to the orphan lambs, because we are organic and cannot use milk powder. Or we make it into cheese.' She had a seductive German accent and spoke with a husky firmness.

'Is there much of a market for the cheese?' Nat had climbed into the car and I fastened his seat-belt, momentarily preoccupied.

'Oh, no, we can't sell it. It would be against EU regulations. We eat it ourselves.'

Nat burst into tears as we drove away, and was violently and repeatedly sick. I had to climb in the back and hold him all the way back to Glasgow. In the front, Ian slowly mulled over what he'd seen. 'She does look younger than you, but I don't think she's as pretty.' 'It's idyllic on that farm now, but what must it be like when it's raining or the midges come out? I've heard the midges can be bad here.' As he said this we passed a boulder in the road on which someone had gone to the trouble of painting a huge face with bared teeth, and the words 'Mighty Midge'.

I felt terrible: as if I had been severely beaten up by someone who left no physical scars, just internal ones. However much I felt I had adjusted to all the changes in my life, I was still stunned by how wrong it felt to see Charlie with another woman. My sister Annabel had been right.

So it was a long while before the significance of the goat-milk conversation sank in. The man who hated goat's cheese more than any other food in the world was now, presumably, eating it every day.

Chapter Twenty-Three

'Luxembourg Fox Stew — Kill a fox, leave it on the roof in a gutter for at least three nights, then skin it, cut it into pieces and leave it to soak overnight in buttermilk. It should then be marinated in red wine for three days, flambéed in brandy and finally simmered for two hours in the sieved marinade, thickened with flour and water. A quarter of an hour before serving, add some chocolate to the sauce.' Recipe loosely translated from *Le Livre de la Cuisine Luxembourgeoise*, by Pol Tousch

I was rather an irritating girlfriend because I was always going on about Charlie. And, worse, I had lost all faith in romantic love. To me, the words 'I love you' just meant 'I enjoy being with you – until someone slightly better comes along'. Ian was very patient (and he knew that the obsessive maundering about one's ex did eventually stop – it had in his case). But sometimes my attitude exasperated him. So he announced that, since I didn't trust words, he would use actions to show how he felt about me. And with that, he began installing central heating in my house.

It was an act of unimaginable kindness. I'd grown used to chilblains, two inches of ice on the insides of windows, black mildew on the walls and a persistent smell of old church hassocks in all the beds, sofas and wardrobes. So the prospect of being warm in the winter was like a wistful dream. I didn't realise, though, that there is an important intermediary stage between being cold and having central heating. This is the purgatory of installation. As boxes of radiators and huge bundles of pipes were lugged into the house I was forced to make impossible choices.

'Would you rather,' Ian would ask, cradling a monster drill in his arms, 'that I cut a hole right through your antique dresser? Or do you want me to run the pipes behind it, so that it tips into the room at an angle?'

Of course, with all the drilling, there were soon holes in all the walls and ceilings, and I found that if I lay down full length beside the bed in Kathy's room I could look down into the kitchen and watch the cat stealing butter off the kitchen table.

Unfortunately, just as the pipes were about to be fitted, it stopped raining and Ian had to go back to Wiltshire and do some muck-spreading and reseeding.

It was sad when he'd gone. In the week he'd been staying with me I'd grown even more attached to him: he was so gentle and unselfish. I wandered forlornly up to the post office and shop, which was full of women. They were all examining packets of sausages and drums of baking soda, just as an excuse to join in the conversation and defer going back out into the rain. It seemed that almost all of them had had central heating or electricity installed by their husbands. One described how she'd cowered in terror as the mains were finally switched on after a refit, sure that her house was going to burst into flames and explode. It hadn't, of course, because though farmers possess few technical qualifications, they have all been plumbing and fiddling with electricity for years. They couldn't keep animals indoors otherwise. The sub-postmaster leaned congenially against his freezer. 'Why don't you persuade Ian to give up farming and become a plumber and handyman?' he asked. 'There's no future in the land any more.'

Plunging prices, and the aftermath of foot and mouth, were having dramatic effects on the countryside. Just as I'd begun to feel properly at home in it, it was changing beyond recognition, and hundreds of farmers were leaving the land. Nick Viney, Farm Project Co-ordinator for the Diocese of Exeter, was one of those trying to stem the exodus. He was touring the West Country, dropping in on different isolated farmers and encouraging them to meet up with their neighbours and form co-operatives, and confessed that he'd been touched by what he found. Typically, he would arrive at a holding where all the animals had been culled, and be invited indoors by a farmer with no cookery experience whatever, who was surrounded by children and fudging up a dinner. 'You know how male chauvinist farmers are?' he said. 'The really old-fashioned sorts have never cooked for themselves. But they are now, because their wives have gone out to work and the whole family is determined to survive financially.'

I was fascinated by the idea of farming husbands and wives being forced, at last, to swap roles, because farmers' wives are an unusual breed. In the past, whenever I interviewed one, we'd inevitably get on to the subject of farming marriages, and they'd start laughing – in an odd, hysterical way – at the complexities of their role. Because, as well as being quite unliberated – in the sense of having to provide a well-run home, and plenty of home-cooking, and do most of the childcare – they were expected to be so tough. As Dee Olof, who runs a highly successful wedding-dress business from an attic on the family farm, put it: 'Farmers tend to be emotionally supportive men who hate weak women. If I had a go at something and failed, my husband, Mark, has never minded. He's just never wanted me to say I couldn't do it. I can remember getting in with the boar and sows (because he told me to), and the boar giving me grief, and Mark saying, "Darling. Perhaps I can give you some advice. When a boar is frothing at the lips it's likely to attack you." But he'd liked my drive and determination in trying to cope. It was that attitude that turned me into a businesswoman.'

So I decided to do some research. First, I went to see Jane, who had got married the same year that I did, and lived on a family farm in Cornwall. I had to park a mile from her house, and creep across darkened fields and through a covered yard where ewes and lambs were muttering to each other, because she was scared of anyone finding out that she had talked to me. I felt like a spy as I slipped through her front door, and in a way, I was. Jane lives in a flat in the same house as her in-laws and everything she does has always been closely observed and criticised by them.

We sat down by the fire. Above us I could hear her in-laws clumping about and having a muffled exchange that, from its tone, bordered uncomfortably on argument. Jane explained that throughout her marriage she had done most of the housework and child-rearing, mainly because her husband simply didn't have the time. He worked at least fifteen hours a day, seven days a week, and was paid less than £500 a month by his father. Because of his low wage, Jane was forced, early on, to earn money in a managerial job. And now, because the farm had become so unprofitable (milk and lambs cost more to produce than they could be sold for), and she'd been promoted, she was effectively subsidising the whole family.

But this was not reflected in her status. If animals were going to market, she had to be up at 5 a.m. to help load them. When she got home from work she was expected to muck in with milking or lambing. Even her sleep was not sacrosanct. 'The other night a cow had a difficult calving. She was really wild, and my husband couldn't get near her, so I had to help. He was skiing across the muddy field with the calving ropes in his hands, and I was running after, a coat over my nightie. We finally managed to calve her under the hedge at two in the morning.'

'Why don't you stand up to your parents-in-law and say you

can't work this hard?' I asked, appalled, but knowing I could never have challenged them myself, if I'd been in her place.

'Because he loves them and he doesn't *want* me to. Does anyone realise, when they marry a farmer, how powerful a grip his family has on him?' She rocked backwards and forwards on the sofa, cuddling a velvet cushion. One side was splitting, and the stuffing was coming out. 'Besides, what could I threaten them with? That we'd leave if they didn't give us an easier time? My husband couldn't leave: he'd shrivel up and die if he had to live in a town.'

After chuckling quietly to herself at the grimness of her predicament, Jane finally said, 'I suppose I stay because I love him so very dearly. I would have walked out years ago if I didn't.'

The next day I called in on Jo Down and her husband Phil, who farm in the Lew Valley, near Okehampton. As Jo showed me round a farmyard like a building site, where a workman was banging nails into ceiling joists under a tarpaulin that flapped in the rain, she explained that they used to keep beef and dairy cows, with a small bed and breakfast business on the side. But after foot and mouth, when all the animals were culled, they looked coldly at their accounts and decided that it would be best to use the compensation money to turn the cow-sheds into holiday homes.

This has caused a monumental shift in their marriage. While there will still be some bullocks for Phil to rear, the type of labour the farm requires has changed dramatically. Instead of Jo helping Phil with farm work, he now has to help her with vast amounts of housework. It is a tough adjustment for a man who, according to his wife, has never used a vacuum cleaner in twenty-two years of marriage.

He has coped by carving a special niche for himself. 'He does PVIs: Pre Visitor Inspections,' Jo laughed. 'My sister and I will have been cleaning all day, and Phil will come in and say "There are some high-altitude cobwebs in Kingfisher cottage." And we will throw things at him.' More usefully, he has taken on the essential task of entertaining visitors.

'Nowadays, if you do not treat your paying guests like friends,' Jo said, 'they do not come back. They love going to the pub with you, and sitting at the kitchen table in the evenings with cheese and port. Phil is very good at opening the port.'

She thinks that a successful farming marriage and working partnership is less about absolute fairness in the amount of work done – and more about each person giving the other what they need most. She described the awful day when her favourite horse, Murphy, had to be put down. She fled in tears to her mother's. When she came back in the evening to cook the guests' dinner she discovered that Phil had buried Murphy and scrubbed every trace of his blood from the stable. 'Phil did that for me, bless him,' she said tenderly.

I'd had such good luck with Feathered Friends that I kept recommending it to single pals, and one of them rang, on an early winter evening close to Christmas, to say that though she hadn't found a lover through it, she had met a number of entertaining people. The latest had a best friend called Arthur Boyt, who had an offbeat hobby: he ate animals he found lying dead beside country roads. Would I like to meet him?

Would I? I rang Arthur's number at once, and he told me he was going away the next day, and if I wanted to see him it would have to be that night. So I sped off to Davidstow, and it was dark when I reached his cottage. He came out to greet me with a tea-towel neatly folded over one arm, a tall, cadaverous man in his sixties, the eyes behind his spectacles sparkling with enthusiasm. There was a strange, intense odour in the air as I took out my notebook. It would have reminded me of farm slurry, if it hadn't been so hot and steamy. Perhaps it was lightly boiled horse-droppings. More ominously still, Boyt ushered me to a table where two places had been carefully laid.

'I've cooked you a badger,' he beamed. 'I'm afraid I didn't have time to marinate it, so it is just simply boiled, with garlic.'

In his unusually high-pitched voice, with its precise turn of phrase, he explained that he was a retired entomologist, and out of curiosity – and thrift – had tasted pretty well every animal that ever gets squashed by a car in Britain.

'Recently, I ate a greater horseshoe bat,' he called from the kitchen, where he could be heard fiddling with saucepan lids. 'It was small, and there was nothing remarkable about the taste, but the romance of eating something so exotic couldn't be denied.'

He came back into the room, and, remembering my day with the survival expert, I asked if he had ever eaten a rat. 'Oh, numerous times,' he said. 'It's a white meat, without a lot of flavour. You could easily mistake it for tasteless chicken. Females are more palatable because the males don't have much of a breast. People say they carry disease, but I would sooner eat a healthy country rat than the raw meat served in restaurants.'

He has even tried fox, though he doesn't recommend it: 'It had a pungent taste that went on repeating long after I had swallowed it.'

He disappeared again at this point, for quite a long time, during which I stared anxiously at the rural scenes on the table-mats and wondered where his wife was. He'd told me (with a twinkling smile) that she'd stormed out before I'd arrived, because she disapproved of his hobby and was, besides, a vegetarian.

'Hedgehog was interesting,' Arthur said, coming back into the room with a tray. 'I didn't cook it in the traditional fashion with clay, which was possibly a mistake. I skinned it, which took off that shield of fatty muscle under the prickles – and inside there was just a little ratty body. It was soft meat with a nice mouth-feel.' He put a plate down in front of me. It contained a mound of reheated fish pie as garnish, and about a kilo of badger meat in a thin, dishwater gravy. 'Normally I would serve badger with a selection of fresh vegetables,' Arthur said, seeing me flinch. He sat down in front of his own plate and began setting about the badger with gusto, carving big chunks off and popping them greedily into his mouth.

'I suppose,' I remarked, carefully slicing off a piece about the size of a thumbnail and examining it – it was dark, and resembled venison in texture, 'that you can only use bodies that are very fresh?'

'Not at all.' Arthur leaned forward. 'I have consumed meat

317

that was blown up like horses on the Western Front. If bodies are swollen, gasified and green they do taste different. But if you cook them thoroughly you can still eat them. I have done it, and there were no repercussions.' Seeing my hesitation he reassured me, most kindly, that our badger hadn't been on the road long, or seethed with maggots.

I had to be brave. So I put the meat in my mouth and chewed. The taste! Imagine a powerful mixture of kidney and liver, with a dash of concentrated musk. It was hard not to retch, but I ate more. After all, I could hardly hide a kilo of badger under my knife and fork. Besides, I had to be polite: Arthur meant well, and had gone to a great deal of trouble on my behalf.

As I stodged through the execrable meal, I did wonder, rather, about all those countrymen who had told me badger was delicious. There are even supposed to be a scattering of pubs in the West Country which specialise in providing illegal badger roasts for selected groups of locals. Was badger like all those other things they'd eaten in the 1930s – pies made of lambs' tails with the wool still on, or rook breasts – a dish you could only stomach if you were used to very grim commons indeed? Or maybe a whole section of humanity just had completely differ-ent taste-buds from me. After all, a few months ago I'd met a Devon farmer's wife who described how her husband's favourite pudding was 'bisky pie': a regional speciality made from sugar and the thick, yellowy-green colostrum that oozes from a cow's teats when it has just given birth. It is baked in an oven until it sets, and served lukewarm. When I wrote slightingly of this recipe, I had reproving letters and e-mails from all over the place, saying how delectable it was. (In Buckinghamshire it is called 'cherry curd pie', and in Sweden *kalvdans*, or 'dance of the calves'.)

But, on the other hand, maybe this badger had been frightened and in pain when it died. I knew that such things could affect meat: one of our lambs had once come back from the butcher suffused with a kidneyish taint, and Charlie had said it was because it had been killed badly.

I swallowed another huge mouthful and washed it down with wine. 'What's the most delicious roadkill you have ever eaten?' I asked.

Arthur put down his knife and fork. He'd almost finished his food. A rapturous expression crossed his face. 'It was dog,' he said. 'I've eaten two lurchers and a labrador and they were all wonderful: a sweet, dark meat with no bitterness or musk, a cross between beef and lamb.'

Suddenly the back door slammed and his wife came in shouting: 'This is a fine time for an interview!' She was a very young, pretty woman, and seemed fearfully cross, so I got up and left. All the way home I kept stopping the car and trying to make myself sick, but it didn't work. My cast-iron stomach wouldn't let me, and I could still taste that badger three days later. Arthur had thoughtfully put some in a bag for me to take home, but Ian's dog backed away when I tried to give it to him.

E-mail from Times *reader Karen Eberhardt Shelton: 'Years ago, in*

California, when we three kids were young, my mum served up a really good Sunday roast, and we did not usually have such things. She confessed that she had found a freshly killed deer at the bottom of our country road, gone home for a knife, and carved off a haunch.'

Chapter Twenty-Four

Do farm animals have a sense of humour? Hilary Joyce, a Dorset farmer's wife, described the day when, with two helpers, she was doing some work in the garden. They got into an easy routine, one hoeing, one digging and one planting, until her boar pig, a Gloucester Old Spot called Tinsel, with a habit of letting himself out of his sty, wandered up. He waited until the latest plant had been snugly bedded in, then leaned forward and ate it. 'It was as if he was saying, "And this is the bit that I do!"'

Because Ian worked for a big landowner he had to help with shooting parties every winter. And besides, he lived in a village where almost everyone was involved in an old-fashioned rural sport. There were meets where he would turn up and talk deferentially to the superior, horsed Master, while I hid behind his capacious green tweed jacket (left over from when he was, briefly, a gamekeeper). And when we went on long walks to check on his crops we would quite often come across the hare-coursers, walking in a long line across the stubble fields. Their beautiful, feathery-eared salukis were in brightly coloured coats, straining on a leash, and a solemn-looking gentleman in a red coat would be riding magisterially ahead, like a figure from an ancient print. When they stopped to talk to us they sounded reasonable. As one of them, Nicki Hill, put it: 'We very rarely ever catch a hare, and those we do are old and sick. And if coursing was banned it would still be legal to go out and bag a hare for the pot, so the hares wouldn't be any better off.' Besides, the hares' real enemy isn't the coursing clubs, but poachers. They don't believe in sportsmanship – or pity – and they often set four dogs on a hare at once. Worse, they are almost impossible to deter. A farm-manager friend of Ian's, David Berridge, explained to me how hopeless it was. The farm he was in charge of, at Fisherton de la Mere, was criss-crossed by footpaths, which meant it was extremely difficult for him to catch poachers in the act. Countless times he had caught up with them, only to have them run to the nearest footpath, leash their dogs, and claim they were simply taking a Sunday stroll on a public right of way. One group even set fire to their van, burning all the evidence, and said cheekily: 'Go on, prove it was ours.' (It had been stolen.) They didn't even seem to care much for their dogs; they'd abandon them, too, if they were being chased.

The area where David works has been plagued by poachers for over twenty years. Some are so persistent that he and his neighbours have learned to greet them by name. One, a stocky sort in his fifties, festooned with gold necklaces and bracelets, and called Fred, has admitted that he has been coming to the same fields for the hares since he was 'knee-high'. David told me that a few months earlier the next-door farm manager had thought he glimpsed Fred's familiar silhouette lurking in a thicket, and called out: 'Come on, Fred. Give yourself up. You've been seen.'

'I'm not Fred,' came the plaintive reply. 'I'm Fred's *nephew*.'

David explained that he had no personal animus against Fred (or his relatives), because at least they weren't violent and always left meekly if caught and asked to do so, but unfortunately modern poachers are far more destructive than the old sort. Increasing obesity and unfitness make them reluctant to walk, so they cut fences and drive across crops in their cars. 'The damage that does is no joke.'

And their tastes are changing, perhaps due to watching too many violent videos. In the West Country there are gangs that hunt deer across fields in cars, and when they finally trap them against a fence they'll leap out and kill them with hammers. They seldom take the carcasses away with them because, if they did, they might get caught. As Derek Crawley of the Staffordshire Rural Policing Liaison Group, who told me he'd come across the same kind of poaching in the north, too, remarked: 'What I'd really like to get across to the public is that wildlife crime is the hobby of town criminals. The city burglar amuses himself at the weekend by doing a bit of poaching or badger-baiting.'

But it was joining the shooting parties that was the real revelation to me. Anyone who went as a beater was paid £20 and allowed to buy as many dead birds as they wanted for 25p each, so I found it pretty well irresistible: it was a chance to see the countryside, earn money and fill the freezer for practically nothing. Sam always insisted on coming too and, the night before, we'd all steal up to Ian's grain stores, bristling with a selection of his guns. (He had them in every shape and size: even Nat was provided with a 9-mm Garden Gun.) We'd peer round the hedge, and on the path beside the store, where grain regularly got spilled as it was brought in or sent out for sale, the ground would be rippling and bouncing with rats. We could just see them in the darkness, whole families of them, plump and squeaking constantly. They were both compelling and slightly disgusting to watch. We'd have one chance to shoot them before they scattered, and then we'd have to wait an hour or two before they slipped back again.

That was the only shooting we did. Early the next morning we'd assemble in a farmyard and find ourselves in the company of a disreputable-looking band of poachers and farmhands, in camouflage, tattered raincoats and an assortment of odd hats, many with bites mysteriously taken out of them. (Bill was always there, with a sullen Louise in tow.) We'd pile into the back of an ancient trailer and perch on mouldy straw bales. And as we rattled across the farm, ominous gaps appearing in the floor beneath our feet, the gamekeeper, thin and hag-ridden, would keep banging on the roof to stop the driver, judiciously picking out a few beaters. (I noticed my family was always chosen last, like the fat, unpopular kids in a playground.) He'd deploy each beater as if they were scouts in a complex infantry battle. And those left behind would boast to each other, recounting astonishing feats of marksmanship. For instance, when one large, genial blond man described killing a hare and a rabbit with one lucky bullet, Bill topped that easily. He described how, in the 1950s, before myxomatosis, his father once got ten wild rabbits with one shot from a .22, they were so thickly clustered together.

We were beating pheasants and French partridge, so we each had a flag, because partridge like running along the ground, and have to be gently stalked for miles, funnelled into a thicket or a patch of shrivelled sweetcorn, and then startled up into the air by enthusiastic flag-waving. They are so responsive to distant movement that often, when we were half a mile away from the guns, we would hear shooting as the birds, anxiously catching sight of the flags in the distance, panicked and bolted.

When it was my turn to climb out into the cold I had to walk to a fixed point and then wait until I heard a whistle. Ahead I could see the faintest blush of sprouting corn against the bare earth of the fields, like a thin green wash of water-colour. Here and there, great sweeps of frost glittered in the shadow under the trees.

The whistle came, and as I walked on, a pair of deer leapt towards me out of the horizon, just small, dark graceful silhou-ettes against the wide, rolling downland. There was another whistle, and I stopped again, rubbing my gloved hands together and stamping my feet to keep warm. I felt like a child again, out on an endless family walk. That same sense of smallness, and wonder – along with a faint, niggling anxiety that I might be doing something wrong and irritating the grown-ups. Now I could see other miniature bright orange flags dotted against the smoky blue sky. Down in a valley ahead of me Sam was standing on the corner of a field in his dark raincoat, like a tiny, animated scarecrow. He kept fidgeting while he waited: sitting down with his legs stiffly in front of him, so he could admire his boots; stretching his arms out and trying to semaphore with his flag. It was odd, but watching this from the shelter of a hedge made me feel totally involved with the landscape in the happiest way.

He was contented, too, I could tell. He'd spent his teens being enraged by the country, and how hard it was to have a lively social life in it. (One New Year's Eve he'd missed the last bus and had to walk twelve miles across country to get home, drinking from streams whenever he got thirsty. 'I don't think anyone else has done that since *Chaucer*,' he complained.) But now that he no longer had to do compulsory farm work he'd started asking for hip-flasks, waterproof trousers and oilskin coats as birthday and Christmas presents. He even talked about how, when he was older and more settled, he'd like a working spaniel like Ian's, and maybe a house in the country. Kathy was the same. From being fiercely pro-city, she now often said wistfully that she'd like to live somewhere where she could ride every day.

Suddenly I noticed that all the other figures in the distance were walking fast towards a wood, and the gamekeeper was signalling

angrily to me to keep up. The guns were so close I could feel
pellets pattering down like metallic rain, and there were birds
everywhere. I'd never been in a wood that was so alive: pheasants were rustling through the fallen leaves, and startling up
into the canopy, complaining throatily as they went, and flights
of songbirds were wheeling round and sweeping back the way
we'd come. There was a real sense of harvest. There were even
deer. A big roe ran in my direction in panic, flinched when it
saw me, and leapt at a fence. It got caught and somersaulted
convulsively, and before I could get there to help it, broke free
and bounded away.

We were almost out of the wood now, and the guns were just
below us. One pheasant flew the whole length of them, being
fired at (and missed) by every single one, and Ian caught hold of
my gloved hand and whispered that when that happened all the
beaters secretly cheered it on. The blond beater had a little terrier that kept pouncing on game birds as they hid under piles of
cut brushwood. It was snapping their necks before bringing
them to its owner (a terrible crime: it cut out the middle-man:
the aristocrats shooting below us). The blond grinned at Ian.
'You'd almost think he was a poacher's dog, wouldn't you?' he
laughed.

Despite their off-puttingly cut-glass accents, the guns had
interesting stories to tell, too. At the end we all talked together
as they went back to their 4 by 4s and we made for the trailer.
An elegant sort in a fox-trimmed hat told me that in her house
her father and brother were so obsessed by shooting that the
cloakroom was full of hanging game, and she always had to

remember to shake the maggots out of her wellingtons before she put them on. Also, in the winter, the U-bend in the downstairs lavatory always clinked with shot, because it was too heavy to flush away. She teased me by saying that in the old days they used to enter any wounded beaters in the game-book along with the lists of birds. And apparently – though I found this hard to believe – one depressed sportsman on a big estate wrote his *own name* in the game-book before going off and committing suicide.

I liked the mad rules. The way you had to do whatever the gamekeeper told you to, whether it was wading waist deep in slurry or plunging head first into a bramble-bush. And the way the cleverest birds could escape. At the end of the day, when the keeper blew his long, lingering final whistle, it was quite start-ling how many mature pheasants crept out from behind trees and started pecking and scratching about calmly, secure in the knowledge that they were safe until the next day. Pheasants, according to the other beaters, were much brighter than par-tridge. One even knew of a pheasant that rode on the front of the keeper's quad-bike every day, as he drove about scattering corn.

Letter from Elizabeth Close, who lives next door to a shoot in County Down: 'One wily cock pheasant round here, the minute he saw more than three cars arrive, went off to my hen-house and sat all day behind a bucket. By the end of January fifteen were doing the same.'

As we waited for the other beaters to climb in the trailer, look-ing north over the Wylye Valley, Ian said: 'Do you realise that all these thousands of trees were planted just to provide cover for game?' Maybe, I reasoned to myself, even hunting wasn't so bad. I might not want to do it myself, but I was beginning to see that without it the countryside would be poorer. And as for the fact that country sports involved killing, well so did eating meat. I couldn't see much difference morally, between helping on a shoot and taking birds home to eat – and keeping a poultry yard.

Country Sporty Rules Nos 2–6

2) *Although women can join in, these sports are mostly about being male. And any small boys are treated with enormous affection. The men always say that they first became gripped by rabbiting, shooting, hunting or whatever when they were six or seven, so it is part of an ongoing initiation process.*

3) *There is a military-style neatness to every detail, even down to the way thick socks are carefully rolled over the bottoms of camouflage trousers.*

4) *Waterproof trews are hugely significant. And that subtle crackle as a whippet-thin countryman executes an important manoeuvre and his waterproofs take the strain.*

5) *There are always overwhelming quantities of at least three of the following: mud, rain, ice and brambles.*

6) *The technical equipment needed to do these sports is treated very seriously indeed, and yet much of it is made of rubbish, like old bits of stick and string. E.g. our partridge-scaring flags were made out of old fertiliser bags, and all countrymen have a thumbstick, handwhittled from a branch, which they take enormous care of, and leave in a special spot outside their back door.*

It was time to meet Ian's parents, and I wasn't looking forward to it at all. I seemed to have trouble getting on with the parents of rural men. Betty had been kind and entertaining company, but laughed at me in private. I was a grotesque, dung-splattered person who thought a healthy bank-balance more important than graceful living. And Wooster's mother had found me appalling in a different way: I was too rude and silly, not nearly county enough.

Ian's parents sounded more promising: they hadn't sent him to boarding school, and when Ian showed an interest in the internal combustion machine aged eleven his father bought him an engine-tuning kit *and allowed him to try it out on the engine of the family car.* They were retired poultry farmers, living on Bodmin Moor.

But when I met them there were awkwardnesses. This was mostly, I discovered later, because they had been very fond of his previous girlfriend. After a while, though, we got on to the subject of wildlife. Ian's mother, Joan, described how, one night, she had heard a terrible screaming and gone up on to the hill above her house to investigate. She followed the noise into a little wood, and saw a vixen rush into the undergrowth. And then the beam of her torch caught a badger. He was standing, frozen on the path ahead of her, a young fox cub dead in his jaws. She hadn't realised, before that moment, that foxes had any natural predators.

There was a small framed photograph in their front room, and something about it was strangely arresting. It showed a delicate, small-boned collie-dog with a black patch over one eye, large pricked ears and a long, bushy tail. The picture, Joan said, was of a dog called 'Waif', which had died ten years earlier. She'd found her one day when she was walking her labradors on the moor. She was just passing an abandoned, overgrown cottage when her dogs ran inside and began yelping. Cowering in a corner was Waif, barely fifteen inches high, starving, and red-raw and almost hairless from mange. She tucked Waif into her coat and took her home. When she called the vet, he said that, from the condition of her teeth, Waif was about a year old.

As the little collie settled into the household and her hair grew back, she displayed a few strange habits. She loved nibbling blackberries, caught squirrels with exceptional ease and, if she saw a rabbit, would chase it, catch it and flip its body with her nose so that it flew, startled, through the air. Once, when they had a plague of mice in the poultry houses, they let Waif in and she caught all the vermin by pouncing on them. She'd study them, back arched, shoulders hunched, head almost vertical, and then jump high in the air, trapping them safely under her two front paws as she came down.

She had a distinctive way of running, too. She'd use her thick, heavy tail (which had much coarser hair than a normal collie's, springing out in all directions rather than hanging straight down) as a rudder to guide her round sharp corners, and twirl it like a mop-head whenever she wanted to stop. She hated the rain, enjoyed gently teasing the farm cat and defended the farm so fiercely that the baker used to throw the bread in through the front door sooner than face her. She was also so highly attuned to Joan's thoughts that she would guess when Joan was about to go on a long ride across the moor and rush to the door expectantly. 'At first I thought it was just because I was getting dressed in riding clothes or collecting up harness. But even if I did none of these things, she would still react the instant the thought of riding entered my head, and race to the door in excitement.'

Although Waif regularly came into season and lived with male dogs, she never got pregnant. And when she was quite old – she died of heart-failure, aged thirteen – a visiting vet took one look at her and suggested she was a cross between a Welsh border collie and a fox. He thought she might have been conceived on one of the many isolated farms in the area, when a female collie came on heat and there was only a fox to take advantage of the situation.

Wondering whether this was possible, I got in touch with Liz Mullineaux, a vet who treats wildlife at a sanctuary in Devon called Secret World. Having never heard of such a cross, she mentioned the subject at a symposium of wildlife vets, and the consensus was that it was unlikely.

'Foxes and dogs belong to two separate genera. Dogs belong to the genus *canis*, and so can mate successfully with wolves, also of the genus *canis*. But foxes belong to the genus *vulpes*, which basically means that they are in a very different group genetically.'

The other vets in the symposium had come across plenty of cases where members of the public had accidentally reared fox cubs thinking they were puppies, or thought they had a fox when what they really possessed was a foxy-looking terrier, so confusion often happens. But given that, a dog-fox cross, though unlikely, is not completely impossible. 'People have managed to cross hawks from totally different gene bases,' Liz told me. 'So you can breed across genera, though what is produced does not live long, and is always infertile.'

If Waif was a genuine collie-fox cross (would she be a 'follie'?), her birth was not an accident. There are many creatures similar enough to interbreed – such as sheep and goats, or horses and donkeys – which, even if they are kept at close quarters, will not mate out of chance. 'It is because,' Liz said, 'what causes them to find a partner attractive is so very different. They have dissimilar pheromones and behaviours, so it only tends to happen in artificial circumstances engineered by humans.' She thought the only way a fox-dog cross could occur would be if a pet fox was deliberately encouraged to mate with a dog. Which makes it odd that someone would go to so much trouble to produce a follie – only to abandon it.

E-mail from Times *reader Lucy Fletcher: 'My dog Clay, found when a grotty Essex farm was bulldozed, trotted like a fox and was fox-marked. She also had some funny habits for a dog, like waiting in the reeds for migrating ducks to settle, and once they had, diving under the water and seizing them by the paddles.'*

Chapter Twenty-Five

Story told by a heating oil supplier, 2002, to illustrate the vast financial gulf opening up between farmers and townies: 'One of my customers is a Dorset farmer, who put his 130-acre holding up for sale at £750,000. Within a day or two, he had a visit from a young bloke in a Porsche, who walked round the farmhouse and said he'd take it. When completion day came the farmer met the buyer again and asked him, curiously, what he planned to do with the land. "Land?" the young bloke said, taking off his sunglasses. "Is there land going with the house, too?"'

The audience in the barn was hushed. The play was about to begin. A ram at the back made a loud, interrogatory blaring noise, and somewhere round the front a broody hen complained, in a muffled way, as she struggled through a blackout curtain. The play, *The Living at Hurford*, had been written by a John Somers, a university professor in the village, and my Ian was in the lead role as 'Mike, the suicidal farmer'.

It was just one in a long line of community plays in my village, which has a passion for them. When Ian and I had first started dating a huge musical had been in production, based on the life and enthusiasms of our local postman, Marty Richards. Marty had played himself, very convincingly and perkily, wearing his normal uniform. And my favourite bit, which I could have watched over and over, was where a group of middle-aged female villagers, wearing extremely short French maid costumes, tickled him with scarlet feather-dusters while he sang a song with the refrain, 'I'm a little postman, short and stout . . . '

I loved the silliness and exuberance that was unleashed by these rural plays. And according to Jon Oram, the artistic director of Claque, who has been involved in this sort of drama since 1982, it always happens. 'When I was doing a community play in Aylesham in Kent, we were trying to find the words of a local song called *Aylesham Sunshine Corner*, when we heard that a local miner called Glyn Goth had had them tattooed on his bum when he was in the army.' Jon and his colleagues tracked down this character, verified that the words were, indeed, preserved on his buttocks, and then wrote the incident into their play. 'We had this moment when the cast turned to each other and said, "Has anyone got the words of the song?" And Glyn would drop his trousers.'

In our musical about Marty, pillars of the community had been persuaded to cross-dress or parade semi-naked on stage, and you couldn't help wondering what long-term effect this extrovert behaviour would have. Would they be able to return to their old, quiet lives after the drama was over? Jon thought not. 'Women, particularly,' he said, 'find their lost selves in com-

336

munity plays. They get listened to – often for the first time in years. They become creative. And when the play is over their husbands either accept these new selves or there is a divorce. I celebrate it, really, but it does cause friction.'

Community plays have such a profound effect because, in most cases, the actors have never performed before. No one is ever turned away. (To make this quite clear, Jon always pins a sign above his audition-room door for people to see before they enter. It reads: 'Congratulations. You've got the part.') And unlike the harsh, professional world, women do not have to be ravishingly beautiful to become stars. In fact it is often the oddest-looking sorts, weathered by a lifetime of rural struggle, who make these dramas work best. When Jon staged a play in Cornwall he needed someone to act the central role of 'Maud'. She had to be powerful and charismatic, and he had almost despaired of finding her when: 'This strange apparition appeared in casting. It got off a motorbike, swathed in leathers and scarves, and it was barely four feet high. It did a sort of motorcycle striptease, and there was our Maud: "All right, my darlings?" It was as if the part had been written for her. In fact, once she appeared, all the other actors started worrying about their accents because she was so very Cornish.'

'But surely,' I said, awkwardly, 'there must be times when people want parts they aren't suited for. How do you handle that?' Jon explained that there was always a way. In one production, a local with a severe speech impediment insisted on being given a central speaking part. 'So we stuck him in a crow's nest at the height of the Battle of Trafalgar and had him call out, over and over, against the sound of a storm: "Nelson is dead". It was incredibly dramatic – and the fact that you could hardly make out what he was saying only heightened the effect.'

As I sat in on our rehearsals (Nat was always in the plays, as either a mouse or a small boy) I used to notice how happy the performers looked in their glamorous make-up and costumes. Surely this was the ideal setting for, well, love affairs? Jon chuckled when I said this. He, his son, and nearly all their colleagues have fallen in love while organising community plays. 'The first one I ever did was in Sherborne and I saw the effect it had on relationships there. In Sherborne there is a boys' school and a girls' school and never the twain shall meet, and both were involved in the play. And there was a huge amount of activity when rehearsals were going on. Always behind the stages. And in the dark.'

The *Living at Hurford* was rather a serious production, though. It was about the aftermath of foot and mouth, the collapse of farming and the painful adjustments the rural community were having to make in order to survive. It was interactive, too. Towards the end the audience – made up almost entirely of local farmers – could question the characters about their motives and feelings. And then they decided how the play should end. Their reactions were almost more interesting than the play itself. One night a celebrated local goose farmer ticked the cast off roundly for the stupidity of their plans. 'The golden rule is: never diversify into anything you don't know inside out,' she hectored, quite forgetting they were actors. Often the audience wept, as the story got uncomfortably close to their own experience. John Carter's wife did. I'd interviewed him at the start of foot and mouth, and though his pigs hadn't caught it, he'd still lost his farm. Mingling with the audience in the interval, I heard news of others I'd interviewed: 'Paul Worden, with the wild boar? Oh – he's gone, too. That's another couldn't ride out foot and mouth.' 'Peter Foster? I think he's growing veg now. The pink veal didn't work out.' There was no doubt everything was changing. Out of the twelve dairy farmers that had been in the village when Charlie and I first moved in, only five were left, and three of those were about to sell up.

And Ian's role had a painful edge to it because he kept saying things on stage that I'd heard him sound off about in my own kitchen. In 2002 the government had allowed Eastern European wheat into the country, and the price of grain, which had always been reliably high, the safest commodity to farm – suddenly plummeted. It cost at least £60 a tonne to grow, and there it was, for sale on Southampton docks at £40. It presented him with an agonising dilemma: with the cost of the sprays and fertiliser he had to buy, and the loans on the heavy machinery he needed, he was sinking deeper and deeper into debt. He couldn't afford to carry on, and yet he adored the five-hundred-acre farm where he worked: its water-meadows, woods and rolling downland. Driving over such a landscape in high-tech machinery was all he'd ever wanted to do. It was agonising hearing him constantly weigh the issues, and fret about his debts. But there were other farmers in the audience who were still hopeful that they could make a living from the land. You didn't feel, listening to them talk, that you were watching the death of British farming – not entirely.

'You know what makes a turkey different from every other kind of fowl?' Steve McCartney asked. He was a builder, and supposed to be fixing the loose bricks on my chimney, but had got side-tracked into having tea.

I could think of plenty of differences, but I knew I wasn't supposed to say anything.

'It's because, however old it gets, you can always eat it with enjoyment. Providing you fatten it first for a month or two.' He went on to describe how, back in September, he'd gone to Hatherleigh market, where they auction poultry every Tuesday. He'd bought an elderly bronze hen turkey for the bargain price of £5, and his problems only began when he went to collect it. He found its owner – also well on in years – cuddling and chatting to it. She was addressing the bird as 'Jennifer', and each time she spoke the turkey would cock her head and reply in a high-pitched twitter, as if she understood what was being said.

When Steve asked why the bird was so tame the old lady explained that Jennifer had been her bosom companion for the last three years. She was only parting with her now because she had to go into a residential home and, most unfairly, they did not allow pet turkeys.

'I hope you are not intending to eat Jennifer,' she said sharply, and Steve had to give an evasive reply.

Back at his smallholding, he became increasingly disconcerted by Jennifer's tameness. She rushed to greet him each time he opened the front door, she engaged him in long, twittering conversations and she insisted on eating from his hand. What he found hardest to bear, he said, was the way the odd little pointed, cocktail-sausage-sized comb on her forehead – bright pink and covered with black bristles – inflated and deflated as she chatted to him, as if reflecting her unease as to the precise nature of their relationship.

'So what happened in the end?' I asked.

He finished his tea. 'I lost my nerve, didn't I? I gave her away to my mate up the road, who's got six little kids.'

I found this story reassuring. It was nice to hear that, by sheer effort of the will, anyone, even a turkey, could escape a dismal fate connected with Christmas lunch. I was still worried by the gypsy's prophecy that I would never eat a Yuletide dinner in my home again. The closer I got to the twenty-fifth the more sinister the omens got. My father-in-law, Michael, died suddenly. And two days before Christmas Eve, while driving his little brother home from a pantomime, Sam hit black ice and, for a few scary seconds, slithered out of control on the brow of a hill. It was a relief when Christmas Day finally began, and I wandered blearily downstairs to put the turkey in the oven. Ian's dog was sleeping by the Aga, and his cat was having a slow-motion fight on the sofa with mine, involving a lot of slapping with a stripy, tabby paw.

The side of my mouth felt decidedly odd, but I thought no more about it until, a few hours later, I glanced in a mirror and saw it was all swollen up like a hamster's. By lunchtime my head had roughly doubled in size, but I insisted on defying the prediction: I squeezed a small amount of potato and half a Brussels sprout into the bit of my mouth that was still working. And then Ian had to take me to casualty, along rutted, icy roads.

They weren't quite sure what was wrong with me, and I spent the rest of the holiday upstairs, in my bedroom, on antibiotics, lying in a mixture of sheets and torn wrapping paper. I was tormented by a present of Nat's: a battery-operated gorilla that burst into song each time the bed moved. 'It's hot, hot, hot,' it sang, in a strong Jamaican accent, celebrating the fact that the central heating was working at last.

While I lay there I thought about how the complications caused by the divorce were gradually smoothing out. Charlie and his girl-friend had bought a different farm, and now lived near enough for Nat to stay with them for a week or two in the school holidays. This made him so much happier, that he was finally starting to gain weight and lose his strained, bony look. Sam had begun talking to his father on the telephone, and maybe Kathy would soon. And Charlie and I had finally hammered out a financial settlement. I'd given him a huge lump sum and promised never to demand any maintenance for Nat, and in return I kept the farmhouse.

The hoover roared into life downstairs, and I heard Nat giggle as Ian chased him with it. It suddenly seemed right that someone so kind and loving – who didn't mind being a surro-gate father to Nat – should move in for ever. I never wanted to be a wife again, though. I hated even the sound of that word – to me it meant the same as 'fool' or 'virtuous drudge'. But I didn't mind being a country girlfriend.

E-mail from Caky – Re Mr Wonderful: 'Well, I thought Ian was just the perfect boyfriend. A really, really nice bloke. I liked him the instant my eyes fell on him. And as for whether it will last: the two of you have what – whether you live in the country or the town – is by far the most important thing: animal warmth.'